THE WONDERS OF FASTING

UNRAVELLING
THE ASTONISHING MYSTERIES
OF BIBLICAL FASTING

VICTOR I. IRUOBE

Copyright © 2016 Victor I. Iruobe

All rights reserved. No part of this publication may be produced, distributed, or transmitted in any form or by any means, including photocopying, recording, or other electronic or mechanical methods, without the prior written permision of the publisher, except in the case of brief quotations embodied in critical reviews and certain other noncommercial uses permitted by copyright law.

For permission requests, write to the publisher, addressed "Attention: Permissions Coordinator" at the email address below:

Life and Success Media Ltd

e-mail: info@abookinsideyou.com

www.abookinsideyou.com

Unless otherwise stated, all scripture quotations are taken from the Holy Bible, New King James Version. Quotations marked NKJV are taken from the HOLY BIBLE, NEW KING JAMES VERSION. Copyright © 1973, 1978, 1984 by International Bible Society. Used by permission of Hodder and Stoughton Ltd, a member of the Hodder Headline Plc Group. All rights reserved. "NKJV" is a registered trademark of International Bible Society.
UK trademark number 1448790.

Quotations marked KJV are from the Holy Bible,

King James Version.

ISBN Number: 978-1-907402-80-7

Cover Design: **MIA**Design.com

TABLE OF CONTENTS

DEDICATION	7
ACKNOWLEDGEMENTS	9
FOREWORD	11
PROLOGUE	13

Part One: Understanding Biblical Fasting — 19

1. FASTING FOR YOUR DESIRED MIRACLE	21
2. PROCLAIMED OR PUBLIC AND PERSONAL FAST	35
3. PERSONAL FAST	51
4. GOD'S PURPOSE FOR FASTING	65

Part Two: Fasting and the present day Church — 79

5. IS FASTING FOR THE PRESENT DAY CHURCH?	81
6. THE BRIDEGROOM HAS DEPARTED: SHALL WE FAST NOW?	101
7. THE PRACTICE OF FASTING IN THE EARLY CHURCH	113
8. TYPES OF CHRISTIAN FASTING	127

Part Three: Principles of Biblical Fast — 141

9. QUESTIONS TO ASK BEFORE FASTING	144
10. THE WRONG AND RIGHT FAST	151
11. THE RIGHT FAST	167
12. WHEN THOU SEEST THE NAKED,	

THAT THOU COVER HIM...	187
13. THE OPEN REWARD OF THE SECRET FAST OF THE BELIEVER	193

Part Four: Fasting Impact — 207

14. REASONS WHY BELIEVERS SHOULD FAST	209
15. FASTING HELPS TO SUSTAIN THE ANOINTING	219
16. FASTING DEEPENS YOUR UNDERSTANDING OF THE WORD OF GOD AND INCREASES YOUR ABILITY TO HEAR FROM GOD	231

Part Five: The Mystery Of Fasting — 241

17. CHANGING THE DESTINY OF NATIONS THROUGH FASTING	243
18. JEHOSHAPHAT GAINED VICTORY OVER HIS ENEMIES	259
19. ESTHER AVERTED NATIONAL CRISIS THROUGH FASTING	271
20. THE DANIEL FAST: FASTING TO OVERCOME THE FLESH	295
21. ELIJAH'S FAST: BREAKING NEGATIVE EMOTIONAL HABITS	307
22. LESSONS FROM ELIJAH'S FAST	311
23. THE HEALING VALUE OF FASTING	327

Part Six: Fasting from the Legend's Perspective — 335

24. QUOTES BY CHRISTIAN LEADERS ON FASTING	337

Part Seven: Diverse issues about Fasting and Prayer — 353

25. ANSWERS TO COMMON QUESTIONS ABOUT FASTING	355
26. FASTING SCRIPTURES: BIBLE REFERENCES OF BOTH INDIVIDUAL AND CORPORATE FASTS	387
27. FASTING SCRIPTURES 2	401
28. BIBLICAL RECORD OF WRONG FASTING	415
29. DURATION OF FASTS	419
30. PRAYER, WHAT IS IT?	429
31. TYPES OF PRAYER	439
EPILOGUE	461
REFERENCES	465

THE WONDERS OF FASTING

Dedication

I would like to dedicate this book to my precious wife, PASTOR ANN IRUOBE. I am a privileged man to be blessed with such a treasure.

I am eternally grateful to God for such an invaluable GIFT.

THE WONDERS OF FASTING

Acknowledgements

I wish to express ardent appreciation to the Author and Finisher of my faith – the King of Kings and the Lord of Lords, from whom the strength, knowledge, wisdom and understanding came to put this work together. My creator, my life is, forever, a living incense of thanksgiving to you!

It is evident that in every new *kairos* (special timing of God), He raises up a voice to speak and declare, in great clarity, His predestined purpose and plans for that hour. There is no question in my mind that you have called me at this momentous hour for this purpose.

Appreciation is also due to my precious wife, Pastor Ann Iruobe. You are a treasure, sweetheart! To my four children – Gloria, Sarah, Joshua and David- Vincent. You are each a special treasure! I pray that our family would continue to grow in the fullness of blessings that comes with beholding His face. Thank you all for the joy you brought into my life.

My profound gratitude to Pastor and Pastor (Mrs) Matthew and Yemisi Ashimolowo (KICC Global), for your love and tremendous encouragement. You are unquestionably, a great inspiration to the Body of Christ, worldwide, not least, the upcoming generation of Ministers of the Gospel. Your lives have taught me humility by experience. May His Grace abound ever more in your lives.

What shall I say of the glorious family of Hope of Glory International Christian Centre? My ardent appreciations go to every one of you. You have all taught me the joy of being a Shepherd. Special thanks to my colleagues in the Ministry Administrative Office, without whose co-operation and hard-work I would not have been able to take time off to write this book. I deeply appreciate you all.

Finally, I will like to register special appreciation to every General in God's Glorious Army, past and present that have taught the invaluable lesson of the clarion call of the Master on His Body to engage in the noble discipline of fasting. May your service be ever remembered.

Foreword

One of the most difficult subjects to sell to people is the subject of fasting along with prayer. We are confronted with a generation which, instead of fasting, is used to fast food.

I will not attempt in this little introduction to ever replicate the work that Pastor Iruobe has done but let me just refer to the fact that the book of Isaiah 58 shows us clearly that if we must experience breakthrough we must fast – Isaiah 58:10

- If we must experience divine revelation we must fast – Daniel 9:2-3

- If we must receive provisions for the work for which we are called, we must fast – Isaiah 58:11

- Divine direction will only be clear to the man who prays and fasts – Isaiah 58:11

- Prosperity is available to the man who fasts – Isaiah 58:11, Psalm 1:3

- Those who pray and fast will possess the future and God will restore to them lost years, lost opportunities and lost favours – Joel 2:25-27

It may not be a practice that is popular today. However, Pastor Iruobe has shown us clearly and the great saints of the past and the great revivals which we have read of have their root in the lives of men and women who disciplined themselves through prayer and fasting – 2 Chronicles 7:14

So brethren, if we must see deliverance from the things that hold us down, we must learn to wait on God – Mark 9:29

May I take this opportunity to celebrate and recommend this book as a book that will go very far in transforming lives, challenging us and possibly aiding us in bringing back the revival we need.

Well done!

Pastor Matthew Ashimolowo

Senior Pastor, KICC GLOBAL

Prologue

Majority of people associate fasting with medieval time and practices which such political leaders like Mahatma Ghandi resorted to as a successful weapon of passive resistance. As a spiritual exercise, many think that fasting is a discipline reserved, only for some fanatics, or at best, ministers of the Gospel.

Fasting goes back to the dawn of life on earth; it is as old as eating. When not eating, the body is fasting, or at least, looking forward to it, revelling in the joy of abstinence and longing to rebuild itself after a thorough 'housecleaning'. Every night we "fast", whether we realise it or not. When we awake, we have 'break-fast'. This is where the name of our first meal of the day is derived from. Fasting is almost as natural as breathing. In the olden days, leaders, people of ranks and others would go into places of solitude to fast for several days on water when they had critical decisions to make. However, as would be seen, the cases of fasting dealt with in this book are different in nature from those that are politically or nutritionally motivated.

When Jesus walked the earth, He was very clear on the subject of fasting: He said,

> *Howbeit, this kind goeth out not except by prayer and fasting (Matt. 7:21)*

Jesus not only spoke about fasting, He authenticated the discipline by fasting Himself. The Bible says:

> *And when he had fasted forty days and forty nights, he was afterward hungry (Matt. 4:2).*

If fasting was that vital to the Lord, it should be no less important to us. It has been to me for many years; and I can attest to its incredible and astonishing power.

In fact, fasting is the most powerful spiritual discipline of all Christian disciplines; *"mighty... to the pulling down of strongholds"* (2 Cor. 10:4).

When exercised with a pure heart and a right motive, fasting could provide us with a key to unlock doors where other keys have failed, and open up new horizon in the unseen world. Indeed, fasting can be a tremendous weapon in our prayer arsenal, if used scripturally.

Jesus warned the Pharisees that their fasting was of religious show; consequently, their attitude would rob them of the ultimate reward God promised those that observe fasting the right way. Likewise, in Isaiah 58: 3-5, God rebuked the people of Isaiah's days for improper fasting:

> *Wherefore have we fasted, say they, and thou seest not? Wherefore have we afflicted our soul, and thou takest no knowledge? Behold, in the day of your fast ye find pleasure, and exact all your labours. Behold, ye fast for strife and debate, and to smite with the fist of wickedness: ye shall not fast as ye do this day, to make your voice to be heard on high. Is it such a fast that I have chosen? a day for a man to afflict his soul? is it to bow down his head as a bulrush, and to spread sackcloth and ashes under him? Wilt thou call this a fast, and an acceptable day to the Lord?*

Obviously not!

Fasting is to be used to draw closer to God and His anointing. True fasting releases the requisite power to deal with crisis, especially, situations with demonic undertone (Matt. 17:21). It is also widely believed amongst Medical Practitioners that fasting is beneficial to the health of the physical body, given its cleansing effect.

Furthermore, Isaiah 58:6-9 claims even greater blessings for those who engage in God's chosen fast – fast that conforms to God's purpose and standard.

> *Is not this the fast that I have chosen? to loose the bands of wickedness, to undo the heavy burdens, and to let the oppressed go free, and that ye break every yoke? Is it not to deal thy bread to the hungry, and that thou bring the poor that are cast out to thy house?*

Unfortunately, for centuries fasting has been unpopular in the churches of the Western nations. The very idea of someone actually fasting today seems strange to present-day believers.

> *When thou seest the naked, that thou cover him; and that thou hide not thyself from thine own flesh? Then shall thy light break forth as the morning, and thine health shall spring forth speedily: and thy righteousness shall go before thee; the glory of the Lord shall be thy reward. Then shalt thou call, and*

the Lord shall answer; thou shalt cry, and he shall say, Here I am. If thou take away from the midst of thee the yoke, the putting forth of the finger, and speaking vanity.

Unfortunately, for centuries fasting has been unpopular in the churches of the Western nations. The very idea of someone actually fasting today seems strange to present-day believers. This is so because not many have taken the pains to teach this very important Christian discipline. However, it must be stressed, that the Bible is replete with clear and unequivocal teachings on the subject, as would be demonstrated in this book.

This book is, therefore, intended to help the believer have in-depth understanding of, not just what fasting is, but the purpose and power of God's chosen fast!

THE WONDERS OF FASTING

Part One

Understanding Biblical Fasting

THE WONDERS OF FASTING

1

FASTING FOR YOUR DESIRED MIRACLE

"Fasting is a medicine. But medicine, as beneficial as it is, becomes useless because of the inexperience of the user. He has to know the appropriate time that the medicine should be taken and the right amount of medicine and the condition of the body which is to take it, the weather conditions and the season of the year and the appropriate diet of the sick and many other things. If any of these things are overlooked, the medicine will do more harm than good. So, if one who is going to heal the body needs so much accuracy, when we care for the soul and are concerned about healing it from bad thoughts, it is necessary to examine and observe everything with every possible detail" - **St. John Chrysostom.**

What an accurate description of the mission and object of this book! The subject of fasting has been the basis of much debate for as long as man has existed. Besides the much readily controversies that surround the very essence of fasting in the present day church, and in the life of the believer generally, the subject is inundated with numerous questions such as: "What is fasting? How do I fast? What is God's purpose for fasting? Is fasting for the present day church? Does God reward fasting? How long should I fast for? How often should I fast? How do I handle the challenges associated with fasting? And how should I successfully break a fast?

Part of the purpose of this book is to address such pertinent issues as these, and to adequately clear up some of the common misconceptions often associated with fasting.

People of faith – people with regenerate minds - would always tie the outpouring of sincere prayer and fasting to miracles.

Fasting is a 'vehicle' with a definite mission leading to an assured destination – MIRACLES! According to Bill Bright, "… fasting as it relates to prayer is the spiritual atomic bomb that our Lord has given us to destroy the strongholds [of Satan]…" For thousands of years, the Household of Faith worldwide have used the discipline of spiritual fasting as a weapon to pound on the doors of heaven for breakthrough. The sceptics may not believe that God exists let alone that He does miracles, and the unbelievers may find ways of explaining away the afflictions they suffer, but people of faith – people with regenerate minds - would always tie the outpouring of sincere prayer and fasting to miracles. In essence, when we abstain from food for spiritual purposes, then God compensates us with life's best, and greatest blessings: breakthroughs, restoration, healing and prosperity – and what is more, the Bible says that God will feed us "with the heritage of Jacob" (Isaiah 58:14). What that means is that fasting will give us a place among other great spiritual heroes throughout history. What an incredible promise! God gives miracles because He has them! James the Apostle says:

> *Every good gift and every perfect gift is from above, and cometh down from the Father of lights, with whom is no variableness, neither shadow of turning (James 1:17).*

However, the scope of the breakthrough we receive from God depends on how serious we are in calling upon Him for His intervention in our lives.

Employing the formidable weapon of fasting would not only turn you into a giant of faith, but would cause you to walk in the footsteps of those that affected their generations for God.

Bill Bright was correct when he said:

Fasting is the most powerful spiritual discipline of all the Christian disciplines. Through fasting and prayer, the Holy Spirit can transform your life.

Fasting is a tool that guarantees a life full of notable miracles. Fasting knows no limit in its operation; ...

Fasting and prayer can also work on a much grander scale. According to Scripture, personal experience and observation, I am convinced that when God's people fast with a proper biblical motive – seeking God's face not His hand – with a broken, repentant and contrite spirit, God will hear from heaven and heal our lives, our churches, our communities, our nation and world. Fasting and prayer can bring revival – a change in the direction of our nation, the nations of the earth and the fulfilment of the Great Commission.

Fasting is a tool that guarantees a life full of notable miracles. Fasting knows no limit in its operation; even the most impossible circumstances receive God's immediate attention through fasting.

The concept is that fasting weakens the body and allows the spirit to receive God's power and direction with greater intensity. While prayer can be seen as a gunshot that helps to penetrate the spiritual world, fasting becomes the 'machine-gun' that makes the discipline even more powerful and effective.

What is Fasting?

Given the much misconceptions surrounding the discipline of biblical fast, I would like to begin with a definition of what fasting is. **Throughout Scriptures, fasting refers to abstaining from food for spiritual purposes. It stands in distinction to hunger strike, the purpose of which is to gain political power or attract attention to a good cause. It is also different from health dieting which stresses abstinence from food for physical, not spiritual, purposes.**

...even the most impossible circumstances receive God's immediate attention through fasting.

That is not to say that these forms of 'fasting' are wrong, but their objective is different from the fasting discussed in this book, which centres on the 'God's-chosen fast', as detailed in the word of God.

Fasting is aimed at withdrawing from food in order to concentrate or focus on God, His holiness, His will and purposes. Biblical fasting always centres on God and His purposes, not on man or the person observing the fast.

In Scripture, the normal means of fasting involves abstaining from all food, but not always from fluid. There were, however, occasions in the Bible where people fasted without food and water for different period of time. For example, Queen Esther fasted without food and water for three days:

Go, gather together all the Jews that are present in Shushan, and fast for me, and neither eat nor drink three days, night or day: I also and my maidens will fast likewise; and so will I go in unto the king, which is not according to the law: and if I perish, I perish (Esther 4:16).

In another instance, we see Saul (Paul) going without food and water for three days during his dramatic conversion on his way to Damascus:

For three days he… neither did eat nor drink –
Acts 9:9

Moses (Exodus 24:18 & 34:28), Elijah (1 Kings 19:8) both fasted for 40 days. On two different occasions, Moses fasted for 40 days, where he abstained from both food and drink. The same holds true for Elijah. It must be noted, however, that these were supernatural fasts spent in the very presence of God. Many people have undergone fasts of this duration without harming themselves, but it should not be done without being certain or convinced that you are in good health and have the assurance that God has called you to undertake a fast of this nature. As a matter of fact, fasts of this length should be the exception rather than the rule. God would not call any of us to do something that is harmful to ourselves.

So far we have seen that biblical fasting has to do with restraining oneself from food for a given period of time in order to engage in specific spiritual exercises.

Common misconceptions

As said, fasting is often a subject of much controversy, indeed, misconceptions. What is pathetic is that, fasting is one of the most misunderstood subjects in the Bible; yet, its practice is associated with incredible benefits, when observed with the right motive and attitude.

It is a well-known fact that when people do not appreciate the plain, literal meaning of a concept or teaching in the Bible, or they simply are against such teaching, they are quick to explain it away, and so rob the church of its valuable blessings. Once the truth becomes confused, it ceases to have any practical meaning. In essence, it loses its objectives and applicability. This is what the present day church has tended to do with the biblical teaching of fasting.

Once the truth becomes confused, it ceases to have any practical meaning. In essence, it loses its objectives and applicability. This is what the present day church has tended to do with the biblical teaching of fasting.

"To fast," we are told, "is not simply or necessarily to abstain from food, but from anything that hinders our communion with God." They contend that "Fasting means to do without, or practice self-denial." In their application of the concept, an individual could 'fast' from watching, not just the television, but from a programme he has been addicted to like the 'East-Enders', for instance. Another could claim to be fasting from attending parties. While it is conceded that fasting involves self-denial in so many respects, due caution must be observed, because we have only to widen the meaning enough and the cutting edge is gone.

It is further acknowledged that there are many things besides food that may hinder true communication with God; however, the fact cannot be contested that fasting simply means an act of voluntary abstention from food for spiritual purposes.

We can draw example from our Lord Jesus Christ.

The Bible says, *"He fasted forty days and forty nights and afterward He was hungry" (Matthew 4:2).*

We shall see that there were three main forms that fasting took in Bible times, but each involved literal abstinence. If at times the word may be widened to include other forms of self-denial, this does not alter the fact of its basic meaning.

Another crucial area of misconception often associated with fasting is in respect of its very purposes or objectives. In some quarters, fasting is regarded as a last resort in times of great crisis. The implication of such notion is that fasting outside times of crisis is both unbiblical and unprofitable. Such believes as these, are particularly erroneous and manifestly dangerous.

Fasting is as important a Christian discipline as prayer! Just as it could not be said that Christian should resort to prayer only in times of great crisis, reserving fasting observance for challenging times only is, in all ramifications, wrong and misleading.

"WHEN YE FAST…"

In the teaching of Jesus, there is an apparent assumption that Christians would fast as indicated by the phrase, "'when' you fast"… in Matthew 6:16. We can arrive at a logical conclusion that the fact that Jesus chose such a phrase and not the opposite – "'If' you fast", indicates that the discipline of fasting has not been left at the discretion of the believer, perhaps, because of its incredible benefits. Fasting is no doubt, the duty of today's believer.

In His response to the seeming accusation levied by the Pharisees against His disciples' refusal to fast - an apparent violation of the Jewish custom - Jesus referred to a time when, after the departure of the Bridegroom (referring to the post - ascension era), the disciples would see fasting as a divine obligation placed on them. Said Jesus:

> *And Jesus said to them, Can the children of the bridal chamber fast, while the bridegroom is with them? as long as they have the bridegroom with them, they cannot fast. But the days will come, when the bridegroom shall be taken away from them, and* **then shall they fast in those days** (Mark 2: 19, 20 emphasis added).

Accordingly, after the Lord's death, his disciples frequently fasted as of necessity, and went through much deprivation and trial. In essence, this prophetic word, as it were, has found fulfilment in the lives of His 'immediate disciples'; and should be also for the His present day 'disciples', until He returns to take to Himself His Bride, when there will be a glad and everlasting feasting.

Fasting is to be a natural outcome of discipleship. We are to fast for the same reason we pray. This does not, by any means, indicate that we are to fast every time we pray.

Jesus addressed fasting in association with both prayer and almsgiving. Jesus declared "when you give alms" (Matthew 6:2), "when you pray"(Matthew 6:6), and "when you fast" (Matthew 6:16). The logical conclusions from these texts are: though, the Bible is silent as to how often we should fast, Jesus intends fasting to be undertaken by the believer as a discipline. Just as Jesus expects us to pray and give alms, He expects us to fast.

In addition, in the Sermon on the Mount, when Jesus spoke about prayer and fasting, He used similar language in addressing both subjects. The main difference, however, is that in relation to prayer; he included a structure of prayer we often refer to as 'the Lord's Prayer'. For the purpose of those who know little or nothing about fasting, but so much about prayer, it may be ideal to highlight some parallels between both disciplines.

Similarities between Prayer and Fasting

Just as we engage in prayers, both privately (individual) (1 Chronicles 4:9, 10; 1Sam.1:11), and corporately (11 Chronicles 20:5-13; Acts 13:1-13), fasting can be embarked upon the same way. A good example of individual fast is seen in the life of Paul in Acts 9:9,

"For three days he… neither did eat nor drink"–
Acts 9:9

As indicated, Moses (Exodus 24:18 & 34:28), Elijah (1 Kings 19:8), and the Lord Jesus Christ (Luke 4:4), all observed what could be tagged 'individual fasts.'

We have example of collective fast in I Samuel 7:6:

When they had assembled at Mizpah, they drew water and poured it out before the LORD. On that day they fasted and there they confessed, We have sinned against the LORD.

Further, there are different kinds of prayer, such as prayer of petition, intercession, prayer of thanksgiving, binding and loosing, prayer of Biblical praise, consecration and dedication; just as there are various kinds of fasting, such as the normal fast, the absolute fast and the partial fast, which would be examined in detail in this book.

THE WONDERS OF FASTING

2

PROCLAIMED OR PUBLIC AND PERSONAL FAST

There are, broadly speaking, two categories of fasting – proclaimed or public fast (Joel 1:14) and personal fast – as Jesus described in Matthew 6:1-18.

THE PROCLAIMED

On a fast day…you shall read the words of the Lord – Jeremiah 36:6

Sanctify a fast; call a solemn assembly… Joel 2:15

Usually, fasting is undertaken occasionally as the believer deems it necessary as a matter between him and God. Public fast is an exception of this notion. Sometimes situations arise in which a church, a group of people or, a nation needs God's divine direction or intervention and, as a result, resort to fasting. This is a proclaimed fast.

> **Usually, fasting is undertaken occasionally as the believer deems it necessary as a matter between him and God.**

Proclaimed and Regular Fast

There is generally a connection between public and regular fasts in that, almost all the regular fasts of the Bible were also public fasts, but not all the public fasts were necessarily, regular.

Regular fasts were those prescribed by God to be observed at specific times of the year. A good example is the Day of Atonement, prescribed by the Mosaic Law. On this day, God required the Israelites to afflict their souls (Lev. 23:27, Psalm 35:13).

In addition to "a fast day" (Jeremiah 36:6), associated with the Day of Atonement, the book of Zechariah contains four other regular fast days:

Thus saith the LORD of hosts; The fast of the fourth month, and the fast of the fifth, and the fast of the seventh, and the fast of the tenth, shall be to the house of Judah joy and gladness, and cheerful feasts; therefore love the truth and peace (Zechariah 8:19).

We have an indication of the observance of the regular fast (Day of Atonement) in the New Testament.

Now when much time was spent, and when sailing was now dangerous, because the fast was now already past, Paul admonished them… (Acts 27: 9).

This was no doubt, in reference to the Day of Atonement. And during the earthly ministry of Jesus, the Pharisees made an empty religious ritual out of this practice as typified by the story of Jesus in Luke 18:11, 12:

The Pharisee stood and prayed thus with himself, God, I thank thee, that I am not as other men are, extortioners, unjust, adulterers, or even as this publican. I fast twice in the week, I give tithes of all that I possess.

Notice Jesus' teaching in verse 9:

Also He spoke this parable to some who trusted in themselves that they were righteous, and despised others.

This is a clear example of religious egotism; the Pharisees were known to despise others, even with their fasts. Fasting was used by the Pharisees at this period of time, as an instrument of oppression against the poor, the needy, and the meek. They despised the very people they ought to be caring for in their seasons of fast (Isaiah 58:7). This was a prototype of the manner and spirit with which the Pharisees held regular fasts in the days of Jesus.

Despite these contemptuous practices by the Pharisees in relation to fasting, there was a revisiting of the practice of collective regular fasting in the second and third centuries. It was widely believed that regular fast was revived among the early Methodists by John Wesley. As a requirement for ordaining Priests in the Methodist Church, prospective candidates were required to fast regularly Wednesdays and Fridays till 4.00 pm.

Arthur Wallis, however, remarks that while caution needs to be taken not to allow regular fasting to become religious rituals, devoid of its spiritual intent, the practice should not be abandoned altogether. "It needs to be stressed", he continues, "that fasting, whether regular or occasional, is a matter between individual and God. Making it a requirement may lead to the same bondage in which the Pharisees were ensnared."

The paramount purpose of a regular fasting is to provide a regular opportunity for spiritual examination and orientation. It is like a spiritual medicine for the soul and body.

Generally, a proclaimed fast is for the purpose of bringing believers together for a special session of collective fasting and prayer. Proclaimed fast operates on the principle of spiritual agreement as taught by Jesus in Matthew 18:18:

> *Again I say unto you, That if two of you shall agree on earth as touching anything that they shall ask, it shall be done for them of my Father which is in heaven.*

However, greater power is released in fasting combined with prayer than in prayer alone. Proclaimed fast offers the believers the opportunity to move in the same direction of faith in one accord. A wonderful, practical example of a proclaimed fast is found in 2 Chronicles 20:1-6.

> *It came to pass after this also, that the children of Moab, and the children of Ammon, and with them other beside the Ammonites, came against Jehoshaphat to battle. Then there came some that told Jehoshaphat, saying, There cometh a great multitude against thee from beyond the sea on this*

side Syria; and, behold, they be in Hazazontamar, which is Engedi. And Jehoshaphat feared, and set himself to seek the Lord, and proclaimed a fast throughout all Judah. And Judah gathered themselves together, to ask help of the Lord: even out of all the cities of Judah they came to seek the Lord. And Jehoshaphat stood in the congregation of Judah and Jerusalem, in the house of the Lord, before the new court, And said, O Lord God of our fathers, art not thou God in heaven? and rulest not thou over all the kingdoms of the heathen? and in thine hand is there not power and might, so that none is able to withstand thee?

A fasting saint is saying to God, 'I have no might of my own, my eyes are upon you'. God takes this level of trust very seriously.

During the reign of King Jehoshaphat, King of Judah, enemies from neighbouring nations invaded Judah. As stated, the Bible says *"Jehoshaphat feared and set himself to seek the Lord, and proclaimed a fast throughout Judah."*

This incident brought the people of Judah together to seek help of the Lord through prayer and fasting. Jehoshaphat prayed, relying on the covenant of protection and deliverance God had given to

Abraham and his descendants. King Jehoshaphat's prayer as recorded in verse 12 is noteworthy:

> O our God, wilt thou not judge them? **for we have no might against this great company that cometh against us**; neither know we what to do: **but our eyes are upon thee** (emphasis added).

In this scripture, we have what drove King Jehoshaphat into fasting: *"no might against this great company that cometh against us…"* Judah was invaded by enemies too great for Jehoshaphat and his people to combat militarily; so they resolved to fight the battle using spiritual weapons – prayer and fasting. The nation of Judah expressed total dependence on God in the midst of this great battle. Said they, "…our eyes are upon you." A fasting saint is saying to God, 'I have no might of my own, my eyes are upon you'. God takes this degree of trust very seriously.

There are definitely valuable lessons to be learnt in the nation's reaction to this imminent threat. Jesus was very succinct when He said that certain situations could not be dealt with otherwise, but with prayer and fasting:

> *Howbeit this kind goeth not out but by prayer and fasting* (Mathew 17:21).

And the Bible says:

He will keep the feet of his saints, and the wicked shall be silent in darkness; **for by strength shall no man prevail**" (1 Samuel 2:9, emphasis added).

Another translation puts it very beautifully thus:

He guards the steps of his faithful ones, while the wicked are made silent in darkness. He grants the request of the one who prays. He blesses the year of the righteous. Indeed it is not by strength that a person prevails (1 Samuel 2:9 International Standard Version).

While these believers were all in agreement, praying and fasting, the Bible records, "Then upon Jahaziel the son of Zechariah, the son of Benaiah, the son of Jeiel, the son of Mattaniah, a Levite of the sons of Asaph, came the Spirit of the LORD in the midst of the congregation…" (verse 14). This is the tremendous power of a proclaimed fast. The spirit of God did not come upon Jehoshaphat – the leader, but on another person in the congregation – how beautiful!

"And he said, Hearken ye, all Judah, and ye inhabitants of Jerusalem, and thou king Jehoshaphat, Thus saith the LORD unto you, Be

not afraid nor dismayed by reason of this great multitude; for the battle is not yours, but God's" (verse 15).

You can imagine how good that sounded to them. The Holy Ghost spoke to them! This was the very purpose of their meeting. The effectiveness of a proclaimed fast rests on the unity and singleness of purpose it creates.

Kenneth Copeland observes that:

"The main reason that a proclaimed fast brings results is that it causes the people's minds [undertaking the fast] to go in the same direction. That direction is toward God. They drop other things and centre their attention on Him. This brings the manifested presence in their midst."

According to Pius Quensnel, "God is found in union and agreement. Nothing is more efficacious that this in prayer."

Ezra likewise exhorted the Jews to conduct a public (proclaimed) fast before their journey back to Jerusalem, with the precious things for the temple. They were returning from their 70 years Babylonian captivity to rebuild the temple (Ezra 8. 21-22); the result? "So we fasted and besought our God for this: and he was intreated of us" (verse 23).

Esther also proclaimed a fast among the Jews in order to avert an imminent danger- total annihilation of the Jewish race being orchestrated by Haman- the Prime Minister of the Land. Esther gave the following instructions:

> *Go, gather together all the Jews that are present in Shushan, and fast ye for me, and neither eat nor drink three days, night or day: I also and my maidens will fast likewise; and so will I go in unto the king, which is not according to the law: and if I perish, I perish* (Esther 4:16)

After this fast, God did not only turn the situation that warranted the fasting around, the king ordered Haman to be hanged *"on the gallows that he had prepared for Mordecai"* (Esther 7:10)

The New Testament example is found in Acts 13:1-2:

> *Now there were in the church that was at Antioch certain prophets and teachers; as Barnabas, and Simeon that was called Niger, and Lucius of Cyrene, and Manaen, which had been brought up with Herod the tetrarch, and Saul. As they ministered to the Lord, and fasted, the Holy Ghost said, Separate me Barnabas and Saul for the work whereunto I have called them. And when they had fasted and*

prayed, and laid their hands on them, they sent them away.

> After this fast, God did not only turn the situation that warranted the fast around, the king ordered Haman to be hanged "on the gallows that he had prepared for Mordecai.

The Holy Ghost spoke in the midst of ordinary men, as they were fasting and ministering to the Lord. This set in motion a great move of God that literally changed the world. "That assignment brought into being two-third of the New Testament…" Kenneth Copeland observed. As instructed, they laid their hands on Saul and Barnabas and sent them forth. The result of their exploits was overwhelming.

Proclaimed fast, as in any well observed fast, requires a great deal of planning and structuring. The following guidelines are offered:

Guidelines for a proclaimed fast

For a proclaimed fast to be effective and achieve its desired purpose, it needs to be well planned, structured and executed. It is not enough to require a group of people or a church to observe a fast for, just the sake of it, without establishing a structure that ensures that all the participants understand what is required of them at any given time, such as the prayer points for each day or prayer section, times of meetings for prayer, venue for prayer, and if it is not an absolute fast, what type of fluids are allowed to be taken.

After this fast, God did not only turn the situation that warranted the fast around, the king ordered Haman to be hanged "on the gallows that he had prepared for Mordecai."

---

1. Explain to all participants the objective(s) of the fast. Make sure everyone understands and is in agreement of such objective(s). A proclaimed fast is valuable and effective only to the degree to which the participants are in agreement about its objectives. We saw a glaring example of this earlier in the case of Jehoshaphat and the nation of Judah (2 Chronicles 20). We saw a firm demonstration of unity at every level: unity of purpose, unity of vision, and indeed, a sense of national solidarity in the way the proclaimed fast was conducted.

2. Make sure everyone in the group is willing to fast. In order words, the fast is not a harsh religious requirement. Note that people with certain illness,

and pregnant women should not, as a matter of caution, fast. Please let this be known ahead of time. Fasting should never be forced on people – it is a matter of choice between individuals and God.

3. If you are leading people to undertake this fast, it is always a good idea to spend time teaching on such topics as the meaning of fasting, God's purpose and power of fasting, well ahead of time. You will be amazed the number of the people in the group that may have been fasting, but do not know reasons why believers are called into the discipline. Teach, for instance, Isaiah 58 and encourage participants to spend valuable time in fellowship with God through-out the duration of the fast. Remember, it is possible to do the right thing wrongly.

4. Explain some unpleasant reactions they could experience in the course of the fast: dizziness, weakness, headaches etc. Do not let the participants experience these unpleasant reactions, not having been told about them ahead of time, and taught how to deal with them in a fast. Otherwise, this could be the basis for which the Devil could tempt the believer to violate his fast. (See chapter three on this).

5. If at all possible, ask all the participants to assemble both mornings and evenings for corporate prayers. In my church, when we declare fasting sessions, meeting early in the mornings to pray is very easy as we use a programme that is already in place which runs between 6.00 am and 7.00 am, Mondays – Fridays for this purpose. If meeting in the mornings is not possible, please emphasise the need to congregate to pray in the evenings. Remember, fasting without prayer is an exercise in futility.

6. Explain the different types of fasts there are: absolute, normal and partial fast; and inform the group what type of fast is being undertaken at any given time.

7. If the fast goes beyond 72 hours, do remember to stress the need for the people undertaking the fast to take as much fluid as possible – i.e. if the fast being observed is not absolute one.

8. Create an atmosphere of faith throughout the period of fasting. Remember that fasting is a weapon of warfare "mighty through God to the pulling down of strongholds" (2 Cor. 10:4).

9. Teach the participants how to break a fast successfully, especially a fast that goes beyond

three days. Emphasise the danger of breaking a fast wrongly.

10. Expose participants to good books on fasting. This has the advantage of helping them learn more about the subject while engaging in the act.

THE WONDERS OF FASTING

3

PERSONAL FAST

The other type of fast is the personal one. The general purpose of this type of fast is self-affliction and repentance. It may be observed in times of personal or communal calamity in order to seek God's divine intervention or, more commonly, as penitence for personal wrongdoing. It could also be resorted to as a means of establishing a fasted-life i.e. taking on fasting as a way of life.

Sometimes, fasting is viewed as an attempt to twist God's arm or to win His approval. But God does not respond to pressure.

It must be stressed, however, that you do not fast to impress God. Fasting changes you, not God. Sometimes, fasting is viewed as an attempt to twist God's arm or to win His approval. But God does not respond to pressure.

One group of people in the book of Acts tried to get God on their side by manipulative fasting:

In the morning some of the Jews made a plan to kill Paul, and they took an oath not to eat or drink anything until they had killed him. They went to the leading priests and the older Jewish leaders and said, 'We have taken an oath not to eat or drink until we have killed Paul (Acts 23:12,14).

But God did not hear their prayer and their plan did not work. In essence, they fasted in vain.

Using fasting in a manipulative way was done by the people in Jeremiah's day too. God said,

Although they fast, I will not listen to their cry; though they offer burn offerings and grain offering, I will not accept them. I will destroy them with the sword, famine, and plague (Jeremiah 14:12).

Edith Schaeffer was emphatic when she said:

"Is fasting ever a bribe to get God to pay more attention to the petitions? No, a thousand times no. It is simply a way to make clear that we sufficiently reverence the amazing opportunity to ask help from the everlasting God, the Creator of the universe, to choose to put everything else aside and concentrate on worshiping, asking forgiveness, and making our requests known-considering His help more important than anything we could do ourselves in our own strength and with our own ideas."

Generally, personal fast is done in secret; a matter between the individual and God. However, this rule might be very difficult to observe in a household setting, where, for example, a wife is undertaking a fast but the husband is not.

In the first place, arrangements need to be made for the family meals. Secondly, as between husband and wife, where only one of them is fasting, it is perfectly in order to let the other party be aware of your intention to observe a fast, and for what duration well ahead of time, as this could mean an abstention from marital relationship for the duration of the fast (1 Corinthians 7:5).

It is also highly recommended for husband and wife to mutually agree to engage in the act of fasting together towards achieving a common goal; that then becomes a proclaimed fast.

In Matthew 6:16-18, in the Sermon on the Mount, Jesus devoted a great deal of time teaching on how to engage on a personal fast:

Moreover when ye fast, be not, as the hypocrites, of a sad countenance: for they disfigure their faces, that they may appear unto men to fast. Verily I say unto you, They have their reward. But thou, when thou fastest, anoint thine head, and wash thy face; That thou appear not unto men to fast, but unto thy Father which is in secret: and thy Father, which seeth in secret, shall reward thee openly.

There are valuable lessons to be learnt from this scripture:

1.   It is to be noted again that Jesus did not say 'if you fast' but "when you fast"; which places a responsibility on the believer to fast.

2.   Jesus warned against using fasting as a hypocritical religious exercise. During the Lord's earthly ministry, fasting had become a very important part of the Jewish life; albeit an empty religious rite. Jesus condemned the "look-at-how-spiritual-I-am" attitude associated with fasting, as depicted by the attitude and motive of the Pharisee spoken of by Jesus in Luke 18: 10 – 14.

Let us now examine the story in some depths.

Two men went up into the temple to pray; the one a Pharisee, and the other a publican. The Pharisee stood and prayed thus with himself, God, I thank thee, that I am not as other men are, extortioners, unjust, adulterers, or even as this publican. I fast twice in the week, I give tithes of all that I possess. And the publican, standing afar off, would not lift up so much as his eyes unto heaven, but smote upon his breast, saying, God be merciful to me a sinner. I tell you, this man went down to his house justified rather than the other: for every one that exalteth himself shall be abased; and he that humbleth himself shall be exalted.

Hypocritical piety will always defeat the purpose and power of a fast. If you publicise your spirituality in order to gain the praise of men, you would have succeeded in exchanging the reward of God for the praise of men.

The verdict of Jesus on fasting conducted with the wrong motive is swift and well delivered: *"…verily I say unto you, They have their reward."* Matthew 6: 16. *"But thou"*, continues Jesus, *"when thou fastest, anoint thine head, and wash thy face;* **That thou appear not unto men to fast,** *but unto thy Father which is in secret: and thy Father, which seeth in secret, shall reward thee openly"* (emphasis added).

3. Jesus spoke of rewards for fasting. Rewards for personal fasting are on two different levels: You have rewards from the admiration of men, as described above, and an open reward that comes from God when you fast in secret. Believe God for

this reward as you go into a fast. Focusing on the reward lessens the pressure fasting has on you. This makes fasting easy. (This subject is dealt with in greater details in chapter 5).

Guidelines for personal fast

Make sure you are medically able to fast before attempting it. According to St John Chrysostom,

"If you cannot go without eating all day because of an ailment of the body, beloved one, no logical man will be able to criticise you for that. Besides, we have a Lord who is meek and loving (philanthropic) and who does not ask for anything beyond our power. Because he neither requires the abstinence from foods, neither that the fast take place for the simple sake of fasting, neither is its aim that we remain with empty stomachs, but that we fast to offer our entire selves to the dedication of spiritual things, having distanced ourselves from secular things... because human nature is indifferent and gives itself over mostly to comforts and gratifications, for this reason the philanthropic Lord, like a loving and caring father, devised the therapy of the fast for us, so that our gratifications would be completely stopped and that our worldly cares be transferred to spiritual works..."

Some people I know can only do a one-day partial fast. They drink different types of juice, but take no food. God knows and understands their medical condition and does not expect them to harm their "temple" (1 Corinthians 6:19) in order to be spiritual.

Prepare your heart, mind and body for fasting. Fasting is not a spur of the moment practice. It needs to be planned, unless on very rare occasions that God instructs the believer to fast as a matter of urgency. Every great endeavour starts with good preparation. Preparation is critical; ask great achievers! See what the Bible says about the value of preparation: *"So Jotham became mighty, because he prepared his ways before the Lord his God"* (2 Chronicles 27:6). As a matter of fact, fasting must be declared – the beginning and duration of any particular fast - must be determined well ahead of time.

Here are some of the things you can do to prepare yourself for personal fast:

1. Begin with short fasts and gradually move to longer periods of fasts if you desire. If you have never fasted before, you need to start gradually. Do not start with a long fast. There is a wealth of wisdom in starting a life of fasting with a moderate approach. The idea behind it is to prepare or

condition the body slowly before moving towards a higher level.

The question I get asked the most by believers and nominal Christians who have heard me teach on this subject is:

How long should I fast for?

As would be seen in our discussion of the "normal fast" (see chapter eight below) fasting, in Bible days, was usually for one day. In addition to the Day of Atonement (Leviticus 23:32), you can see examples of one day fasts in Judges 20:26; 1 Samuel 14:24; 2 Samuel 1:12; and 2 Samuel 3:35. The Jewish day was counted from sunset to sunset, so this meant that the fast would be broken (that is, food could be eaten) after sundown. However, some fasts were longer. The fast of Esther continued 3 days, both day and night. At the burial of Saul the fast was seven days (1 Samuel 31:13) and David also fasted seven days when his child was ill (2 Samuel 12:16-18). The longest fasts we find in the Bible are for forty days: Moses (Deuteronomy 9:9, 18; Exodus 34:28), Elijah (1 Kings 19:8), and Jesus (Matthew 4:2). The biblical principle here is that the length of time you fast is determined by your own desires and the occasion or purpose of the fast. The duration can be that which the individuals or groups feel led to set.

It is been stressed throughout this book that some fasting could be injurious to the body if wisdom is not applied. For instance, unless one is divinely sustained, fasting for more than three days without water is highly dangerous. It is to be discouraged!

Let me quickly add that you do not have to go on a particularly long fast in order to get the attention of God. Neither do long fasts get you more benefits than short ones.

Arthur Blessitt's opinion on the subject can be of tremendous assistance to the believer:

"In my personal life, fasting has been for specific purpose and for a long duration. After three days, there are no hunger pains or desire for food. From twelve to fourteen days later, there seems to be a sense of cleanliness and mental clarity. After twenty-one days, there seems to be an outpouring of spiritual power and creativity that is indescribable, but continues until the fast is ended. It seems especially after the third week that one is no longer even remotely interested in the trivial physical world around. One's mind is filled exclusively with profound spiritual ideas and truths. One of the most profound things is that the mind will concentrate for hours on the same subject without once wavering or being distracted. There is no question that there is awesome power in fasting. If the fast is controlled by the Holy Spirit and Jesus is foremost, then it is a beautiful and powerful experience."

It is very common for people to experience significant improvement in their health from fasting between 3 and 30 days. The idea is to fast as briefly as possible, but as long as is necessary to allow the body to restore health.

Of course, if you are to derive maximum health benefits from your fasting, you must drink good amount of water, in order to get rid of toxins.

I often encourage those just beginning the act of fasting to start with very short fasts, for instance, fast a meal, and get used to that, and gradually move on to a fairly longer fasts, say, a day, three days, before attempting longer fasts. Fasting with water is an added benefit for you. You can also consider some juice fasts. (See further details under the 'Question and Answer' section in chapter twenty-five of this book).

2. Eat smaller meals before starting a fast. Avoid high fat and sugary foods. Eat raw fruit and vegetables for, at least, two days before starting a

fast. Physical preparation makes the drastic change in your eating routine a little easier, so that you can turn your full attention to the Lord in prayer.

3. Do not be put off by negative reactions such as dizziness, headache, or nausea in the early stage of your fast. Most people have never gone without food for longer than a few hours; this causes some negative reactions in the early days of their fasting. Further, nausea and headaches, during a fast can also result from caffeine withdrawal. So, I recommend, if you are a heavy soda or coffee drinker, start withdrawing about a week before the start of your fast. This should make it much easier and less headaches to grapple with. Headaches during early days of fasting are also indication that you have left fasting for too long.

4. Drink sufficient water before the fasting begins. The loss of fluids during the fast takes a toll on the body and creates problems in completing the fast successfully. Of course, if you are to derive maximum health benefits from your fasting, you must drink good amount of water in order to get rid of toxins.

The use of natural diuretics (substance that reduces the body's water volume by increasing the kidneys' urine production and output) helps in losing the excess fluids, which in turn helps in losing body weight. Ginger has been found to be very useful for this purpose. Thus, using the natural diuretics forms one of the important tips to lose weight fast.

5. Take adequate rest before and during a fast. The smaller the responsibilities and work pressure you are involved in during a fast, the better for the successful completion of the fast. This also helps you to be focused on the assignment at hand.

6. Read good books on fasting, especially those that contain testimonies of people that have had amazing breakthroughs through fasting. I particularly find this very helpful when I am fasting. Study scriptures on fasting; major on God's miraculous intervention through fasting.

7. Meditate, go for a walk, take lots of naps, journal, and listen to music, take long, warm bathes and relax, above all, be sensitive to the Spirit of God.

8. Enter into a fast with a positive faith, expecting God to reward you. Jesus promised, "… thy Father, which seeth in secret, shall reward thee openly" (Matthew 6:18).

9. Avoid distractions at all cost. Disconnect from television, radio, newspapers and the Internet,

for the duration of your fast. This will help you stay focused on the Lord, His word, and the object of your fast.

10. Take a retreat. Though fasting is not necessarily a 'holiday', in the true sense of the word, experience has, nonetheless, shown that if maximum benefits are to be derived from any period of fasting, time needs to be taken away from people and the daily routine that have dominated our entire life, to spend time in quietness and stillness with the lord; gazing at His love, might, glory, beauty and power.

11. Some people experience vast mood swings during a fast. One moment they are totally focused on God and the next they are wallowing in pity. Knowing that this is likely to happen will help you react properly. Learning to refocus on God and His goodness during this tough emotional time will help when your fast is over and you experience similar emotions. Most of us use food to stay alive physically, but also eat to cover up frustration, anger, stress and other negative emotions. So when we stop feeding the body, the suppressing factor of food is eliminated from the equation and many hidden feelings can often surface that you were not fully aware of. But it may not be limited to anger. You may also feel a lot of sadness, fear and even

sorrow. The solution is learning to always refocus on God. You must also rely on the Holy Spirit to strengthen you at this crucial time. Generally, these could be signs of the enemy's revenge. Stand your ground, be resolute, and continue with your fast. Note that the devil would do everything possible to cause you to give up as he feels uncomfortable with your fast.

12.   Fasting is a time to study God's Word, meditate and pray. To achieve this, have a structured plan for prayer and Bible study. Spend quality time talking to God and allow Him to reveal Himself to you in His Word.

13.   Break a prolonged fast gradually with meals that are light and easy to digest, preferably, raw vegetables, fruit, or some soup. Trying to eat too much following a fast will only make you sick and leave you with an unpleasant memory of fasting.

4

GOD'S PURPOSE FOR FASTING

Fasting should always have a special object in view. No one should fast just for fasting sake. Every true fast is purpose – driven.

David Livingstone said,

"Fastings and vigils without a special object in view are time run to waste. They are made to minister to a sort of self-gratification instead of being turned to good account."

Fasting is not to be some religious ritual we go through. When we fast, we should have a specific purpose in view, a reason for it, something we want to accomplish as a result of our fast. It can be for something very simple as well as something complex and desperate. So, why fast? Why should a person set apart a specific time where he denies himself the basic necessities of life, for the purpose of seeking God? Let us examine some specific purposes of fasting.

Specific Godly reasons for fasting

Fasting, as in every Christian discipline, is meant to be purpose-driven, as said. It is said that if we aim at nothing, we achieve nothing! Our objectives need to be well defined as we take up a fast.

In times of physical or spiritual needs Christians realise their inadequacy and in humility and repentance look to the Lord.

Since fasts in the Old Testament were in response to calamities and were to demonstrate humility and repentance, it would seem that the same purpose and attitudes would hold true for New Testament believers. Jesus hinted that this should be the purpose for fasting among His disciples. His disciples would fast after the bridegroom was taken away (Matt. 9:14-15; Mark 2:18-20; Luke 5:33-35). The removal of the bridegroom from his bride would normally be looked on as a tragedy that would evoke a felt need. In times of tragedy and heartache, Jesus' disciples would fast. Fasting then is a legitimate response to dangers, trials, heartaches, or sorrows. In times of physical or spiritual needs, the believer realises his inadequacy, and in humility and repentance looks up to the Lord.

Fasting As a Means of Self-Humbling

However, it would be wrong to limit the purpose of fasting to just a means to averting crisis. For instance, David sees fasting as a means of self-humbling. He says "I humble myself soul with fasting" (Psalm 35:13). Humility is not a transcendent experience, or a vague emotional experience. Humility is a way of life that becomes part of our 'being' as we make conscious, determined effort to incorporate it as part of the qualities that define us. We must bear in mind that God will not humble us, because He has given us the responsibility to work out humility for ourselves. David, in the scripture just quoted, has shown us the 'way to achieving humility'. The Bible is replete with the Lord's teachings on the value of humility. It is an established principle of God that whoever goes the way of humility receives the master's lifting or promotion.

Humble yourselves, therefore, under God's mighty hand, that he may lift you up in due time (1 Peter 5:6).

And in Matthew 23: 12, the Bible says,

And whoever shall exalt himself shall be abased; and he that shall humble himself shall be exalted.

From these two Bible passages, it is very safe to conclude that in life, the 'way up' is 'down'. The choice, therefore, is whether to be exalted or abased.

It was the choice of John the Baptist to humble himself before the Master.

He must increase, but I must decrease (John 3:30)

John was saying in essence, 'This is the assigned moment for the Master to take the centre stage, while I slip off to the side-line'.

However, it would be wrong to limit the purpose of fasting to just a means to averting crisis.

Since John's mission was to go before Jesus and prepare the way for Him (Mark 1:2-3), the time came when John needed to fade into the background of the Bible account and allow Jesus His place. It is with considerable grace and humility that John says, *"He must increase, but I must decrease" (John 3:30)*. What can we learn from this statement? In another instance he said, *"I indeed baptize you with water unto repentance, but He who is coming after me is mightier than I, whose sandals I am not worthy to carry. He will baptize you with the Holy Spirit and fire"(Matt 3:11)*. John had no pretensions of greater glory than the coming Christ. The Pharisees sent a list of questions to John—whether he was the prophet, or the Christ, or Elijah resurrected—and John never rashly agreed to any inaccurate designation (John 1:19-26). John knew who He was—and that he was inferior to Jesus—and that did not bother him. Instead, *"He must increase, but I must decrease"* reflects a mind-set of complete humility in the face of one greater.

John shows us that passing the torch is natural—yet still requires humility. "He must increase, but I must decrease" is the thought of each passing generation of God's leaders who are looking to the future of Christ's cause. It was the thought of Moses preparing Joshua, and David preparing Solomon, and Paul preparing Timothy and Titus. Yet we should never think that the need for a new generation to take the reins of leadership in God's work means that relinquishing those reins is easy for a generation accustomed to them! We desperately need the humility to say that we are not as important as the fate of a local church, or the development of leaders in worship and preaching, or the confidence of young believers. Let us promote and encourage them; acknowledging that they must increase, and we must decrease.

John reminds us that God's word is more important than any one person. Surely his followers warned him to be quiet about Herod's adulterous marriage (Matt 14:4) so that he could stay out of trouble and keep preaching—yet the word of God was more important than what happened to John. Further, consider what might have happened had John not stepped aside for Jesus—a power struggle, competing teachers and disciples, and a prevention of many disciples from coming to Jesus. Yet John conceding to Him enabled Jesus to say,

> *"Assuredly, I say to you, among those born of women there has not risen one greater than John the Baptist..."* (Matt 11:11).

Why? Because God gives us more grace when we humble ourselves before Him. The Scripture says: "God opposes the proud but gives grace to the humble." We may advance the gospel, or detract from its advancement —yet it remains far bigger than we are, individually! We must guard against an inflated sense of self in spiritual matters! "He must increase, but I must decrease" is a distillation of a humble heart. Are we pursuing this humility?

Another motive for fasting is to mourn sin, i.e. in repentance and confession: Examples of these are found in Deuteronomy 9:18; 1 Samuel 7:6; 1 Kings

21:27; Ezra 10:6; Jonah 3:5; and Acts 9:3-9. In the Old Testament, when people wished to demonstrate that they were serious about repenting from their sin, they fasted. Our willingness to sacrifice shows the depth of our commitment and in this case fasting is a pictorial way of saying to the Lord, "I care more about getting right with You, God, than I do about even my own life." So a good occasion for fasting is when we are truly grieving over our sins.

A further motive for fasting is that it draws us closer to God. God wants us to become one with Him. The Scripture says that if you *"draw near to God... He will draw near to you"* (James 4:8)

Fasting is also an effective tool in dealing with demonic forces. Specifically, Jesus recommends fasting in dealing with satanic forces. He said, *But this kind goes not out but by prayer and fasting* (Matthew 17:21).

Fasting is also instrumental for interceding for those who are sick. There are two examples in Scripture of fasting on behalf of those who are sick: 2 Samuel 12:15-23; Psalm 35:13. Both of these examples come from the life of David. In Psalm 35:13 David says, *"Yet when they were sick, I put on clothes of sadness and showed my sorrow by going without food."* David saw fasting as a means of asking God for physical healing in the lives of other people.

> **Fasting also helps us find God's will. If we expect God to reveal His direction for our lives, we must put Him first.**

A situation of impending danger calls for fasting. There are occasions when death or danger threatens us. We see from the Scripture that it is certainly appropriate to employ fasting as a means of receiving God's protection during these times. When Ezra was carrying a large consignment of gold and silver to the temple in Jerusalem along a route infested with bandits, he records: *"I proclaimed a fast...that we might humble ourselves before our God, to seek from him a straight way for ourselves, our children, and all our goods" (Ezra 8:21,23,31)*. Other examples of fasting for protection are found in Jeremiah 36:9 and Esther 4:3.

Fasting also helps us find God's will. If we expect God to reveal His direction for our lives, we must put Him first. Often this means putting aside the fulfilment of our physical appetites, so that we can focus our attention on Him. We find an example of fasting for direction in 2 Chronicles 20:1-30. Three nations were coming against Judah to destroy them.

King Jehoshaphat, the king of Judah, proclaimed a fast for the whole nation and they asked the Lord what they should do. God heard their prayer and their fast and gave the people prophetic direction through one of the choir members! God told them what to do.

Acts 13:2 is another example of direction being given by God during a fast. Here we find the leaders of the church of Antioch worshipping and fasting. The Holy Spirit used this occasion to tell the church leaders to choose Paul and Barnabas from among their group and send them out to spread the gospel among the Gentiles. So fasting is one of the ways we seek God's guidance and direction in our lives.

Fasting appears to have been a regular part of the ordination of church leaders and missionaries. We have already looked at Acts 13, the calling of Paul and Barnabas for missionary service. Verse 3 tells us that after they received this direction from the Lord, the apostles ordained Barnabas and Paul for missionary service by prayer, fasting and laying their hands upon them.

We find the same thing later on in the same book of Acts — Paul and Barnabas - fasted prior to the selection of the first elders for the new churches they planted (Acts 14:23). It would appear that fasting in these cases is a way of seriously seeking God's blessing, anointing, and power upon the leaders of the church.

Fasting is also ideal when we want to intercede on behalf of others, especially when believing God for the salvation of others.

All the above issues in relation to the purpose of fasting are dealt with more comprehensively in later chapters.

Prophet Isaiah's Discourse on fasting

Isaiah 58 outlines the pattern of the fast that is acceptable to God, its purposes or objectives (what it is designed to accomplish).

Prophet Isaiah takes us on an exhilarating analytical journey on the subject of fasting on several fronts. In the 58th Chapter of his book, Isaiah offers a comprehensive discourse on key issues associated with fasting. In the first instance, he gives a detailed analysis of God's purpose for fasting. According to Prophet Isaiah, God is to be the centre figure of our fasts; otherwise, the whole exercise is futile. Second, he spells out the motives that could defeat the purpose of fasting. And of course, he examines the fast that is acceptable to God.

God's ordained purpose for fasting

Our immediate focus, as the heading suggests, is to consider God's ordained purpose for fasting according to prophet Isaiah. In verses 6-7 of the chapter under consideration, after condemning the wrong approach the people of his days had had towards fasting, he went ahead and spelt out God's purpose for fasting. He says,

> *Is not this the fast that I have chosen? to loose the bands of wickedness, to undo the heavy burdens, and to let the oppressed go free, and that ye break every yoke? Is it not to deal thy bread to the hungry, and that thou bring the poor that are cast out to thy house? when thou seest the naked, that thou cover him; and that thou hide not thyself from thine own flesh?*

The primary purpose of fasting, according to the above text, is to gain spiritual empowerment – the anointing - to break every yoke. We hear so much today of "The anointing breaks the yoke" (Isaiah 10:27):

> *And it shall come to pass in that day that his burden shall be taken away from off thy shoulder and his yoke from off thy neck, and the yoke shall be destroyed because of the anointing.*

This has become one of many Pentecostal clichés. This extra anointing is presented to be greater than the baptism of the Holy Spirit; it is able to break all the bondages, everything that hinders one's success in life.

Jesus, after He was baptised in water, was led by the Spirit into the wilderness, there He fasted forty days and nights. What happened thereafter was outstanding! Phenomenal and Inspirational! The Bible says He returned in the power of the Holy Spirit into Nazareth and exploded!

> *And Jesus being full of the Holy Spirit returned from the Jordan, and was led by the Spirit into the wilderness…And Jesus returned in the power of the Spirit into Galilee: and there went out a fame of him through all the region round about* (Luke 14:2,14).

According to Bishop David Oyedepo, fasting is to

"enhance your strength, so you can loose the bands of wickedness, undo the heavy burdens and break every yoke. This is God's kind of fast… When you engage in this God-ordained fast, you build yourself up spiritually to a point where Satan steers clear of you and issues that concern you…when you fast, you are creating an atmosphere for your spirit-man to grow. If you therefore, must stay in power, fasting must be a part of your life…"

God uncovered the self-seeking and the self-pleasing motives which underscored their show of religious piety by the people of Isaiah's days. They had accused God of not responding to their fasts. God addressed their self-indulgence by their abuse of employees and even fighting. As long as the people's attitude remained this way, God regarded their fasting as an abomination. God gave Israel conditional requirements to be set free or He would not respond to them.

The first thing to be done for their fasting to be acceptable to God was to let the oppressed go free. The idea is that they were to unbind their fellowmen, they were to break the bonds of slavery (yokes) they had on others, not on themselves. God was prepared to reward their sacrifice, only on the condition that they had a change of heart.

THE WONDERS OF FASTING

Part Two

Fasting and the present day Church

THE WONDERS OF FASTING

5

IS FASTING FOR THE PRESENT DAY CHURCH?

The Bible regards fasting as a normal part of Christian living, and Church history indicates that the Church practised regular fasting for several centuries after the Ascension of Jesus. Fasting is as vital to the believer today as in the Bible days. It occupies the same spiritual position in the believer's life as prayer and giving.

Since the time of Moses, the Israelites had been required to fast annually on the Day of Atonement (Leviticus16:29; 23:29). The Old Testament also speaks favourably of other special fast days in which the entire nation humbled themselves before God (1 Sam. 7:5-6; Jer. 14:12). In fact, at least once, God even commanded an emergency fast (Joel 2:12).

By New Testament times, fasting had been encumbered by additional regulations – religious rituals. The Jews fasted two days each week throughout the entire year (Luke 18:12), and required this from everyone. These traditional regulations by the Pharisees defeated the very purpose and objective of fasting, from God's perspective.

As seen, the practice of fasting was revisited and rightly engaged amongst the disciples in the early Church era and throughout the epistles.

Thank God, the torch passed to the great revivalists and bible scholars who shaped Church history, with astonishing exploits for God in their time and generations - all of whom attributed such amazing accomplishments to the tremendous power gained through fasting.

God's 'Generals' and their fasted-lives

Men of the same generation that served God with fervent prayer and fasting, like Anna (Luke 2:37) includes Charles G. Finney, Andrew Murray, and Charles Spurgeon. History had it that when Finney felt devoid of the power of God, he would fast and pray for a day. Spurgeon once announced, "Our seasons of fasting and prayer at the Tabernacle have been high days indeed; never has Heaven's gate stood wider; never have our hearts been nearer the central Glory."

Matthew Henry, for instance – a pastor, scholar, and writer expressed regret that fasting was generally neglected among Christians of his days. He assumed that it was a duty required of believers. He listed four reasons why fasting is important: it secures God's power to assist us; it sharpens prayer; it demonstrates humiliation before God; it controls the body.

Jonathan Edwards - the leader of the Great Awakening in New England had multitude attracted to his meetings in which his sermons were accompanied by fainting and outcries. Many communities were spiritually changed. He fasted three days prior to the revival in which he preached his powerful sermon, "Sinners in the Hands of an Angry God." Often when he arose from praying and entered the pulpit, his countenance reflected God's presence.

John Wesley preached and practiced fasting - each Wednesday and Friday. He later encouraged all Methodists to observe fasting the same days, because he believed that the early church kept these days. He said that if he failed to fast and pray, he quickly lost his spiritual fervour.

To further answer the question whether fasting is for the present day church, we would examine its practice in the New Testament under distinct headings:

Fasting as Practiced and Taught in the Gospels

Anna's fasting (Luke 2:37)

The first mention of fasting in the New Testament is in connection with the presentation of the infant Jesus at the temple (Luke 2:37), in keeping with the Mosaic Law (Exodus 13:2-15; Numbers 18:15-16). Two Godly people, Simeon and Anna, were attracted to the infant. Anna's constant service to God is described as "fastings and prayers."

According to Luke 2:37,

> ... *she was a widow of about fourscore and four years, which departed not from the temple, but served God with fastings and prayers night and day.*

In this instance, fasting is looked on as a special service unto God. There is no indication that she was required to do this. Rather her "fasting and prayers" were prompted by a felt need. Perhaps she was so burdened to see the birth of the Messiah that she spontaneously devoted her entire life to fasting and prayer. To appreciate her tremendous work, you need to recall the great conflicts that preceded the birth of our Lord Jesus Christ; all the fierce battle of the devil to thwart God's programme for the redemption of the human race. Child of God, for every move of God, somebody, somewhere, at a definite point in time, must pay the ultimate price! Anna paid a costly price; and did it gloriously!

Remember, Jesus came through the linage of Abraham. Sarah, Abraham's wife, was barren for a number of years before Isaac, the promised child was born. Then almost like a pattern, or should I say satanic pattern, Isaac married Rebecca, and Rebecca was also barren. It was obvious that the devil wanted to use barrenness to destroy God's redemptive plan for mankind that was rooted in the Lord Jesus.

Then down the line, we read of the most awful, abominable practices engaged in by some of the people of this linage: for instance, Judah (remember the kingdom belonged to Judah), went as far as impregnating his daughter-in-law, Tamar (Gen. 38:18). Then look at the immoral life of David. So the devil used every weapon available to stop the birth of our Lord Jesus Christ.

This was the reason Anna had to withdraw for a good number of years to contend with the forces of darkness before our saviour was born. She could not fight this battle otherwise. But through prayer and fasting she prevailed! God gave her a great burden; the burden of paving a way for the birth of the promised Messiah. The Bible says she never departed from the temple; she took this heaven-ordained assignment with zest, and through her glorious labour the Messiah was born. But where are her 'kinds' in our generation today? Where are her 'types' in our Church today? May God inspire us to offer our utmost for Him.

JESUS AND HIS TEACHINGS ON FASTING

"…*and when ye fast*" – Matthew 6:16

In His teaching – Sermon on the Mount – Jesus stated clearly and without qualification to His audience, "when ye fast…" leaving the believer in no doubt that, when occasion demands it, he is to take up the discipline of fasting.

The Lord's teaching on fasting, no doubt, offers the present day church an explicit theological standard to adhere to in fasting.

Said Jesus:

Moreover when ye fast, be not, as the hypocrites, of a sad countenance: for they disfigure their faces, that they may appear unto men to fast. Verily I say unto you, They have their reward. But thou, when thou fastest, anoint thine head, and wash thy face; That thou appear not unto men to fast, but unto thy Father which is in secret: and thy Father, which seeth in secret, shall reward thee openly (Matt. 6:16-18).39

A detailed analysis of the above scripture presents us with pearls of wisdom that can significantly revolutionise, not just our fasted life, but every facet of our relationship with God.

First as already pointed out, Jesus, in His "… when you fast…" choice of words in preference to "if you fast" seems to make fasting as a necessary and vital condition for a breakthrough living, both physically and spiritually. He implied by His choice of words that all who truly believe in Him would and should fast.

The Appearance of the fasting Saint

Further, in the said scripture Jesus dealt with the issue of how one should look during a fast. In dealing with this significant matter, Jesus categorises the observers of fasts into two groups – the hypocrites and the Saints. The Lord's categorisation of the observers of fasts has huge implications, not least because fasting is not an automatic evidence of genuine spirituality, but because its practice is validated in all religions of the world – Islamic, Buddhism, Hinduism etc. These all fast for various reasons.

For the hypocrites, Jesus directed His comments at the Pharisees, and His remarks were without reservations:

Moreover when ye fast, be not, as the hypocrites, of a sad countenance: for they disfigure their faces, that they may appear unto men to fast. Verily I say unto you, They have their reward (Matt. 6:16).

The reality is that there are no groups of people or nationals in modern world particularly tagged 'hypocrites'. Hypocrisy is a product of the mind!

How many times have you heard non - Christians joke about the hypocrisy of Christians? How many disillusioned people have you met that have been burned by fake Christians and Christian leaders, who preach one thing and practice another – the exact opposite.

Hypocrisy seems to touch a raw nerve in Jesus. Jesus did not just speak out against it he went on a full-on assault. Jesus assaulted it; He attacked it over and over again throughout his ministry here on earth.

However, for far too many people, being a Christian and being a hypocrite go hand in hand. We could try to say that the outsiders just have misunderstood those in the church, but sadly, most of their perceptions are true.

Religious artificiality is a disease of the soul that can only be healed by having an authentic relationship with the great healer.

Let us examine the Old Testament on the same subject:

The Lord says:

These people come near to me with their mouth and honor me with their lips, but their hearts are far from me. Their worship of me is made up only of rules taught by men (Isaiah 29:13 NIV).

I have been around Christians my entire life, it is true that authenticity is rare.

In Ezekiel 33:30-33

As for you, son of man, your countrymen are talking together about you by the walls and at the doors of the houses, saying to each other, 'Come and hear the message that has come from the LORD.' My people come to you, as they usually do, and sit before you to listen to your words, but they do not put them into practice. With their mouths they express devotion, but their hearts are greedy for unjust gain. Indeed, to them you are nothing more than one who sings love songs with a beautiful voice and plays an instrument well, for they hear your words but do not put them into practice.

Scary isn't it? God was condemning them because they came, heard the words of the Lord, expressed devotion with their mouths but in their hearts nothing was changing, they put nothing into practice.

Do we act one way with some people and another with others?

Now let us go back to the passages we have been considering.

At the time this was written, there were three significant disciplines among the Jews…giving, praying, and fasting. We need to understand that Jesus did not dispute these as good works. He was all for giving, praying and fasting. His concern was that this had degenerated into a masking of evil motives. He was against, not the observance of these disciplines, but the motives for observing them.

Let look at the relevant verses again:

But when you give to the needy, do not let your left hand know what your right hand is doing... (verse 3).

And when you pray, do not be like the hypocrites, for they love to pray standing in the synagogues and on the street corners to be seen by men... (verse 5)

When you fast, do not look sober as the hypocrites do, for they disfigure their faces to show men they are fasting... (verse 16)

When we give, pray, or fast, we are warned not to be hypocritical.

We are encouraged, for instance, to give generously (Luke 6:38), but it must be a matter between the believer and God. When you announce it in your own ways no matter how subtle it may be, that is your reward. Motivations can be so deceiving. What is at the heart of your giving?

Praying is great. But when you pray, go into your room, close the door and pray! Take a look at your prayer life. How much of it is real? In my view, it is almost insane to spend hours in prayer just to be noticed by men, and earn their admiration.

The following cardinal points are worth noting:

1. Constantly evaluate your private life against your public life. If you are practicing any or all of these disciplines: giving, praying, or fasting in public only, something is wrong. Evaluate your heart. Why do you do the things you do? What is the motive behind it? Do not hide behind a mask. Be real. Ask for help. Admit your weaknesses. Jesus loves when we admit our weaknesses and ask for help but he hates hypocrisy.

2. Probe yourself of the result you desire to be the outcome of your engaging in any of the disciplines as analysed - giving, praying, and fasting. If you cannot pinpoint any benefits flowing directly from God, then the motive is likely to be wrong. There would, undoubtedly, be some rewards, but they are likely to emanate from the wrong source – man.

The Lord said in unambiguous terms of the second group – His saints:

> *But thou, when thou fastest, anoint thine head, and wash thy face; That thou appear not unto men to fast, but unto thy Father which is in secret: and thy Father, which seeth in secret, shall reward thee openly* (Matt. 6:17-18).

The fast of the Saints of God is to be different. They are to honour and please God with their fasting; never for personal aggrandisement. They are to wash and anoint their faces. Accordingly, their external appearance is to be given serious consideration, so that the fasting believer does not draw undue attention to himself. As seen, this has grave consequences.

In the words of Zac. Fomum,

"…believers who fast must pay special attention to their physical appearance. They should be clean. They should bathe at least once a day. They should brush their teeth once every two hours. Fasting people have a special mouth odour. They cannot afford to burden other people with it."

Who Should See the Fast?

Another great lesson from Jesus's teaching on fasting has to do with: who should see the fast. Here again, Jesus identifies two categories of people with varying attitudes- the hypocrites and the Christians. The hypocrite's fast in order to catch the attention of men. They put the admiration of men and personal aggrandisement ahead of the legitimate objectives of fasting. They possibly think of a class of people who they want to impress with their fasting.

The question of 'who sees the fast' carries an expensive implication when we examine the ultimate issue in relation to the outcome of the fast – reward!

However, for the precious saints of Christ, they are to fast, not to be seen by men, but by the Almighty – who alone rewards fasting. They are to fast as a sacrifice, offered on the altar of incense, to be seen and smelt by their father who is in heaven! Can you see the enormous difference between fasting to attract the praise of men, and fasting in praise and honour to the Lord? If He is the Lord of your life, He is to be Lord over your fast!

To the praise and Glory of the Lord, I have observed fasts of various lengths and durations; the longest so far being twenty-one days straight fast. Can you imagine how foolish it would have been to embark on such a long fast, with the sole objective of letting men see what a 'fasting guru' I have become? God forbid!

The question of 'who sees the fast' carries an expensive implication when we examine the ultimate issue in relation to the outcome of the fast – reward!

Who Rewards the Fast?

The fourth vital issue raises the question of who rewards the observer of the fast. Jesus stated very categorically, *"... thou appear not unto men to fast, but unto thy Father which is in secret: **and thy Father, which seeth in secret, shall reward thee openly.*** (Matt. 6:17-18 emphasis added). A logical conclusion to be drawn from this is: ***whoever sees the fast, rewards the fast!*** The hypocrites fast to catch the eye of man; so man is the rewarder of the fast of the hypocrites. Whoever fasts to be seen by man is a hypocrite! He receives his reward from the people who see his fast and sing his praise.

A logical conclusion to be drawn from this is: whoever sees the fast, rewards the fast!

The Saints of the Most High, on the other hand, fast so as to be seen by their Father, who is in secret. He is Omnipresent! Nothing escapes His surveillance! David asks brilliantly:

> *Whither shall I go from thy spirit? or whither shall I flee from thy presence? If I ascend up into heaven, thou art there: if I make my bed in hell, behold, thou art there. If I take the wings of the morning, and dwell in the uttermost parts of the sea; Even*

there shall thy hand lead me, and thy right hand shall hold me (Psalm 139: 7 – 10).

Every transaction of man is within the watchful eyes of the all-knowing God. Child of God, He sees your fast! Those who fast for His glory and honour labour to ensure that their fasting is seen only by Him, so as to draw the reward He promised! For the hypocrites, God's verdict is that they receive their rewards by the 'congratulations' they receive from men. He received it when people looked at his disfigured face and exclaimed, "What a fasting expert!" Notice that he – the hypocrite receives his rewards instantaneously. But the righteous – the ones whose fasting are channelled to please and honour God, have their rewards both now and in the future.

I have drawn significant encouragement from the wealth of wisdom in Zac. Fomum's brilliant teachings on the rewards that await the fasting believers on the judgment day:

He said:

There is, however, a reason for fasting that has nothing to do with the current age or getting things from God **now but has to do with the age to come.** When the Lord comes He will reward His servants according to their works. This book shall be opened. There shall be the book of prayer, the book of giving to the Lord, the book of self-denial, the book of fasting, the book of obedience, etc, and believers shall be reward according to what has been recorded in those books. My dear brother and sister the book of fasting shall be opened. What [do you have] recorded in that book against your name? Is there anything at all? Are there only partial fasts? Are there only a few complete fasts? Are there any absolute fasts? Are there any long fasts? Are there any fasts that satisfy the heart of God? It is possible to know now so that no one will be surprised on that day." He warned, "there will be no reward for any fast by any believer that was carried out to draw attention to himself. God does not record such fasts, since the fasting person has already received his reward from the one whose attention he drew to his fasting. This should make believers think… There will be rewards only for those who fasts were meant to catch the eye of God alone. What does this all mean? I think that the first thing that it means is that any reward that may be received now, like power for service, divine visitation, etc., is only a foretaste of what will be in the future. The central issue will be the reward by the One Who sees in secret. Those who may not receive any visible reward for their fasting in time need not be discouraged. The Lord is keeping their reward for [the] judgment Day.

What a prophetic insight into the glorious reward God has in store for those who worship the Master with fasting; highly motivating! A rare gem!

Finally, some fast with the intention of drawing the attention of God and man at the same time? It is clear from our teaching so far that God does not record such fasts, because He cannot be involved in a mixture. It is either entirely God's or man's. God will not share His glory with any man!

Are Prayer and Fasting, Distinct Disciplines?

In other words, can prayer and fasting be engaged in as two separate disciplines?

It has been argued by some that Jesus dealt with fasting as a spiritual exercise distinct from praying, contending that though, fasting and prayer are often linked in Scriptures and experience, this is not necessarily the case. On the contrary, they argue, that fasting stands on its own ground and may, occasionally, serve a spiritual purpose of its own. Fasting and prayer are two distinct weapons; two instruments of spiritual warfare. They can work independently.

According to the proponents of this argument, just as there may be praying without fasting, so there may, on occasions, be fasting, truly acceptable to the Lord, without praying – at least in the sense of intercession. They argue there was no mention of prayer accompanying the fasts recorded in the book of Esther. The prophets and teachers in Antioch, they contend, were worshipping and ministering unto the Lord with fasting, rather than prayer and fasting (Acts 13:2). Therefore, they conclude, 'the fact that one in not able to give oneself to long prayers during a long fast does not mean that the period not accompanied by specific prayer is devoid of spiritual power'.

This line of reasoning contains a degree of credit, given that at the height of a lengthy fast is a common experience of physical weakness that makes lengthy and fervent prayer impossible on occasions. At such times, however, direct communication with God should still be maintained in whatever form: both the short prayers that are uttered in short and dis-jointed phrases throughout the day and night, and the groanings which cannot be uttered (Romans 8:26), still serves as booster rocket, lifting our prayers beyond the boundaries of earth into the heavenlies. That said, it must be stressed, however, that fasting accompanied with prayers have stronger power to undermine the enemy's stronghold than either of them on its own.

It is to be noted that fasting without the study of the word of God and communication with God through prayers, is an exercise void of its full potentials. Stripped of these disciplines, 'fasting' seizes to be 'fasting' but a hunger strike!

6

THE BRIDEGROOM HAS DEPARTED: SHALL WE FAST NOW?

The second important statement Jesus made on fasting came as an answer to a question the disciples of John the Baptist asked Him:

> "Why," they asked, "do we and the Pharisees fast, but your disciples do not fast?" (Matthew 9:14).

The first thing to be noted about this question is that, though directed at Jesus, it was not about Jesus not fasting. They did not say Jesus did not fast. They were rather 'mad' at the disciples of Jesus not fasting. They knew that Jesus authenticated the discipline of fasting by engaging in the act Himself. They regarded the disciples' attitude in this regard as a flagrant violation of the Jewish tradition.

To this important question, Jesus gave a powerful and intriguing answer:

> *When the Bridegroom is taken from them... then they will fast* (Mathew 9:15)

On the surface, this answer seems straightforward and simple, yet more has been written on this incident than about any other New Testament reference on the practice of fasting.

In Matthew's account the question is asked by the disciples of John the Baptist. Luke attributed the question to the Pharisees (Luke 5:30, 33), and Mark wrote that the questions came from both groups (Mark 2:18).

Whereas Matthew and Mark record a question that calls for an answer, Luke's account records a simple statement that has the force of a question. In all three accounts there is the clear assumption, by human judgement, that Jesus' disciples were doing something wrong.

An important explanation, however, is that Jesus and His disciples did not conform to the common customs of traditional Judaism. Their conduct reveals a clear-cut breach with existing religious practice. This issue concerning fasting brought into focus the whole question of Jesus' attitude toward Jewish tradition. This is also evident in the two following analogies of placing a new patch on old cloth and putting new wine in old wineskins (Matt. 9:16-17; Mark 2:21-22; Luke 5:36-38). Christ's teaching could not be blended with rabbinic traditions.

Fasting was embarked upon as a religious duty among the Jews in the days of Jesus' earthly ministry. However, both the Pharisees and the disciples of John the Baptist were appalled that while they observed the traditional rites of the time (fasted, according to the Jewish tradition), the disciples of Jesus did not. They decided to confront Jesus with the matter. They asked:

> ...Why do the disciples of John and of the Pharisees fast, but thy disciples fast not?... Mark 2:18.

Jesus's response was of profound significance! In a sense delivered with a prophetic tone! Said Jesus,

> ...Can the children of the bride-chamber fast, while the bridegroom is with them? as long as they have the bridegroom with them, they cannot fast (verse 19).

As often His custom, Jesus responded to this important question by way of a parable. He spoke of three significant issues: the "bridegroom," "children of the "bride-chamber," and the appointed "time to fast."

All three are remarkably important:

In the first place, as always in the New Testament, the bridegroom is Christ Himself. The children of the bride-chamber are the disciples of Jesus (now present day believers).

However, while this is perhaps the most crucial statement as recorded in the New Testament on the subject of fasting, however, the question remains, what period could Jesus be referring to? It is very clear that the days of His absence indicated by the words "when the Bridegroom is taken away from them," refer to the period of this present church age, from the time of His ascension to the Father, until His return to rapture His Bride.

This is, undoubtedly, how His disciples understood Him. It was after His Ascension to the Father that we read of them fasting (Acts 13:2,3; 14:23).

So, the days of fasting are finally upon us! The departure of the bridegroom signals the beginning of this glorious discipline. Because the prophecy of the "bridegroom being taken away" has been fulfilled, the accompanying responsibility vested on the Saints to engage in fasting as a result, must be fulfilled also. However, before the Bridegroom left, He promised to come again to receive the believers unto Himself. While the Church awaits His glorious return, fasting must continue. The time is now!

The early Church fulfilled this prophecy. The Bible says,

> *Now there were in the church that was at Antioch certain prophets and teachers; as Barnabas, and Simeon that was called Niger, and Lucius of Cyrene… As they ministered to the Lord, and fasted…* Acts 13:1-2,

No doubt, Christ's answer is also deeply pertinent to the question of whether fasting is relevant to the believer today. He asks, "Can the wedding guests mourn as long as the Bridegroom is with them?" (Matt. 9:15). Then, quite prophetically, He added, "But the days will come when the bridegroom is taken away from them, and then they will fast." As said, the bridegroom has long been taken from us, therefore, fasting must continue. In His statement, Jesus viewed fasting as a sign of mourning, which is inconsistent with the joy of the bridegroom's presence.

There were times when Jesus and His disciples went hungry; times when, due to the heavy demands of Kingdom assignments, they had no time to eat. A very glaring example is in Mark 11: 12 – 14:

> *The next day as they were leaving Bethany, Jesus was hungry. Seeing in the distance a fig tree in leaf, he went to find out if it had any fruit. When he reached it, he found nothing but leaves, because it was not the season for figs. Then he said to the tree, "May no one ever eat fruit from you again." And his disciples heard him say it.*

But there is no evidence of Jesus and His disciples undertaking a definite voluntary fast together. (Jesus, of course, fasted forty days and nights in the wilderness before his public ministry). Reason? The Bridegroom was still with the wedding guests! The occasion called for feasting, not fasting, rejoicing, not mourning. Although the disciples would fast when the bridegroom was taken from them, it would be for a different purpose and in a different spirit from that which characterised the fasting of the Pharisees. There would be no return to the legalism of the old order. However, by and by, fasting would be replaced by feasting (Revelation 22:17, 20):

> *And the Spirit and the bride say, Come. And let him that heareth say, Come. And let him that is athirst come. And whosoever will, let him take the water*

of life freely. He which testifieth these things saith, Surely I come quickly. Amen. Even so, come, Lord Jesus.

JESUS 'EMPOWERED' THROUGH FASTING

Jesus not only taught fasting, as discussed, he validated the practice by His forty-days fast. Immediately after His baptism, Jesus was led by the Holy Spirit to spend forty days and nights fasting in the wilderness:

And Jesus being full of the Holy Ghost returned from Jordan, and was led by the Spirit into the wilderness, Being forty days tempted of the devil. And in those days he did eat nothing: and when they were ended, he afterward hungered, (Luke 4:1-2).

Of course, during these days Jesus was tempted of the devil.

However, there is a significant difference in the description of Luke of Jesus before and after His fast. Luke's record of Jesus before the fast was: "And Jesus being full of the Holy Ghost returned from Jordan…" (Luke 4:1). But at the end of the fast, Luke 4:14 asserts, "Then Jesus returned in the power of the Holy Spirit to Galilee, and news of Him went out through all the surrounding region."

When Jesus went into the wilderness, He was already "full of the Holy Spirit." That was outstanding! In other words, He started out 'full' of the Holy Spirit. But look at verse 14. At the end of the wilderness experience - the 40 days fast, He became 'empowered' by the Holy Spirit! Of course, how could Jesus accomplish the astonishing miracles we see throughout the Gospels?

In the light of evidence such as this, is it any wonder that Derek Prince concludes:

"It would appear that the potential of the Holy Spirit is power, which Jesus received at the time of his baptism in Jordan, only came forth into full manifestation after He had completed his fast. Fasting was the final phase of preparation through which he had to pass, before entering into His public ministry."

There is, therefore, a significant difference between being filled with the Spirit and operating in the power of the Spirit. For Jesus, a transformation took place; a transition that took Jesus from being filled with the Spirit, to walking in the Spirit. He got empowered with that which had possessed Him.

Moving Beyond the "In-filling" process

This has been clearly exemplified for us by the Master. Being filled with the Spirit alone does not guarantee empowerment.

The way to empowerment involves a process; never by accident! And there are no short-cuts involved. In the life and ministry of Jesus, we see a clear-cut process, right from His baptism at river Jordan, *"And it came to pass in those days, that Jesus came from Nazareth of Galilee, and was baptized by John in the Jordan And immediately coming up out of the water, he saw the heavens opened, and the Spirit like a dove descending upon him"* (Mark 1:9 -10) to another phase where He was led by the Spirit into the Wilderness, and was *"full of the Holy Spirit."* (Luke 4:1). And, of course, to the final and ultimate phase of His empowerment – being the stage where he began to perform astonishing miracles (Luke 4:14). This was precipitated by a remarkable event that bridged the earlier phases with the ultimate phase, and that was His forty days fast.

The disciples and the divine process

The same spiritual laws that applied in Christ's ministry were applicable also in the ministry of His disciples. In John 14:12, Jesus said, 'He that believeth on me, the works that I do shall he do also.' By these words, Jesus opened the way for His disciples to follow the pattern of His own ministry. If fasting was a necessary part of Christ's preparation for ministry, it must play a vital part also in the disciple's preparation and execution of ministerial duties.

Having exemplified it in His own ministry, Jesus went on to stress the significance of fasting in achieving spiritual breakthroughs when prayer by itself proved inadequate (Matthew 17:21): He said to His awe-stricken disciples:

> ... *this kind goeth not out but by prayer and fasting.*

What a lesson! No one had ever taught them that before. Neither had experience in ministry led them that way before this time. However, with this revelation about the incredible power of fasting as, impacted by the Master, the disciples had acquired an asset – a piece of armoury that would significantly impact their lives and ministry, forever, if utilised. If they were ever going to *"make full proof of [their] ministry" (2 Timothy 4:5)*, and make their *"calling and election sure"* (2 Peter 1:10), they had been given a vital key, an infallible weapon (the knowledge of fasting) to accomplish all these.

The early church suddenly became a force to

> reckon with. The 'outburst of power' that resulted from the empowerment process could not be curtailed, not even by the Sanhedrin Council.

Similarly, the disciples were with the Master for a period of three years, during which they were trained, and impacted. The life and ministry of Jesus was replicated in them. Yet it was not until after the Upper room experience, with the combined ministry of prayer and fasting (as will be fully discussed in the next chapter), and the wilderness experience of having the bridegroom taken away from them that they pressed into both the in-filling and the empowerment stages of their ministry.

Signs and wonders authenticated this process! Pandemonium hit the streets of Jerusalem like a thunder-bolt on the Day of Pentecost! The disciples were visited with the most amazing power of the Holy Spirit, amidst extra-ordinary demonstration of the same power that shaped and defined their ministry thereafter.

The early church suddenly became a force to reckon with. The 'outburst of power' that resulted from the empowerment process could not be curtailed, not even by the Sanhedrin Council. (The Sanhedrin was the supreme council, or court, in ancient Israel).

> **Outstanding miracles were a living proof of this phenomenal outpouring of the Spirit of God in, not just the Antioch Church, but in Jerusalem and beyond.**

Outstanding miracles were a living proof of this phenomenal outpouring of the Spirit of God in, not just the Antioch Church, but in Jerusalem and beyond. This was the birth-place of the unprecedented move of God which 'flames' suddenly spread and engulfed the whole world.

This power is still available today! It belongs to our time and generation! However, the secret key that opens the reservoir of power, or should I call it the flood-gate of heaven, is fasting and prayer. The combined effect of prayer and fasting are adorable. They produce undeniable results. Have you noticed that men may criticise methods or principles, but never are able to deny or critique results? It is often said that if you do not appreciate your harvest, all you need to do is to change your seed. Fasting is a tremendous seed that yields astonishing dividends in the life of the believer.

7

THE PRACTICE OF FASTING IN THE EARLY CHURCH

Fasting Associated with Saul's Dramatic Conversion

"And he was three days without sight, and neither did eat nor drink." Acts 9:9

The first reference to fasting in the Book of Acts is in connection with the dramatic conversion of Saul on the road to Damascus. After his unusual experience Saul was left blinded. He was led into the city of Damascus, where for three days he was *"without sight, and neither ate nor drank" (Acts 9:9)*. It has been argued by some that this experience lacks the essential elements of a true fast. In the first place, they contend, the experience appears to have been imposed on Saul (Paul); he did not of his free will abstain from food and drink, which fasting entails. Second, the experience, they argue, was more of Paul falling into a trance than it being a voluntary abstinence from food and water. Be that as it may, it cannot be denied that Paul later became one of the greatest advocates of the discipline of fasting (2 Corinthians 6: 3-10, 11: 23-27), as would be seen in the next chapter.

Fasting Associated with the First Missionaries

The New Testament Christians, not only practiced fasting individually, they took fasting as a corporate discipline also. Significantly, in the early church, prayer and fasting were the means by which the first missionaries were commissioned. This was attested to by Luke in Acts 13:1-3:

> *Now there were in the church that was at Antioch certain prophets and teachers; as Barnabas, and Simeon that was called Niger, and Lucius of Cyrene, and Manaen, which had been brought up with Herod the tetrarch, and Saul. As they ministered to the Lord, and fasted, the Holy Ghost said, Separate me Barnabas and Saul for the work whereunto I have called them. And when they had fasted and prayed, and laid their hands on them, they sent them away.*

As these leading ministers – prophets and teachers - were ministering to the Lord with fasting, the Holy Ghost gave a clear leading concerning God's mandate for two of the leading ministers in their midst.

*Separate me Barnabas and Saul for the work whereunto **I have called them** (Emphasis added).*

The phrase *"...the work unto which I have called them"* is noteworthy.

God had called Barnabas and Saul to the work of the ministry; they did not know it for a fact, until it was revealed to them through this corporate fasting of the leaders of the church.

Thank God, these leaders obeyed the leading of the Spirit and fasted, otherwise Barnabas and Saul (Paul), could have been out of the perfect will of God for their lives. Thank God for leaders that led the right way; paving a way for upcoming leaders to be impacted and released into God's assignment.

This meeting – the corporate fast – of the leadership team of the church could be said to be the birthplace of all the exploits the Bible attributes to Paul.

Having experienced the formidable power of prayer and fasting first-hand, Paul and Barnabas later employed the same tool in the establishment of churches, and appointment of their leaders thereafter. After Paul and Barnabas completed the first officially church-sponsored foreign missionary effort, they visited each church they had established to be sure proper leadership was set in place.

> *And when they had preached the gospel to that city, and had taught many, they returned again to Lystra, and to Iconium, and Antioch, Confirming the souls of the disciples, and exhorting them to continue in the faith, and that we must through much tribulation enter into the kingdom of God. And when they had ordained them elders in every church, and had prayed with fasting, they commended them to the Lord, on whom they believed* (Acts 14:21-23).

It should be appreciated that everything we have read about the practice of fasting in the early church had a beginning or foundation to it. First, was the outpouring of the Holy Spirit which was ushered in through the prayer and fasting of the disciples. In Acts 1:13 we read:

And when they were come in, they went up into an upper room, where abode both Peter, and James, and John, and Andrew, Philip, and Thomas, Bartholomew, and Matthew, James the son of Alphaeus, and Simon Zelotes, and Judas the brother of James.

This became the tradition of the disciples after the ascension of Jesus; giving themselves "continually to prayer and the ministry of the word" (Acts 6:4). They put prayer first! Prayer gives an edge and weight to the word. And the dispensation of the Holy Ghost was born. This marked the beginning of an outstanding ministry for the disciples – a ministry characterised with notable miracles and amazing wonders. Indeed, God's church has always waited more on prayer than on anything else for its success. This was clearly demonstrated by the early church. From this humble beginning grew the practice of fasting. With fasting, a new lease of life was birthed, that shaped the spiritual landscape of Jerusalem and its environs. Everyone acknowledged that a force to reckon with had been born – the church.

Fasting as Practiced and Taught in the Epistles

Fasting played a vital role in the life and ministry of Paul. Immediately after his dramatic encounter with Christ on his way to Damascus, Paul spent the next three days without food and water (Acts 9:9). Later he referred to fasting as one of the signs of the legitimacy of his missionary ministry. In 2 Corinthians 6:3-10, Paul listed various ways in which he had proved himself as a true minister of God. It is noteworthy that in verse 5, two of the ways identified by Paul are: "in watchings, in fastings".

> *Giving no offence in anything, that the ministry be not blamed: But in all things approving ourselves as the ministers of God, in much patience, in afflictions, in necessities, in distresses, In stripes, in imprisonments, in tumults, in labours, in watchings, in fastings; By pureness, by knowledge, by long suffering, by kindness, by the Holy Ghost, by love unfeigned, By the word of truth, by the power of God, by the armour of righteousness on the right hand and on the left, By honour and dishonour, by evil report and good report: as deceivers, and yet true; As unknown, and yet well known; as dying, and, behold, we live; as chastened, and not killed; As sorrowful, yet alway rejoicing; as poor, yet making many rich; as having nothing, and yet possessing all things.*

Again, in 2 Corinthians 11: 23-27, Paul revisited this all important subject of fasting, and said,

*Are they ministers of Christ? (I speak as a fool) I am more; in labours more abundant, in stripes above measure, in prisons more frequent, in deaths oft. Of the Jews five times received I forty stripes save one. Thrice was I beaten with rods, once was I stoned, thrice I suffered shipwreck, a night and a day I have been in the deep; In journeyings often, in perils of waters, in perils of robbers, in perils by mine own countrymen, in perils by the heathen, in perils in the city, in perils in the wilderness, in perils in the sea, in perils among false brethren; In weariness and painfulness, in watchings often, in hunger and thirst, in **fastings often,** in cold and nakedness"* (emphasis added).

In verse 27, Paul again joined watching with fasting. More significantly, the plural form, "in fastings often," proves that Paul devoted himself to a life of fasting. As a matter of fact, for the early church and Apostle Paul fasting was a normative practice. Why did Paul fast so often? Paul saw fasting as a POWER-BOOSTER, and had proofs that validated this. This is a clear example for today believer to emulate.

FASTING: a refilling process.

Whatever you do in the kingdom, at whatever time you no longer sense that 'cutting edge unction', be it in preaching, singing, praying, or you sense that the more you pray, the less results you actually have, or you face a situation of outright 'power-seizure', what is required is simply, to suspend all the 'labouring' and seek the 'unction to function' – go for "a-refill". So fasting is a tool devised by God that offers the opportunity to reconnect to your power source for fresh supplies of the anointing.

A problem that has persistently invaded the Household of Faith today is that those committed to ministry assignments are so 'busy' that they find little or no time to get in their closet to undergo this 'refilling' process. The Bible – the source of all of our inspirations – leaves us with no doubt as to the legitimate source of the anointing. Let us consider this scripture together:

> *How God anointed Jesus of Nazareth with the Holy Ghost and with power: who went about doing good, and healing all that were oppressed of the devil; for God was with him (Acts 10:38).*

First, as seen in this scripture, God is the source of the anointing, and gives it to whosoever He wills; in this case, to Jesus.

Further, the anointing is the enabling power (supernatural power) that is needed by the believer to operate in the kingdom. Jesus could not discharge His kingdom mandate without it, and you should not either.

And it shall come to pass in that day, that his burden shall be taken away from off your shoulder, and his yoke from off your neck, and the yoke shall be destroyed because of the anointing (Isaiah 10:27).

In addition, those endued with the anointing of the Holy Ghost, are propelled (inspired) to do exploits for God.

... but the people that do know their God shall be strong, and do exploits (Daniel 11:32).

Finally, the phrase, *"...for God was with him..."* is noteworthy! Its significance is sadly, often overlooked. While Jesus was engrossed with the work of the ministry, 'doing good, healing all that were oppressed of the devil' - He maintained contact with His source - the source of His anointing, God. The busy nature of His ministerial itinerary did not affect, in the least, the grip Jesus had on His source. The busier He was, the greater His grip on His 'power-source' for the requisite anointing to fulfil the task at hand.

> **For today's believers, and a good number of kingdom labourers, the moment we sense a level of success in ministry, we disassociate or disconnect from the very source of the anointing that enabled us to achieve that degree of success.**

Martin Luther was once quoted as saying,

"I have so much to do that I shall have to spend the first three hours in prayer."

For Martin Luther, the divine ability to carry out Kingdom responsibilities is derivable from the presence of God.

For today's believers, and a good number of kingdom labourers, the moment we sense a level of success in ministry, we disassociate or disconnect from the very source of the anointing that enabled us to achieve that degree of success. This is the sad reality!

While we may not consciously take a decision to severe our relationship with the power-source, we very often discover that, unless we keep constant watch in this regard through unceasing fellowship with God, there exists a great distance between us and 'the' God we claim to be 'working for'. Consequently, we are left operating, not with the optimum level of power God intends for our lives, but a latent residue of that power. Of course, this has far- reaching consequences.

The idea of working for God is, sadly, one of the greatest misconceptions of our time! Acts 10:38 does not say that Jesus was working for God. It says rather that: '…God was with Him.' My understanding of this phrase is that Jesus did all His exploits in ministry in active partnership with God. He was in constant touch with His base; in prayer and fellowship with God. Too many ministers and ministries are no longer in partnership with the God that called them into the work of the kingdom in the first place. They may have started out working in partnership with God, but in the process of time, they severed that relationship. They are now, as it were, 'doing their own thing.' How sad!

For too many, they are so busy working for God that they have lost contacts completely with Him; no more time for prayer, scripture meditation, fasting and the likes. They have, consequently disappeared from God's radar! Dear Servant of God, what God are you working for? You have no right to engage in any work of the kingdom without daily examining your relationship with God.

Paul succinctly declares: *"I die daily"* (1 Cor. 15:31), and emphatically enjoins the believer to examine himself daily:

Examine yourselves to see whether you are in the faith; test yourselves. Do you not realize that Christ Jesus is in you—unless, of course, you fail the test? (2 Corinthians 13:5-6).

Both 'the dying daily' and 'the self-examination' requirements are part of the same indispensable process that aids and culminates in conforming to the image of the Master (Romans 8:29, 2 Cor. 3:18).

If the signs that are to approve us in ministry are to be evident in our churches and ministries (Mark 16: 17-18), we must stay close to the the 'sole owner' of His work and His anointing.

Dr. Kenneth Boa leaves us with some golden nuggets on the subject. He said:

"What does a relationship with God look like and how do we obtain it? It is vital for church leaders to grapple seriously with this question, for part answers no longer suffice. Lives well-lived, not just words eloquently spoken, must become our response. The quality of our relationship with God is what will influence the health, potency, and witness of the church in an increasingly complex and hostile world..."

If the signs that are to approve us in ministry are to be evident in our churches and ministries (Mark 16: 17-18), we must stay close to the 'sole owner' of His work and His anointing. This is what helps us build our lives on a fully biblical perspective, and build a work that last for God.

Remember, the Bible says, "…not by might, nor by power, but by my spirit", says the Lord (Zech. 4:6).

THE WONDERS OF FASTING

8

TYPES OF CHRISTIAN FASTING

Now that we have explored the Old and New Testament principles and teachings about fasting, it is important to now examine the different kinds of fasting revealed in the word of God.

Generally, we have three types of fastings which were substantially practiced in the Bible days under different circumstances. These are the normal fast, the partial fast, and the absolute fasts.

The Normal Fast

The most common form of fast is generally known as the normal fast. There are very few rules when it comes to this fasting under the Old Testament. This fast was conducted on the Day of Atonement, and it was from sunset of one day to sunset of the next (Leviticus 16:29; 23:32).

However, what the normal fast entails is very clear from the 40 days fast of the Master.

He fasted forty days and forty nights and afterwards He was hungry" (Matthew 4:2).

This type of Christian fast makes our definition of fasting more vivid which is, abstaining from all form of food but not from water or fluid. It is very clear from the details given that Jesus' fast was this type. The passage says, "He ate nothing" (Luke 4:2), 'not that He drank nothing'. Afterwards "He was hungry", 'not that He was thirsty'. Again, Satan tempted Him to eat bread, but not to drink. These all suggest that our Lord's fast was an abstention from food, not from water. It is also suggested that in a hot desert climate like the wilderness where Jesus was, someone died in twenty-four hours if they drank no water. And for many, their body could not survive forty days without food apart from being supernaturally sustained.

Fasting and Sleep

Despite the broad definitions given to fasting by some, there is nothing to suggest that fasting involves abstaining from sleep. God may require it as part of the sacrifice involved in fasting for some reasons, albeit for a short period of time, but not necessarily required as part of the overall activities we must be involved in as part of the fast. Paul speaks of "watchings" as distinct from "fastings" (2 Cor. 6:5; 11:27).

It is argued that if abstaining from sleep were a requirement of fasting, no long fast would ever be possible without some supernatural interventions, as the body craves sleep as much as water, and is bound to succumb at some point during the fast.

There is, however, a strong indication in 1 Corinthians 7: 3-5 that, for married couples, fasting entails abstention from marital relations:

> *Let the husband render unto the wife due benevolence: and likewise also the wife unto the husband. The wife hath not power of her own body, but the husband: and likewise also the husband hath not power of his own body, but the wife. Defraud ye not one the other, except it be with consent for a time, that ye may give yourselves to fasting and prayer; and come together again, that Satan tempt you not for your incontinency.*

Having established that the normal fast involves abstaining from all forms of food, but not from water, it must now be distinguished from the other two forms of fasts – the absolute and the partial fasts - which we must now consider.

The Partial Fast

This type of fast is based on the fasting practices of Daniel as recorded in Daniel Chapters 1 and 10. There is no complete abstinence from food in this kind of fast. The emphasis here is on restriction of diet rather than complete abstention. This type of fast is highly recommended for beginners to the discipline of fasting, and those with health needs (having obtained their physician's permission to fast).

There are many forms of partial fasts. The observer of this fast could take just one meal every twenty-four hours. A word of caution, though! The single meal should be light and not the size of three meals in style, which would be gluttony. Yet another type of partial fast is to drink, throughout the duration of the fast, fruit juice or milk. A classic example of this fast, as seen at the commencement of the Book of Daniel is with regards to Daniel, and his three companions (Shadrach, Meshach and Abednego), who ate only vegetables and drank only water (Daniel 1:15). They had been selected from among the Hebrew exiles as a result of their noble birth and intellectual attainments for special training. They served before the King of Babylon.

These Hebrew men had resolved not to defile themselves with the King's meat or wine, as these would have first, been offered to the Babylonian gods. Instead, they requested for vegetables for food and water, instead of wine.

The steward over their affairs agreed to test the effect of this simple diet on them for ten days. And the Bible says:

> ... *at the end of ten days their countenances appeared fairer and fatter in flesh than all the children which did eat the portion of the king's meat.* Daniel 1:15.

Whether or not there was supernatural intervention in this particular fast is difficult to ascertain, however, it could be argued, especially from a nutritional perspective that a simple and wholesome diet is far more beneficial than a rich and elaborate one. It is also true that those who live where there is constant dining and wining are, often than not, beset with ailments. All forms of fasting practiced in a sensible biblical manner are physically beneficial, as will be discussed later.

However, the value of partial fast, or any other fast, is not confined to the physical benefits. Later in the Book of Daniel, we read how this prophet received a revelation from God about the future of his people Israel. He describes how he sought the Lord for the understanding of this vision:

> *In those days I Daniel was mourning three full weeks. I ate no pleasant bread, neither came flesh nor wine in my mouth, neither did I anoint myself at all, till three whole weeks were fulfilled* (Daniel 10:2,3).

While we are not told reasons why he did not engage in a normal fast as we see him do in the previous chapter, there is, undoubtedly, a definite spiritual value in a special season of seeking God with such restricted diet. For Daniel, it resulted in a great spiritual victory over the powers of darkness as well as the unfolding of the vision by an angelic messenger.

Something akin to a partial fast could be said to be the period of Elijah's spiritual preparation. At cherith the raven brought him bread and meat morning and evening and he drank from the brook. Later, in the home of the widow of Zarephath, he was sustained with simple cakes made from meal and oil (1 Kings 17).

The advantages of this kind of fast are numerous: First, it allows a great many variations which have been tried with tremendous benefits. Further, a partial fast is known to be beneficial where circumstances make it impossible or inconvenient to undertake a normal fast. It is also of tremendous benefits, and highly recommended for people who have health problems that prevent them from undergoing complete fasts. It has been seen as a stepping-stone to the normal fast by those who have never fasted before. A case for partial fast may also be made for people whose nature of jobs are very demanding, and consequently make long complete fasts impossible.

The Absolute Fast:

This type of fast is one in which the person refrains from both food and water for an extended period of time. Usually this is never for more than three days, perhaps, because of the medical implications associated with such abstention. The body can function many days, even weeks without food, and can be tremendously beneficial physically and medically; but the body can survive only for a very limited time without water - seventy-two hours being the maximum.

Queen Esther

A pattern for the duration of absolute fasts (without food and fluid) could be said to have been set by Queen Esther, in Esther 4: 15-16:

Then Esther bade them return Mordecai this answer, Go, gather together all the Jews that are present in Shushan, and fast ye for me, and neither eat nor drink three days, night or day: I also and my maidens will fast likewise; and so will I go in unto the king, which is not according to the law: and if I perish, I perish." Esther decided to fast for three days abstaining from both "food and water" both "day and night.

A critical situation warranted this measure.

According to Arthur Wallis,

"a crisis of the utmost gravity threatened the whole Jewish race with extermination. Even Esther herself could expect no immunity because she was queen. She called this absolute fast because desperate situations require desperate measures."

Other patriarchs that resorted to this kind of measure in dealing with crisis of great magnitude include:

Prophet Ezra

Driven by overwhelming concerns over the shameful compromise of the Priests and Levites of his days, Ezra fasted absolute for three days (Ezra 9:3):

> And when I heard this thing, I rent my garment and my mantle, and plucked off the hair of my head and of my beard, and sat down astonished.

This significant act is frequently mentioned in the sacred writings, and was common among all ancient nations. Shaving the head and beard were signs of excessive grief; much more so the plucking off the hair, which must produce exquisite pain. All these expressed his abhorrence, not merely of the act of taking strange wives, but of joining affinity with these strange women in their idolatrous practices. Also in Ezra 10:6 we see his deep abhorrence over the evil practices of his days expressed in the following words:

> ...and when he came thither, he did eat no bread, nor drink water: for he mourned because of the transgression of them that had been carried away.

The only way Ezra knew best to deal with these acts of apostasy among his people, and evoke God's intervention, was to seek God through fasting.

Saul of Tarsus (Paul)

Saul of Tarsus- the great persecutor of the Church- got supernaturally blinded with his encounter with Jesus, and the Bible says, "And for three days he... neither ate nor drank" Acts 9:9. The outcome of this supernatural encounter marked a milestone, not just for his personal life, but for the Church as a whole.

King David

David was another observer of the absolute fast. He fasted seven days as a plea to God to save the life of his illegitimate child with Bathsheba (2 Samuel 12:15-20):

> *And Nathan departed unto his house. And the Lord struck the child that Uriah's wife bare unto David, and it was very sick. David therefore besought God for the child; and David fasted, and went in, and lay all night upon the earth. And the elders of his house arose, and went to him, to raise him up from the earth: but he would not, neither did he eat bread with them. And it came to pass on the seventh day that the child died. And the servants of David feared to tell him that the child was dead: for they said, Behold, while the child was yet alive, we spake unto him, and he would not hearken unto our voice: how will he then vex himself, if we tell him that the*

child is dead? But when David saw that his servants whispered, David perceived that the child was dead: therefore David said unto his servants, Is the child dead? And they said, He is dead. Then David arose from the earth, and washed, and anointed himself, and changed his apparel, and came into the house of the Lord, and worshipped: then he came to his own house; and when he required, they set bread before him, and he did eat.

Absolute fasts, of a protracted nature – extending beyond three or seven days, are also found in the Bible, but these exceptions were based upon direct guidance from God.

Fasting Beyond Three Days Absolute

Absolute fasts, of a protracted nature – extending beyond three or seven days, are also found in the Bible, but these exceptions were based upon direct guidance from God. Readers are, therefore, advised that the people involved in these fasts were supernaturally sustained, and loss of lives have resulted from long fasts that were not cautiously undertaken. You must not undertake a fast for periods longer than your body can survive!

Moses

Examples of the observers of these extreme fasts are: Moses - (Exodus 34:28, Deuteronomy 9:9-18). On two separate occasions of forty days and forty nights, Moses was in the presence of God, neither eating nor drinking.

And he was there with the Lord forty days and forty nights; he did neither eat bread, nor drink water. And he wrote upon the tables the words of the covenant, the Ten Commandments (Exodus 34: 28).

And I fell down before the LORD, as at the first, forty days and forty nights: I did neither eat bread, nor drink water, because of all your sins which you sinned, in doing wickedly in the sight of the LORD, to provoke him to anger (Deuteronomy 9:9-18).

Elijah

Another person who undertook a protracted fast without food and water was Elijah (1 Kings 19:8):

And he arose, and did eat and drink, and went in the strength of that meat forty days and forty nights unto Horeb the mount of God.

Arthur Wallis draws a striking parallel between these two leading Old Testament figures:

while Moses was the law giver, Elijah was its restorer (Mal 4:4-6; Mark 9:12). Secondly, both had a supernatural ending to their lives, and hundreds of years after they died, both appeared on the mountain of transfiguration with Christ (Matt. 17:1-8). It is perfectly in order to attribute such deep encounters both of them had with God to the fasted life they lived.

Finally, as discussed, Jesus also exemplified a protracted fast:

And Jesus being full of the Holy Ghost returned from Jordan, and was led by the Spirit into the wilderness, Being forty days tempted of the devil. And in those days he did eat nothing (Luke 4: 1,2).

The length of the fast a believer observes is, no doubt, a matter between him and God, as said. However, due caution should be observed not to choose fasting, of a duration too long that he cannot complete, or too gruesome to cause him harm.

THE WONDERS OF FASTING

Part Three
Principles of Biblical Fast

THE WONDERS OF FASTING

9

QUESTIONS TO ASK BEFORE FASTING

Before we go further, it is pertinent to stress that Christian fasting must be embarked upon with clear objectives in mind. Just as it is unwise to pray just for the sake of praying, fasting void of purpose is a waste of time, and yields no results whatsoever. Accordingly, we would like to examine very crucial matters that must be fully resolved before a believer undertakes a fast.

What are your objectives or Goals for fasting?

Why are you fasting? Is it for spiritual renewal, for guidance, for healing, for the resolution of problems, for special grace to handle a difficult situation? Ask the Holy Spirit to clarify His leading and objectives for your fast. This will enable you to pray more specifically and strategically.

Through fasting we humble ourselves before God to deal with situations in our lives, homes, awaken our churches, and heal our land according to 2 Chronicles 7:14. Make this a priority in your fasting. Be specific about the purpose of your fast from the onset. If you do this, and set your heart on the reward, the pressure of fasting on your body is lessen. Personally, just reminding myself of the gains of my fasting from the Lord makes fasting a pleasurable exercise for me.

Is your fast God – ordained?

It is vitally important to ask yourself this question before undertaking any fast. It must be the fast that God has ordained. Notice in Isaiah 58:5, God asked "…wilt thou call this a fast, an acceptable day to the LORD? Dear Saint, God has His chosen fasts! It is this fast that God rewards; not just any fast. God has no responsibility whatsoever, blessing what He has not initiated or ordained. A believer's fast that is not God ordained, invariably attracts no reward from Him, because God should be the focus of everything we do: in prayer, in fasting, and indeed, in all our Christian service. As earlier observed, in the parable of the Pharisees and the Publican, Jesus condemned the fasting of the Pharisees because it was born out of pride and tradition. He fasted for personal aggrandisement – an ego boosting exercise! It was not 'God-ward.' According to the said parable recorded in Luke 18:11,12, the Pharisee commended his deeds (works) before God, as he 'assassinated' the character of his praying partner – the Publican. The motive of his fasting was clearly revealed in his prayer:

> *The Pharisee stood and prayed thus with himself, God, I thank thee, that I am not as other men are, extortioners, unjust, adulterers, or even as this publican [tax collector]. I fast twice in the week; I give tithes of all I possess.*

It is highly recommended that one follows God's leading in fasting. Be certain that it is the Lord, and not your ego leading you to undertake a fast, and that it will honour and glorify God.

Have you set a time for prayer and meditation of the word of God?

As fasting is often undertaken in association with prayer, it is of utmost importance that before the believer commences a fast that he sets out a rough time-table for sessions of prayer and scripture meditation. This has been of immense benefit to me. This ensures that sufficient time is devoted to prayer and scripture meditation. We understand that as we speak to God in prayer, He speaks to us in return, very often through scripture meditation.

As Judah fasted and prayed under the leadership of Jehoshaphat against her enemies, the Bible says, the spirit of God rested upon a Levite by the name of Jehaziel and said,

> ... listen all you and you inhabitants of Jerusalem, and you, King Jehoshaphat! Thus says the Lord to you: Do not be afraid nor dismayed because of this great multitude, for the battle is not yours, but God's... (2 Chronicles 20:14).

This was in response to the prayer of Jehoshaphat and his people. It is vitally important to set time for prayer and meditation before undertaking any fast. It must not be left to chance!

It is recommended that prayer accompanies fasting for maximum results. Bishop David Oyedepo remarks that when Jesus was in a fast, he was "busy stuffing Himself with the Word of God; so that when it was battle time, He fought valiantly, using the word-weapon..."

It should be noted that prayer, fasting, and the word of God are all weapons of warfare. Studying the word of God in the course of observing a fast is specifically required by God:

"On your fast day…you shall read the words of the Lord" (Jeremiah 36:6).

Accordingly, fasting coupled with prayer and the study of the word of God puts you at an advantage.

Jentezen Franklin was right when he said that fasting, when combined with prayer…creates a cord that is not easily broken (Eccl. 4: 12).

Fasting Journal: Do you have a fasting journal?

When we say "Fasting Journal," we are referring to a notebook specifically purchased for the purpose of writing your fasting experiences. Yes, it is that serious!

> Yet, no two fasts are ever the same! Every fast brings its distinct physical and emotional experiences.

How prepared are you to hear from God during your fast? Do you have plans to 'document' what you hear the Lord say to you? Note that whatever the Lord speaks to you during your fast may not be for now or the immediate future. You must keep a record of the leading the Lord is giving you concerning the subject-matter of your fast, and indeed, other specific areas of your life. These may well be in relation to issues that could take years to come to fruition; indeed, the vision could yet be for a time and season, very well into the future.

Habakkuk was admonished by God to:

"...write the vision and make it plain on tables, that he may run that readeth it. For the vision is yet for an appointed time; but at the end it will speak, and it will not lie. Though it tarries, wait for it; because it will surely come, it will not tarry," says Prophet Habakkuk – (Habakkuk 2:2,3).

Every great vision requires 'writing down', and every great vision requires a 'run'. Yet, how do you run if you have no clear leading? It is therefore, important that you keep a detailed record of the subject-matter of your fast, and what you receive from the Lord as a result. Your physical and emotional reactions to the fast should also be documented. Yet, no two fasts are ever the same! Every fast brings its distinct physical and emotional experiences. Having a fasting journal will ensure that your objectives for the fast are well defined. Yet, on a wider perspective, a life worth living is a life worth recording.

When after the fast, you return to read what you wrote. I guarantee that in retrospect, you will be amazed at some of the things you would have put on paper.

How long will your fast be?

It is advised that before you embark on a fast, you decide the duration of the fast. There are no perpetual fasts. In scripture, as seen, the duration of fasts people engaged in were for definite and pre-determined period of time. Esther, for instance, fasted for three days.

> *The inhabitants of Jabesh-gilead fasted for seven days, after the death of Saul* (1 Samuel 31: 11-13),

When the inhabitants of Jabesh-gilead heard that which the Philistines had done to Saul; all the valiant men arose, and went all night, and took the body of Saul and the bodies of his sons from the wall of Beth-shan, and came to Jabesh, and burnt them there. And they took their bones, and buried them under a tree at Jabesh, and fasted seven days.

Moses, Elijah and Jesus fasted for 40 days. It is an important decision to be made with God, as to the duration of your fast.

The wisdom in making this decision resonates in the following words of Richard J. Forster:

"As with all the Disciplines, a progression should be observed; it is wise to learn to walk well before we try to run. Begin with a partial fast of twenty-four hours' duration; many have found lunch to lunch to be the best time. This means that you would not eat two meals. Fresh fruit juices are excellent to drink during the fast. Attempt this once a week for several weeks. In the beginning you will be fascinated with the physical aspects, but the most important things to monitor is the inner attitude of worship."

There are no hard and fast rules governing the length of any type of fast you may choose to engage in; however, it is always advisable to begin with a day fast, from sunrise to sunset. There is no wisdom in a beginner attempting a 40 day fast. Start small and walk your way up to longer fasts. Moderation should be the guiding principle.

This then leads us to a very pertinent issue which has to do, not just with having the right motive for fasting, but what I call the wrong and the right fast.

10

THE WRONG AND RIGHT FAST

The Wrong Fast

We must never think of fasting as a hunger strike designed to force God's hand and get our own way! We do not need to strong arm God. God is always eager to answer our prayers.

David gives the assurance that God answers prayers:

O you thou that hearest prayer, unto thee shall all flesh come (Psalm 65:2).

Gill Exposition of the Bible puts it wisely:

".... So as to answer it sooner or later, in one way or another, and always in the fittest time, and in the best way; so as to fulfil the requests and supply the wants of men, so far as may be for their good, and God's glory; which is a proof of the omnipresence, omniscience, and all sufficiency of

God; who can hear the prayers of his people in all places at the same time, and knows all their persons and wants, and what is most proper for them, and can and does supply all their needs, and causes all grace to abound towards them; and it also shows his wondrous grace and condescension, to listen to the cries and regard the prayers of the poor and destitute…"

God is good! He is generous (James 1:5) and eager to give us 'good things' (Matthew 7:11). Do not use fasting to try to push God into a corner. Fasting does not change God; it changes man!

According to Elmer Towns, "Even if we wanted to, we could not manipulate God…"

An in-depth study of the word of God makes it clear that God's standard for dealing with man cannot be compromised by the personality or sacrifice of man. As a matter of fact, God is no respecter of persons. Pauls establishes:

> … *the foundation of God standeth sure, having this seal, the Lord knoweth them that are His…" (2 Timothy 2:19).*

So, no fasting of a man can alter God's standard. The words "standeth sure" speak of the irrevocability of that standard. For example, in 2 Kings 17:16-17 the Bible tells us that:

"Israel... left all the commandments of the LORD their God, and made them molten images, even two calves, and made an idol pole and worshiped all the army of heaven, and served Baal. And they caused their sons and their daughters to pass through the fire, and used divination and enchantments, and sold themselves to do evil in the sight of the LORD, to provoke him to anger.

They sacrificed their sons and daughters by burning them alive. They practiced black magic and cast evil spells. They sold themselves by doing what the LORD considered evil, and they made him furious- (verse 17, The Word Bible).

How did God react to Israel's state of apostasy? God's judgment was swift and harshly delivered! In verse 20, the Bible records:

And the LORD rejected all the descendants of Israel, and afflicted them, and delivered them into the hand of plunderers, until he had cast them out of his sight.

In the Word Translation Bible reads,

So the LORD rejected all of Israel's descendants, made them suffer, handed them over to those who looted their property, and finally turned away from Israel.

God's reaction to sin is consistent through-out the Bible. For instance, in Judges 2:14, we read:

In his anger against Israel the LORD gave them into the hands of raiders who plundered them. He sold them into the hands of their enemies all around, whom they were no longer able to resist."

God would always judge sin because, in His sight and His Holiness, He cannot endure to "look toward iniquity":

"You are of purer eyes than to behold evil, and cannot look on iniquity..." (Habakkuk 1:13).

Sin separates us from God. Prophet Isaiah lays the blame squarely on the sins of the sinner:

Behold, the LORD's hand is not shortened, that it cannot save; neither his ear heavy that it cannot hear: But your iniquities have separated between you and your God, and your sins have hid his face from you, that he will not hear (Isaiah 59:1,2)

When the Wrong Person Fasts...

Accordingly, when a wrong man or a man out of tune with God fasts, the fast is wrong, and it bears no consequence with God. As a matter of fact, before a man fasts or prays, he must qualify to engage in the act. In other words, he must have recognition in heaven for his sacrifices to be acceptable to God. The sacrifice of the wicked is an abomination before God. Both the prayer and fasting that proceed from a wrong heart are a futile effort at taking the persons of God for granted. They bear no spiritual fruits whatsoever.

The kind of fasting that God is pleased with, includes a desire to live an upright life, and help the poor and the oppressed.

Martin Luther argues:

… genuine Christian fasting is a fruit of repentance… it helps keep the flesh in check and is a fine outward training in preparing to better receive God's grace.

He was not alone in the condemnation of wrong attitude to fasting. John Calvin – exposing the abominable fasting habits of the Catholic Church in his time - taught that fasting is of no value to God unless the heart is right and unless fasting is accompanied by genuine repentance, humiliation, and sorrow in the presence of an awesome God.

The 58th chapter of Isaiah presents us with a clear picture of what God regards as wrong attitude in fasting, and, of course, the wrong fast.

Isaiah took to task those who go through the motions of religious observance while at the same time committing sins and promoting corruption. The kind of fasting that God is pleased with, includes a desire to live an upright life, and help the poor and the oppressed.

The Lord instructed Isaiah to proclaim loudly the sins of the nation. This includes the outward righteousness of the people as they went to the temple, obeyed God's laws, fasted, and appeared eager to serve the Holy One of Israel. But the Lord, who sees the heart (1 Sam. 16:7), was not impressed with the external religious rituals. Says God:

> *What are all your sacrifices to Me? ... I have had enough of burnt offerings and rams and the fat of well–fed cattle; I have no desire for the blood of bulls, lambs, or male goats.... Stop bringing useless offerings. I despise [your] incense.... I hate your New Moons and prescribed festivals. They have become a burden to Me; I am tired of putting up with [them]. When you lift up your hands [in prayer], I will refuse to look at you; even if you offer countless prayers, I will not listen* (Isa. 1:11-15).

Quoting Isa. 29:13, Jesus offered a similar rebuke to the religious leaders of His days:

These people honor Me with their lips, but their heart is far from Me. They worship Me in vain, teaching as doctrines the commands of men (Matt. 15:8-9).

These are important passages that speak to Christians today. The question should be constantly asked, is our worship a humble response to God's grace, or a self-centred effort to draw attention to ourselves or to curry God's favour?

Warren Wiersbe notes,

When we worship because it is the popular thing to do, not because it is the right thing to do, then our worship becomes hypocritical.

The Jews were commanded to observe only one fast per year, on the Day of Atonement (Lev. 16:29-31), but they were permitted to fast personally at other times. Somehow, the permission to fast devolved into a contest among God's people to gain His attention. Now they complained that the Lord did not see or notice their fasting.

Hear the outcry of the people:

Wherefore have we fasted, say they, and thou seest not? wherefore have we afflicted our soul, and thou takest no knowledge? Behold, in the day of your fast ye find pleasure, and exact all your labours (Isaiah 58:3).

These people were apportioning blame to God for not being just. They wanted to gain God's attention at all cost, while buried in their evil practices.

God's response was swift:

Behold, you fast for strife and debate, and to strike with the fist of wickedness: you shall not fast as you do this day, to make your voice to be heard on high. Is it such a fast that I have chosen? a day for a man to afflict his soul? is it to bow down his head as a bulrush, and to spread sackcloth and ashes under him? will you call this a fast, and an acceptable day to the LORD? (Isaiah 58:4-5).

The people in Isaiah's days were fasting for all the wrong reasons! They fasted to get things from God, and hypocritically appeared righteous.

The problem with the people's fasting here, of course, is that it was an empty religious ritual observed to satisfy some religious requirements. It was fasting characterised with injustice to others, and of course, it ended in strife and contention. This was the kind of fasting practiced by the Pharisees in Jesus' days. There was no repentance or self-humbling!

The kind of fasting that God is pleased with, includes a desire to live an upright life, and help the poor and the oppressed.

Fasting is meant to encourage believers to respond positively to God's commands. As we deprive ourselves of certain physical needs – food, sleep, sexual relations, for example, we are better able to see the weakness of our flesh and to hear God's voice. Although the people of Israel were fasting, they had clearly neglected the instructions from the Lord to care for the less fortunate among them and treat them as members of their own family who, at one time, had been slaves in Egypt. In others words, they were overlooking the very essential elements of a true fast. Fasting should result in self-denial, not self-indulgence. When believers share with others it serves as a reminder that all they own ultimately belongs to God.

There is undoubtedly, a clear message for today's believer in this passage: there is no amount of cry by man, any group of persons that would move God to alter His standard. God rejected their fasting because God is looking for fasting that meets His requirements. If the fasting fails to meet God's criteria, He is not interested.

Abstaining from food alone, therefore, is not what makes and defines the fast. There is a weightier matter that has to do with the condition of the heart. Failure at this level means outright failure! Once the heart is wrong, fasting becomes impotent. The heart is the foundation of everything we do for God. The Bible says, *"If the foundation be destroyed, what can the righteous do"* (Proverb 11:3). Absolutely nothing!

There is a pathetic account in the book of Zechariah 7: 1-3 that further highlights or elucidates the great premium God places on His pre-ordained standard set, as prerequisite for accepting the fasts of the believer:

> *And it came to pass in the fourth year of King Dairus, that the word of the Lord came unto Zachariah in the fourth day of the ninth month, even in Chisleu, when they had sent unto the house of God Sherezer and Regemelech, and their men, to pray before the LORD of hosts, and to the prophets; saying Should I weep in the fifth month, separating*

myself, as I have done these so many years?

The people of Zechariah's days had fasted, albeit ritualistically for a staggering period of seventy years - every fifth and seventh month of the year. The people would have carried on with this ritualistic practice - wrongful attitude towards God's holy and sacred sacrifice (fasting), had God not intervened! In verse 5, after a practice that had spanned through a period of seventy years, God finally expressed His disgust at what the people regarded as "a fast unto the lord." Says God,

Speak unto all the people of the land, and to the Priests, saying, When ye fasted and mourned in fifth and seventh month, even those seventy years, did ye at all fast unto me, even to me?

Fasting for seventy years without approval from God? How awful! Indeed, these people were fully persuaded that they were fasting unto the Lord those seventy years. The length of time these people had engaged in a wrongful fast did not move God to condone their practice. God would always distance Himself from whatever is at odd with His purpose and pattern of doing things. What is the implication of this, you may ask? A man could choose to fast for a 'century,' if he so wishes, but if that fasting is conducted in defiance to God's criteria, the fasting is wrong, and the duration or length of the fast is irrelevant. Further, if a wrong man or a man out of tune with God fasts, his fasting is an abomination to God; he receives no reward but condemnation in return. How tragic!

> *The sacrifice of the wicked is abomination: how much more, when he bringeth it with a wicked mind?* (Pro. 21:27, KJV).

> *The sacrifice of the wicked is detestable - how much more so when brought with evil intent!* (Pro. 12:27, NIV)

Here exists a fundamental principle: while man looks at 'his fast', God looks at the heart of the 'faster'. If the heart is right with Him, then God looks at the fast.

> *For the LORD sees not as man sees: man looks on the outward appearance, but the LORD looks on the heart."* (1 Samuel 16:7).

The same goes for prayers, giving, and indeed, all our services in the kingdom. If our heart is right then God considers our service. But when the heart is wrong or is in opposition to His will, then God takes His eyes away from us. The first pre-requisite for fasting, therefore, is a heart that is pleasing to the Lord.

Can you imagine two sisters or brothers in the same fellowship who keep malice with each order? On a service day, they sing praises to the Lord, but immediately after the fellowship is over, they continue being enemies. On the fellowship fasting days they participate fully, and pray fervently, expecting God to hear their prayers; then they wonder why God is not 'moving'. We wonder why we labour so much with little or no results. Dear Saint, God is not mocked! David said *"If I regard iniquity in my heart, the Lord will not hear me" Psalm 66:18*. The master is looking for His life reflected in the believer that fasts; a life fully yielded to Him.

This was recorded concerning a beloved saint – Gaius.

> *The elder unto the wellbeloved Gaius, whom I love in the truth. For I rejoiced greatly, when the brethren came and testified of the truth that is in thee, even as thou walkest in the truth* (3 John 1, 3).

And of Demetrius the testimony runs:

> *Demetrius hath good report of all men, and of the truth itself: yea, and we also bear him record; and ye know that our record is true* (3 John 12).

These exemplify the hearts that the Master is seeking. *"Those that will worship [serve] the father in spirit and in truth."* John 4:23.

Still on the subject of wrong fast, Jesus said

Moreover when you fast, be not as the hypocrites, of a sad countenance, for they disfigure their faces, that they may appear unto men to fast. Verily I say unto you. They have their reward. But thou when thou fastest anoint thine head, and wash thy face. That thou appear not unto men to fast but unto God thy father which is in secret, shall reward thee openly" Matt. 6: 16-18.

In this passage, Jesus tells the believer how to engage in fasting that would meet God's standard and attracts His blessings: they are to anoint their heads and wash their faces. In Jewish custom anointing one's head and washing one's face was not done for daily hygiene or cosmetic reasons. Rather they were reserved for joyous occasions. So unusual religious sorrow within should be compensated for by outward signs of an opposite sort. Reality in the sight of God rather than appearance in the sight of man must be the believer's desire.

And the words "your [singular] Father," used twice in verse 18, point to the personal relationship between the individual and God. This is elsewhere expressed powerfully by the use of the Aramaic term "Abba", which can be translated, "Daddy" (Mark 14:36; Rom. 8:15). Acts of piety such as fasting must be performed solely and exclusively for the believer's "Father" with no concern for one's reputation before others. God "is in secret," and He "sees in secret." The double use of the word "secret" in Matthew 6:18 emphasises the hiddenness of the virtuous act of fasting, in order to be performed for God alone. These secret acts are noticed by God and will be rewarded by Him. The passage closes with the assuring words "thine father …will reward you…"

As with almsgiving and prayer, the believer should practice fasting as an act of private piety. His main concern was their inner spirit with which fasting was performed. They were to be pure in motive as they fasted and not to fast as a means of gaining approval from others.

THE WONDERS OF FASTING

11

THE RIGHT FAST

Having examined the negative fast, we must now turn our attention to consider the positive fast – the kind of fast that honours the Master, which consequently attracts His reward! Let us examine this in the life of Jesus Himself.

And ... being full of the Holy returned from Jordan, and was led by the Spirit in the Wilderness. Being forty days tempted of the devil. And in those days he did eat nothing, and when they were ended, he was afterward hungered (Luke 4:1-2).

After the Lord's fast, the Bible says, "And Jesus returned in the power of the Spirit..." (v.14). What are the implications of the verse just quoted? First, being full of the Holy Spirit does not necessarily cause one to walk in the power of the Spirit. One of the ways to walking in power as a believer is fasting and prayer. Second, Jesus was full of the Holy Spirit when He entered into forty days fast. But how did He come out of it? The Bible says,

> *And Jesus returned in the power of the Spirit into Galilee, and there went out the fame of him through all the region around about (LK 4:14).*

Notice that Jesus was already full of the Holy Ghost when he entered the fast, but he was overflowing with the Holy Spirit when he finished. He was already filled, but now he was empowered; an overflowing of what filled Him – The Holy Spirit.

As discussed, in Isaiah 58: 6-7, God told what the fasting that is pleasing to God entails:

> *Is not this the fast that I have chosen? to loose the bands of wickedness, to undo the heavy burdens, and to let the oppressed go free, and that ye break every yoke? Is it not to deal thy bread to the hungry, and that thou bring the poor that are cast out to thy house? when thou seest the naked, that thou cover him; and that thou hide not thyself from thine own flesh?*

What Does Isaiah 58:6-7 mean?

1. God is not impressed with your religious performance. "You cannot fast as you do today and expect your voice to be heard on High."

2.   If you want God's attention, then you need to live the true fast: seek justice for the oppressed, share your resources with those in need, break the structures that enslave the weak, honour the Sabbath, and pour yourself out for the hungry.

3.   If you live the true fast, then God will guard, guide, strengthen, and listen to you. God will give you life, beauty, and joy. These are not empty promises of prosperity. They are promises with substance.

Isaiah stressed that the fast that is acceptable to God has in focus the breaking of the chain of injustice and the destroying of yokes of oppression, wickedness, and setting of captives free. This anointing comes from fasting, not just praying. Jesus was emphatic on the subject when He said that certain demonic oppressions could only be overcome with the power that is generated through prayer and fasting. " ... Howbeit this kind goeth not out but by prayer and fasting" Matthew 17:21.

In summary, the God - chosen fast will make you want to love and give to people and not to take from and mistreat people.

EIGHT CHARACTERISTICS OF GOD'S CHOSEN FAST

"Is not this the fast that I have chosen? to loose the bands of wickedness, to undo the heavy burdens, and to let the oppressed go free, and that ye break every yoke? Is it not to deal thy bread to the hungry, and that thou bring the poor that are cast out to thy house? when thou seest the naked, that thou cover him; and that thou hide not thyself from thine own flesh?" (Isaiah 58:6-7)

The above scripture lists seven key characteristics of the kind of fast that is pleasing to God. In other words, these are the conditions that must be met by every fast that attracts the attention and rewards of God.

They are to:

1. Loose the bands of wickedness
2. Undo the heavy burden
3. Let the oppressed go free
4. Break every yoke
5. Deal thy bread to the hungry
6. Bring the poor that are cast out

into thy house

7. Cover the naked

8. Not hide thyself from thine own flesh.

The issues raised in these verses of scriptures are fundamental and significant. They further buttress the need to combine faith with works. It is not enough to have faith. Our faith must have practical works in our relationship with others, to be genuine. From the expository teaching of Apostle James on the subject, we can conclude that emphasis on faith at the expense of works renders faith ineffective, as our fasting.

> *What does it profit, my brethren, if someone says he has faith but does not have works? Can faith save him? If a brother or sister is naked and destitute of daily food, and one of you says to them, "Depart in peace, be warmed and filled," but you do not give them the things which are needed for the body, what does it profit? Thus also faith by itself, if it does not have works, is dead.*
>
> *But someone will say, "You have faith, and I have works." Show me your faith without your works, and I will show you my faith by my works. You believe that there is one God. You do well. Even the demons believe—and tremble! But do you want*

> to know, O foolish man, that faith without works is dead? Was not Abraham our father justified by works when he offered Isaac his son on the altar? Do you see that faith was working together with his works, and by works faith was made perfect? And the Scripture was fulfilled which says, "Abraham believed God, and it was accounted to him for righteousness." And he was called the friend of God. You see then that a man is justified by works, and not by faith only. Likewise, was not Rahab the harlot also justified by works when she received the messengers and sent them out another way? For as the body without the spirit is dead, so faith without works is dead also (James 2:14-26 NKJV).

The church, to be effective in its mission, cannot afford to be in isolation and out of touch with the needs of the people it is called to serve.

We see incredible consensus from the writings of various Bible authors on the subject.

Paul says,

> As we have therefore opportunity, let us do good unto all men, especially unto them who are of the household of faith (Galatians 6:10).

And Apostle John was emphatic in his view:

But whoever has this world's good, and sees his brother have need, and shuts up his bowels of compassion from him, how dwells the love of God in him? My little children, let us not love in word, neither in tongue; but indeed and in truth (1 John 3:17).

Loose the bands of wickedness

According to Webster's New Explorer Encyclopaedic Dictionary, a band is "something that confines or constricts while allowing a degree of movements; something that binds or restrains legally, morally, or spiritually…"

When the enemy wants to have his way, alter the course of an individual, family, or, even, a church's life and take full control of the affairs of their destiny, he uses bands – the bands of wickedness.

Too many of God's people are in one form of bondage or another. Some are experiencing fiery trials that have defiled prayers, many are drowning in depression. Some believers are under the bands that bound them long before they met Christ and are still being haunted. These individuals, families, even churches find themselves under the weight of bands of afflictions, yokes of set-backs and frustration in life. Jesus said this kind only comes out by prayer and fasting. I believe He is referring to the type of prayer and fasting described in the book of Isaiah, as discussed, to lose the bands of wickedness and destroy the yokes of depression. Today, churches are full of well-meaning people and families who Satan has limited, confined and restrained to a life of misery and reproach. How sad! These people have prayed all kinds of prayers and attended all kinds of special meetings: conventions, conferences, seminars, all-night prayer meetings, to mention but a few, seeking solutions, but to no avail. The church can no longer ignore the command to loosen the bands of wickedness and undo the heavy burdens. To do so is to shy away from God's mandate for the church. Our fasting destroys the yoke the enemy has placed on people both in the church, our cities and nations. God's prescription for losing the bands of wickedness is His "chosen fast". Men and women must rise in the power of the Holy Ghost to bring deliverance and freedom from the bands of wickedness.

Let the oppressed go free

One of the greatest objects of fasting is to set the oppressed free. To be oppressed means the following:

1. Burden with cruel or unjust impositions or restraints; subject to a burdensome or harsh exercise of authority or power: for example, a people oppressed by totalitarianism.

2. To lie heavily upon (the mind, a person etc.)

3. To weigh down, as sleep or weariness does.

4. To put down; subdue or suppress.

5. To press upon or against; crush.

According to Strong's Exhaustive Concordance of the Bible, the Greek word for oppression – katadunasteuo – means "to exercise dominion against." The Hebrew word for oppression or to be oppressed "ratsats" means "to crack in pieces, to break, bruise, crush, discourage, oppress, struggle together."

Thank God! The Bible says:

*How God anointed Jesus of Nazareth with the Holy Spirit and with power, who went about doing good and healing all who were **oppressed** by the devil, for God was with Him* (Acts 10:38, emphasis added).

There is healing for the oppressed! God has mandated His church to set the oppressed, hurting people free. Jesus says:

> *The Spirit of the Lord is upon me, because he hath anointed me to preach the gospel to the poor; he hath sent me to heal the brokenhearted, to preach deliverance to the captives, and recovering of sight to the blind, to set at liberty them that are bruised* (Luke 4:18).

> *"… the Lord is that Spirit: and where the Spirit of the Lord is, there is liberty"* (2 Cor. 3:17).

There is freedom for you if you are in any form of oppression in Jesus name.

Break every yoke

Literally, a "yoke" is a device laid across the necks of animals to harness them together so they can work as a team, and their load is attached to it. It was also widely used by slave traders in the transportation of slaves.

A yoke was a sign of absolute slavery and captivity. In a sense, they played the role of modern day "hand-cuffs", often used by the police on some suspects. Yokes are designed to restrain movements.

They were also used as vindictive instruments to humiliate, despise, and enslave prisoners.

If a yoke was not properly attached to the animals, or if the load was too heavy for them to pull, the yoke would chafe the animals painfully and hinder their productivity.

However, its use gave rise to a couple of figurative meanings in the New Testament.

Jesus employed its use when He taught His audience: *"My yoke is easy and My burden is light"* (Matthew 11:30), wherein He was contrasting the "difficulties" of following Him with the difficulties of keeping the Law of Moses.

Also, Apostle Peter described the harsh requirements of the Law the young converts in Antioch were asked to satisfy as pre-requisite for being accepted into the Christian faith, as a yoke.

He said:

*Now therefore, why do you test God by putting a **yoke** on the neck of the disciples which neither our fathers nor we were able to bear?"* – (Acts 15:10, emphasis added).

The other major figurative meaning refers to the way a yoke places animals side-by-side. This is to compel them to move together in order to accomplish anything. This aspect is the basis of the teaching, "Do not be unequally yoked together with unbelievers." (2 Corinthians 6:14). This teaching is not exclusive to marriage; in fact, Paul was not even talking about marriage in this passage. It more broadly applies to any relationship that would compel two people to "work together as one."

The only weapon, according to the Bible, that destroys yokes is the anointing of the Holy Spirit working through a human vessel.

> *And it shall come to pass in that day, that his burden shall be taken away from off your shoulder, and his yoke from off your neck, and the yoke shall be destroyed because of the anointing* (Isaiah 10:27).

Nothing fuels the anointing as much as biblical fasting. The vessels of God are empowered to the degree that they submit themselves to God. It is God that fills His vessels with the divine ability that is needed to accomplish kingdom assignments. The Word says, "… we have this treasure in earthen vessels, that the excellency of the power may be of God, and not of us. (2 Cor. 4:7).

Sadly, despite the authority Christ has given the church, countless numbers of people live in perpetual darkness under the yoke of satanic bondage. The same applies to millions of Christian homes. Child of God, you do not have to bear that burden any more. The Bible says,…his [Satan's] burden shall be taken away from off your shoulder (Isaiah 10:27). Every yoke, no matter its intensity or duration, is destroyable.

Fasting and Good deeds

Is it not to deal thy bread to the hungry, and that thou bring the poor that are cast out to thy house? when thou seest the naked, that thou cover him; and that thou hide not thyself from thine own flesh? (Isaiah 58: 7).

The seventh verse of Isaiah 58 is extremely vital to our study, as it takes our discussion to an altogether new dimension. It must be stressed that God greatly blesses generosity to the needy.

To have adequate understanding of what this verse conveys, it is important to examine its various segments or requirements distinctly.

Most translations of the Bible take an interpretative approach, taking "flesh" to mean, significantly, 'one's own family.' For examples:

...and do not hide from relatives who need your help (NLT)

... and not to turn away from your own flesh and blood? (NIV)

... and to not ignore your own flesh and blood? (HCSB)

I must admit, for a number of years, Isaiah 58, verse 7 was one of those scriptures I found very difficult to understand – at best it read like one of the Shakespearean poetry works. Bless God, a revelation got dawned on me, and I have regarded it as one of my favourite fasting scriptures ever since. Saint, if we must engage in the fast that God has prescribed for His Church, we must go about it His way, following every detail closely.

Let us now examine the various components of the said verse:

Is it not to deal thy bread to the hungry...

Christlikeness is more to do with how we treat the poor. It sounds like what our modern societies have labelled 'charitable work.' Yes, God teaches that if our fasting must meet His criteria, it must have something to do with taking care of the poor. The greatest 'charity worker' that ever lived is Jesus;

He healed the sick, raised the dead and fed the poor, all for nothing in return. The Bible says:

He that has pity upon the poor lends unto the LORD; and that which he has given will he pay him again (Proverbs 19:17)

He that giveth unto the poor shall not lack: but he that hideth his eyes shall have many a curse (Proverbs 28:27).

John Kilpatrick was emphatic when he said:

"The Church has grown accustomed to letting soup kitchens and relief agencies feed the hungry...There is something about hand-on ministry and sharing that transforms the heart and the soul. There is something about rubbing shoulders with the hungry, the lost, and the wounded that keeps our eyes on Jesus Christ and our egos on the ground, where they belong. God planned it this way because He knows that when we personally share our bread with another person, we also share love, encouragement, and reassurance that the person we serve is valuable and precious in the sight of both God and man....our religion becomes a lifestyle of Christlike sharing, loving, and redeeming. After all, if Jesus were to walk among us today, where would we find Him-with the satisfied or the hungry?"

Bring the poor that are cast out into thy house...

It must be noted that concerning these requirements, God is not looking for something we do just when we are fasting, but an act that is habitual – a lifestyle!

Knowing or recognising the poor does not require prayer and fasting. You do not need a special word of knowledge to know who is poor and who is not. The poor are easy to identify. Jesus says, *"For you have the **poor** always with you..."* (Matthew 26: 11, emphasis added).

I know it could be very risky sharing your shelter with people you do not know so well, but you know what? Be led by the Spirit of God. The dividends of sharing our bounty and shelter with others are immeasurable. We are enjoined by Scriptures *"not to forget to entertain strangers: for thereby some have entertained angels unawares* (Hebrews 13:2).

There is great joy and fulfilment in the lives of people that have made it a practice to open their home to the needy. They are tremendously rewarded. The Bible says,

> *For God is not unrighteous to forget your work and labour of love, which ye have shewed toward his*

name, in that **ye have ministered to the saints, and do minister** (Hebrews 6:10, emphasis added).

David –A Case Study

1 Samuel 30 contains some golden nuggets that would help us appreciate the significance of sharing the love of Christ with the poor and needy.

In this biblical account, David and his men had just had a devastating incident – what would have been an act of terrorism in modern times.

The Bible says:

And it came to pass, when David and his men were come to Ziklag on the third day, that the Amalekites had invaded the south, and Ziklag, and smitten Ziklag, and burned it with fire; And had taken the women captives, that were therein: they slew not any, either great or small, but carried them away, and went on their way. So David and his men came to the city, and, behold, it was burned with fire; and their wives, and their sons, and their daughters, were taken captives (1 Samuel 30:1-3).

In an act of reprisal against the enemies, David resorted to a military conflict (battle) – quite reminiscent of the September 11, 2001 (9/11) terrorist attacks on America, and the consequent "War on Terror" campaign against Afganistan and Iraq, by the American Government.

And David enquired at the Lord, saying, Shall I pursue after this troop? shall I overtake them? And he answered him, Pursue: for thou shalt surely overtake them, and without fail recover all (verse 8).

Initially, David engaged in this conflict with six hundred Soldiers. However, with time, two hundred of them got so weak they could not continue with the battle. Knowing that these men were ready prey for the enemies, David decided to carry on with the conflict without them, and continued in the battle with the remaining four hundred soldiers.

So David went, he and the six hundred men that were with him, and came to the brook Besor, where those that were left behind stayed. But David pursued, he and four hundred men: for two hundred abode behind, which were so faint that they could not go over the brook Besor (verse 9, 10).

At the end of the battle God gave David and his four hundred warriors victory over the enemies.

When David was to share the spoils they gained at the end of the conflict, watch how he dealt with the two hundred soldiers that fainted on the way, as a result of which they could not actively engage in combat with the enemies:

> *Then David came to the two hundred men who had been too exhausted to follow him and who were left behind at the Besor Valley. They came out to meet David and the men with him. As David and his men approached, he asked them how they were.* **But all the evil men** *and troublemakers among David's followers said, "Because they did not go out with us, we will not share with them the plunder we recovered. However, each man may take his wife and children and go* (verses 21, 22 NIV, emphasis added).

It takes an evil mind to rob the poor and the less privileged in our midst.

It is amazing how David resolved this commotion right within his camp:

> *David replied, "No, my brothers, you must not do that with what the Lord has given us. He has protected us and delivered into our hands the raiding party that came against us. Who will listen to what you say? The share of the man who stayed*

> with the supplies is to be the same as that of him who went down to the battle. All will share alike." David made this a statute and ordinance for Israel from that day to this (verse 23-25 NIV).

Interestingly, David demonstrated the act of Christian generosity that seems to be missing in the Church today. He touched not just his immediate friends and neighbours with his generous heart, but those that had no alliance or affiliations of any sort with him. He sent the spoils from this battle far and near.

> When David reached Ziklag, he sent some of the plunder to the elders of Judah, who were his friends, saying, "Here is a gift for you from the plunder of the Lord's enemies." David sent it to those who were in Bethel, Ramoth Negev and Jattir; to those in Aroer, Siphmoth, Eshtemoa and Rakal; to those in the towns of the Jerahmeelites and the Kenites; to those in Hormah, Bor Ashan, Athak and Hebron; and to those in all the other places where he and his men had roamed (verses 26-31 NIV).

Fasting, to be effective, must go hand-in-hand with good works. We cannot engage in one without the other.

12

...WHEN THOU SEEST THE NAKED, THAT THOU COVER HIM...

In our world today, too many people are naked. With the present global economic melt-down, millions of people, families, and even churches are faced with gruesome challenges. Many live with the excruciating pains of lack and abject poverty daily. Notice this scripture says 'when thou seest the naked'; not 'if' thou seest the naked'. Dear saint, the present economic climate has claimed its victims; the destitute are all around us! People are hungry! It is our responsibility – the church - and not that of any formal institutionalised system to feed the poor and needy both within and outside our churches. Multitude of people are naked – exposed to the elements and eyes of the world. The church must step in and show these people that someone cares.

The naked also includes those who are damaged by the words and criticisms of the accusers and the self-righteous – fellow believers. We need to learn to stand together in times of trouble and crisis. Unfortunately, the sad reality is that believers who are going through painful situations find more assistance and sympathy out in the world than in the Body of Christ.

Mahesh Chavda called it acting like sharks. He said:

"We have trained ourselves to act more like sharks than believers when we see someone who is wounded, bleeding and floundering in the waters of adversity or failure. The members of the Body of Christ seem more determined to attack and cut up their wounded members than to rush to their side with support, healing, and gentle correction if needed. We are to support each order in grace and mercy because we are yoked together and united in Christ. If one falters, we all falter. That is why the fasting family of God wants to see every individual family in its body blessed. If one is affected, we are all affected, so it behoves us to stick together."

Hatred stirs up strife: but love covers all sins (Prov. 10:12).

…and that thou hide not thyself from thine own flesh?

The saying: "you can choose your friends, but cannot choose your family members" holds true in all ramifications – in relation to our earthly family and the family of believers. We cannot pick and choose our family members.

Majority of Christians have not come to terms with the huge significance God has placed on the family structure. As a result, many have accepted the wander and roam plan of the world system, casting off all obligations to family members, as well as the local church. This is quite dangerous! Family life and church life are paramount in God's plan. This is true because the character of God is best formed in the heat and pressure of long-term, mandatory fellowship with other people who may or may not agree with you on every detail. Family is important to God! Well-structured learning and long-term character formation and growth takes place in the crucible of family life than in any other area of human institutions.

In the words of John Kilpatrick:

"The family is God's safety net for a lifetime. Modern society, in its wisdom, has tried to dismantle the family. However, the family structure has worked for thousands of years in every culture on earth. Long before there were welfare agencies, government assistance programs, and Social Security, there was family. The family not only provided for the physical necessities of its members but also policed those among them who were not diligent about seeking work or meeting their responsibilities… Even the Church has fallen into the "let the government do it" mentality."

Personal responsibility and duty were once at the heart of all family relationships. Children knew that they had an inherent responsibility to care for the parents in old age, just as their parents had cared for them in infancy. The sick, the disabled, and failing were never abandoned…after all they were family. Where personal responsibility and duty are discarded, the family safety net fails. It is time for the Church to restore God's standard of responsibility to every Christian home and congregation.

Paul was explicit in his declaration on the subject:

But if anyone does not provide for his own, and especially for those of his household, he has denied the faith and is worse than an unbeliever (1 Timothy 5:8).

Progression of the verse

Let us look at the progression of the verse, (Isaiah 58:7):

First, is to give bread: Is it not to share your food with the hungry

Second, is to give shelter: and to provide the poor wanderer with shelter

Third, is to give clothing: when you see the naked, to clothe them, and

Fourth, is the mandatory responsibility to one's family: not to turn away from your own flesh and blood? (NIV).

Giving bread is the easiest of the three, you could say. Giving shelter is more dangerous, and most definitely not convenient. Giving clothing (keep in mind, we are talking about people in ancient times, not people with massive modern wardrobes) is a permanent, significant material sacrifice.

I believe that the text is using "flesh" in the normal, literal sense, not in the figurative sense. The figurative sense "relatives" is used in scripture, but not nearly as much as the literal sense. Giving to the needy is not only to be engaged in when we are enjoying prosperity; we are to give even if it seems like such giving will place us in need. As a matter of fast, it is such sacrificial giving that breaks the yokes of poverty off the life of the giver and release abundance (Luke 6:38).

13

THE OPEN REWARD OF THE SECRET FAST OF THE BELIEVER

Moreover, when you fast, do not be like the hypocrites, with a sad countenance. For they disfigure their faces that they may appear to men to be fasting. Assuredly, I say to you, they have their reward. But you, when you fast, anoint your head and wash your face, so that you do not appear to men to be fasting, but to your Father who is in the secret place; **and your Father who sees in secret will reward you openly** (emphasis added, Matthew 6: 16-18).

There is a dimension to this scripture that needs to be appreciated. Whereas we fast to achieve specific blessings from the Lord, we see from this scripture that God has His reward for those that fast. Yes, the Lord will answer your prayer concerning the subject-matter of your fast, but He has His own reward for you in addition, just for fasting. This is my firm belief; that those that fast have special reward from God apart from God's commitment to reward them also with whatever motivated them to fast. "Shall reward them openly" is an emphatic promise of the Master to those that fast, whatever be the subject-matter of the fast (so long as it is within the confines of God's word).

Kenneth Copeland remarks that reward for personal fast are on two different levels:

"One is from the admiration of men…[but] "an open reward comes from God when you fast in secret. You can believe for this reward when you go into the fast. Be specific about its purpose. If you believe for the reward from the onset, the pressure on your physical body will lessen."

Notice that these rewards also apply to proclaimed fast. You can fast as a congregation and claim the benefits (rewards) of fasting for that congregation. God calls us to fast to bring the spirit of man in authority over the flesh. This enhances intercession and sets the captive free.

In Zechariah 8:19 God pronounced a blessing on the people for their dedication and devotion to fasting:

Thus saith the LORD of hosts; The fast of the fourth month, and the fast of the fifth, and the fast of the seventh, and the fast of the tenth, shall be to the house of Judah joy and gladness, and cheerful feasts; therefore love the truth and peace.

These blessing are still available today for the people of God that worship and honour Him with fasting.

Personal reward for fasting according to Prophet Isaiah

In the 58th chapter of his book exclusively dedicated to the subject of fasting, prophet Isaiah dealt comprehensively with the rewards that are accruable to people (believers) who set out time to fast with the right motive.

In verse 6 Isaiah spells out the attitude and motive that characterise the fasting that is pleasing to God:

Is not this the fast that I have chosen? to loose the bands of wickedness, to undo the heavy burdens, and to let the oppressed go free, and that ye break every yoke?

Indeed, as earlier established, there are many bands of wickedness that cannot be undone, many yokes that cannot be broken, and many oppressed that cannot be set free, until believers take their God-given position of authority and deal with these manifestations of the devil through prayer and fasting.

The Psalmist prayed,

"Oh let the wickedness of the wicked come to an end..." Psalm 7:9.

Isaiah continues by describing the attitude that is required by the fasting believer towards people – especially toward the needy and the oppressed, as stated:

Is it not to deal thy bread to the hungry, and that thou bring the poor that are cast out to thy house? when thou seest the naked, that thou cover him; and that thou hide not thyself from thine own flesh? (verse 7).

You see, fasting is man getting into a very serious business with God! Every fast must be God-ward (toward God). Therefore, if it must have the approval of God and attract the desired reward, it has got to be done God's way – with the right commitment and attitude. On the contrary, if we do as we please when we fast, like the Pharisees in Jesus' days, He will ask the same question he put to the Israelites in Prophet Zechariah's days:

> "... When ye fasted and mourned ... those 70 years, did ye at all fast unto me, even to me?" Zechariah 7: 5-6

Fasting of the kind that God is pleased with must be associated with sincere and practical charity in our relationships with those close to us – especially the poor and needy- who need our help in material and financial matters.

In subsequent verses Isaiah once again re-visited the issue in relation to the attitudes associated with the "God kind of fast", and contrasted these attitudes with genuine practical charity:

> "...If thou take away from the midst of thee the yoke, the putting forth of the finger, and speaking vanity; And if thou draw out thy soul to the hungry, and satisfy the afflicted soul..." (Verse 9-10)

This is very crucial, and must be adhered to if our fasting will ever achieve the desired result.

"The yoke, the putting forth of the finger, and speaking vanity", according to Derek Prince could be "summed up in three words: legalism, criticism, and insincerity." An important requirement for the God chosen fast is to avoid judging and accusing others. Our words must be with grace and seasoned with salt as believers,

> *"Let your speech be always with Grace, seasoned with salt, that you may know how to answer"* Colossians 4:6.

Isaiah lists numerous blessings promised by God to those who practice the kind of fasting that is acceptable to God. Fasting is a requirement for victorious living.

Special Fasting Blessings

Derek Prince observes that these blessings are listed in successive stages:

1. Isaiah described the blessing of **health and righteousness:**

> *Then your light shall break forth like the morning, your healing shall spring forth speedily, And your righteousness shall go before you; The glory of the Lord shall be your rear guard"* (verse 8).

The NIV appears to paint the picture more clearly:

> *"Then your light will break forth like the dawn,*

and your healing will **quickly appear**; then your righteousness will go before you, and the glory of the Lord will be your rear guard"(emphasis added).

This is in consonance with Malachi 4:2, *"But to you who fear My name The Sun of Righteousness shall arise With healing in His wings; And you shall go out And grow fat like stall-fed calves"* There is 'a dealing (degree of relationship) with God' that provokes divine healing. Fasting gives you opportunity to activate your faith for healing.

Fasting guarantees outstanding results where prayer is limited.

Notice the phrase, "then your righteousness will go before you." What has righteousness got to do with it; you may ask? Jesus said, "But seek first the kingdom of God and His righteousness, and all these things shall be added to you." (Matthew 6:33).

"...the glory of the Lord shall be thy rereward." The word "rereward" literally means rare protection or uncommon protection. He Lord Himself becomes your protector, such that if people try to ensnare you, God will fight on your behalf because you are one of His consecrated saints. This puts us on the

offensive in the battle against the enemy of our souls.

Why will God answer your prayer when you fast? It is because when you fast, you are open to Him. Your spiritual capacity to hear and receive from Him is significantly increased.

---

2. In verse 9, Isaiah describes the blessing of **answered prayer**:

"Then you shall call, and the Lord will answer; You shall cry, and He will say, 'Here I am.'"

Here God commits Himself to answer your prayers and supply your needs. Are you tired of praying without results? Fasting guarantees outstanding results where prayer is limited. God has committed Himself to answer your prayers when you fast. Why will God answer your prayer when you fast? It is because when you fast, you are open to Him. Your spiritual capacity to hear and receive from Him is significantly increased. Fasting puts you in readiness to be filed by God.

3. Further, Isaiah described the blessings of guidance and fruitfulness:

"And if thou draw out thy soul to the hungry, and satisfy the afflicted soul; then shall thy light rise in obscurity, and thy darkness be as the noon day: And the Lord shall guide thee continually, and satisfy thy soul in drought, and make fat thy bones: and thou shalt be like a watered garden, and like a spring of water, whose waters fail not" (vv.10-11). Notice, *"then shall thy light rise in obscurity."* What an amazing promise both of God's continual guidance and unceasing supply of His blessing. Promise of prosperity and abundance in the middle of recession! It must be noted, however, that these things have already been provided in Christ, fasting merely puts us in a better position to receive them.

4. Next, Isaiah describes the blessings of **restoration**:

"And they that shall be of thee shall build the old waste places: thou shalt raise up the foundations of many generations; and thou shalt be called, The repairer of the breach, The restorer of paths to dwell in" (verse 12).

In fasting people's lives are restored. Nations have their destinies changed miraculously. Nineveh is a good example of this.

5. Finally, Isaiah describes the blessing of **upliftment, promotion and exaltation:**

"...Then shalt thou delight thyself in the Lord; and I will cause thee to ride upon the high places of the earth, and feed thee with the heritage of Jacob thy father: for the mouth of the Lord hath spoken it."

What is the "heritage of Jacob" which we are to receive through fasting? Kenneth Copeland believes that Deuteronomy 32: 9-14 provides an answer to the pertinent question:

"For the Lord's portion is his people; Jacob is the lot of his inheritance. He found him in a desert land, and in the waste howling wilderness; he led him about, he instructed him, he kept him as the apple of his eye. As an eagle stirreth up her nest, fluttereth over her young, spreadeth abroad her wings, taketh them, beareth them on her wings: So the Lord alone did lead him, and there was no strange god with him. He made him ride on the high places of the earth, that he might eat the increase of the fields; and he made him to suck honey out of the rock, and oil out of the flinty rock; Butter of kine, and milk of sheep, with fat of lambs, and rams of the breed of Bashan, and goats, with the fat of kidneys of wheat; and thou didst drink the pure blood of the grape."

The heritage of Jacob, Kenneth Copeland, remarks, "ensures that we hear the voice of the Good Shepard and that we are not led astray by the evil one..."

God is the source of true promotion. *"Promotion cometh neither from the east, nor from the west, nor from the south; but God is the Judge. He putteth down one, and setteth up another."- Psalm 75:6,7.*

Like Joel, Isaiah establishes a connection between fasting and the restoration of God's people. Isaiah ends his discussion on fasting with the theme:

> *"Thou shall build the old waste places: thou shalt raise up the foundations of many generations; and thou shalt be called, The repairer of the breach, The restorer of paths to dwell in* (verse 12).

The work of restoration is, no doubt, an agenda that is uppermost in the heart of God in this hour. David's prophesy in this regard could not be more accurate. In Psalm 102:13, he says:

> *"Thou shalt arise, and have mercy upon Zion: for the time to favour her, yea, the set time, is come".*

A summary of the benefits of fasting is listed (below) in this form for quick and easy reference:

1. Then shall your light break forth like the dawn (Revelation).

2. Your healing shall spring up speedily (Divine healing and wholeness).

3. Your righteousness shall go before you (Righteousness).

4. The glory of the LORD shall be your rear guard (His shekinah glory illuminating your paths).

5. Then you shall call, and the LORD will answer; you shall cry, and he will say, Here I am. Then your light shall dawn in the darkness (answered prayers).

6. And your darkness shall be as the noonday (Divine wisdom).

7. The Lord will guide you continually (Continual guidance).

8. And satisfy your soul in drought (supernatural supply).

9. And strengthen your bones (Divine strength).

10. You shall be like a watered garden (Refreshment).

11. And like a spring of water, whose waters do not fail (Constant supply of life).

12. Those from among you shall build the old waste places (divine supply of labourers – the Aholiabs, and Bezaleels).

13. You shall raise up the foundations of many generations (Raising of future generations).

14. And you shall be called the Repairer of the Breach (A new name, restorer).

15. The Restorer of Streets to Dwell In (Restoration).

OTHER PROMISED BLESSINGS ASSOCIATED WITH FASTING

Joy, Gladness and Cheerfulness

"Thus saith the Lord of hosts; The fast of the fourth month, and the fast of the fifth, and the fast of the seventh, and the fast of the tenth, shall be to the house of Judah joy and gladness, and cheerful feasts; therefore love the truth and peace" (Zech. 8:19)

God's Open Reward

"But thou, when thou fastest, anoint thine head,

and wash thy face; That thou appear not unto men to fast, but unto thy Father which is in secret: and thy Father, which seeth in secret, shall reward thee openly" (Matthew 6:17, 18)

Spiritual Powers Over Demons

"But this kind goes not out but by prayer and fasting" (Matthew 17:21)

Divine Empowerment and Supernatural Publicity

"And Jesus returned in the power of the Spirit into Galilee: and there went out a fame of him through all the region round about."

Part Four
Fasting Impact

THE WONDERS OF FASTING

14

REASONS WHY BELIEVERS SHOULD FAST

This section centres on the value of fasting in the believer's life. The purpose is to demonstrate the inestimable impact fasting has on the people who occasionally set everything aside to seek God through prayer and fasting. In scriptures, we find several occasions where the people of God fasted, both as individuals, groups or nations, and the astonishing outcome of such sacrifice.

It must be stressed that certain levels in life cannot be scaled, or victories achieved in our lives and the church without the combined force of prayer and fasting being applied. Over the years, the Church has been inundated with teachings on the subject of prayer. Indeed, it has been a popular conference topic, and a lot of literature exists on the subject. But not so much has been propagated about fasting. This account, to a great extent, for the much controversy that has bedevilled this time-honoured weapon God has blessed the church with.

For the present day church, fasting is like a hidden treasure that has been purposely ignored over the years; yet its significance cannot be overemphasised as a formidable weapon of warfare (2 Cor. 10:4). With the discovery of this all-powerful weapon, the Body of Christ must now, like a treasure hid in the field that has been found, sell everything to buy it.

It must be stressed that certain levels in life cannot be scaled, or victories achieved in our lives and the church without the combined force of prayer and fasting being applied.

Again, the kingdom of heaven is like unto treasure hid in a field; the which when a man hath found, he hideth, and for joy thereof goeth and selleth all that he hath, and buyeth that field (Matthew 13:44).

The obvious question is: 'When is it appropriate to fast?' "What are good biblical reasons for going without food, to seek the Lord?' 'What types of situations should induce fasting?' The Bible has answers to those questions.

This section has too broad headings: (a) **How fasting changes us,** and (b) **Changing the destiny of people and nations through fasting.**

HOW FASTING CHANGES US

Fasting helps the believer to seek and gain God's attention.

Describing the fast that God has ordained, God says, *"Then you shall call and the Lord will answer" (Isaiah 58:9).* According to Arthur Wallis,

"Fasting is designed to make our 'prayer mount up with wings as the eagle.' It is intended to usher the supplicant into the audience chamber of the King, Who will then extend the Golden sceptre (which means the request is granted). Fasting may be expected to drive back the oppressing powers of darkness and loosen their hold on the prayer objective; it is calculated to give an edge to his petitions. Heaven is ready to bend its ear to listen when someone prays with fasting..."

This is the way it works: when a man in tune with God fasts, he can proceed to tell God: 'I have done my utmost, there is nothing left for me to do; if there was anything else, I would have done it'. This moves God to act. Fasting is the believer's utmost. When the saint of God has prayed and fasted, He can then challenge God to move on his behalf. Paul says, *"...having done all, to stand, stand therefore"*

(Ephesians 6:13). When we come to the end of ourselves, God rises to the challenge. In the words of Pauline Harthern,

"...Fasting intensifies prayer. A man who prays with fasting gives heaven notice that he is very serious about his petition. Prayer and fasting become the catalyst to change the impossible into victory."

Fasting is the believer's utmost

According to Andrew Murray,

"Fasting helps to express, to deepen, and to confirm the resolution that we are ready to sacrifice anything, to sacrifice ourselves to attain what we seek for the kingdom of God." Closely related to the above is the fact that fasting gives the believer's request the requisite strength and urgency – "And shall not God avenge his own elect, which cry day and night unto him, though he bear long with them" (Luke 18:7). R.A Torrey puts it quite succinctly, "If we would pray with power, we should pray with fasting. This of course does not mean that we should fast every time we pray…"

Mahesh Chavda gives an exquisite description of the astonishing potency of fasting when combined with prayer, thus:

"If prayer is the capsule containing our gifts and requests to God, then fasting is the booster rocket that lifts our prayers beyond the boundaries of earth and into the heavenlies. Fasting provides the "oomph" of the Spirit needed to catapult us beyond the gravity of the flesh and into the very purposes of God! When the corporate prayers of the many joined in the name of [Jesus] are mounted on the booster rocket of our corporate fasting, our prayers suddenly take on a supernatural power that few on earth have ever seen! You can be sure that Satan fears this holy combination as no other. Every time God's people have dared to lay aside their differences or personal concerns long enough to seek God in prayer and fasting together in one mind and one accord, terrible things have happened to his dark kingdom, while wonderful and miraculous things have happened to mankind!"

To answer the above questions, the believer should resort to fasting when he needs to seek God with greater intensity.

FASTING AS A MEANS OF SUBDUING THE FLESH.

Eating is something we must do for survival – we have to eat. If we can, on a periodic basis deny ourselves what is a necessity of life, then we surely will be able to master our flesh in other areas. Paul said, "I discipline my body and bring it into subjection, lest, when I have preached to others, I myself should become disqualified" (1 Corinthians 9:27 NKJV). He said all those who are able to master the flesh would be granted an incorruptible crown as reward for their discipline. Fasting is a way of mastering our flesh. It is an exercise of self-denial. Jesus said, *"If any man will come after me, let him deny himself, and take up his cross daily, and follow me"* (Luke 9:23 KJV).

If we can deny ourselves food and drink for a period of time we should be able to deny our flesh in the realm of sinful desires and in the disciplines of the Christian life such as prayer. When the disciples were asked by Jesus to stand with Him in prayer, they fell asleep and Jesus said, "Could you not watch with Me one hour? Watch and pray, lest you enter into temptation. The spirit indeed is willing, but the flesh is weak" (Matthew 26:40-41 NKJV). If we can take control over the flesh in the area of eating, then, we can control it in every other area of life.

FASTING INTENSIFIES PRAYER.

Fasting is an effective aid to meaningful prayer. Through fasting prayer is intensified, spirituality is sensitised, and ministry is more powerfully effective. Fasting draws you closer to God, and gives you such a profound hunger for His presence that overcomes struggle in prayer, and leaves a lasting impact of the anointing upon your life.

If prayer is the fire, fasting is the high-octane fuel that makes that fire rage!

If prayer is the fire, fasting is the high-octane fuel that makes that fire rage!

Fasting deepens and strengthens your prayer life.

Fasting makes you a better intercessor. It enables you to engage in more serious, heart-felt intercessory prayer. (Nehemiah 1:3-4)

In the words of Hallesby:

"Fasting helps to give us that inner sense of spiritual penetration by means of which we can discern clearly that for which the spirit of prayer would have us pray in exceptionally difficult circumstances."

Unceasing, incessant prayer is essential to the vitality of your relationship with the Lord, and your ability to function in the world.

In the Old Testament, God said:

Command Aaron and his sons, saying, This is the law of the burnt offering: It is the burnt offering, because of the burning upon the altar all night unto the morning, and the fire of the altar shall be burning in it." (Leviticus 6:9).

Further, we read in the law that the fire on the altar should burn always and ever. After God has lighted the fire, the priest was to ensure that the fire burned always, and never extinguished. How did the priest discharge this onerous responsibility? He was to *"...burn wood on [the altar] every morning, and lay the burnt offering in order upon it; and he shall burn thereon the fat of the peace offerings. The fire shall ever be burning upon the altar, it shall never go out." Leviticus 6:12-13 (emphasis added).* Fasting is the wood that needs to be added to the fire of prayer to keep it burning.

This charge is still for believers today. Paul enjoins the believers to "pray without ceasing" (1 Thessalonians 5:17).

Leonard Le Sourd remarks:

"Fasting is designed to make prayer mount up as on eagles' wings. It is intended to usher the supplicant into the audience chamber of the King and to drive back the oppressing powers of darkness, thereby loosening their hold on those being prayed for. Fasting definitely will give an edge to (a person's) intercession and power ...petition."

> **When your prayer life needs revitalisation, embrace the grace of fasting.**

When your prayer life needs revitalisation, embrace the grace of fasting. Your heart will be touched more easily, your spirit will soar higher, and your awareness of His presence will increase.

Oswald Sanders was succinct when he said,

"... but in addition to this flex value, fasting has direct benefits in relation to prayer as well. Many who practice it from right motives and in order to give themselves more unreservedly to prayer testify that the mind becomes unusually clear and vigorous. There are a noticeable spiritual quickening and increased power of concentration on the things of the spirit."

This means that spiritual reality is more easily discernible through fasting. In a long fast, you are so overwhelmed with His presence that the desires of the flesh are significantly reduced and the spirit rises and soars, controlling the soul. In fact, the things of the world become absolutely meaningless. One cannot but agree with Oswald Sanders obvious view that one of the values of fasting lies in the fact that its discipline "helps us keep the body in its place. It is a practical acknowledgment of the supremacy of the spiritual".

Fasting is still God's chosen way to deepen and strengthen prayer. Without it, your prayer life will lack the requisite vitality and 'fire' to confront the gate of hell, and put the enemy on the run. Answers to prayer, guidance, direction, insight – all flow more freely when fasting is freely and willingly embraced with grace in the heart. Fasting will remove roadblocks and distractions in your prayer life and thus will intensify your prayer life, drawing you closer to God, to hear Him clearly. Fasting has established a new spiritual dimension in my life, lifting me to a higher plane of spiritual authority.

15

FASTING HELPS TO SUSTAIN THE ANOINTING

Fasting plays a vital role in releasing and sustaining the anointing. Fasting has a direct link with the measure of the grace of God that operates in a believer's life. The same is true for the ministers of God. For me, fasting has been the secret to obtaining open doors, miraculous provision, favour and the tender touch of God upon my life. This is because fasting helps the believer to tune into the spirit realm where all his inheritance already exists. When the believer feels dry spiritually or needs a fresh release of the unction of God, fasting is the secret key that unlocks the flood-gate of heaven and releases such level of grace that nothing else can. Fasting is for spiritual empowerment; without fail, it culminates in the release of power – greater power for outstanding achievements.

This is the secret of excelling in the work of the kingdom. The surpassing power of God is available to everyone who desires it and can pay the price for it; fasting is one infallible instrument for obtaining it. As said, Jesus the son of God fasted for forty days and night. If Jesus could have accomplished all His earthly assignment without fasting, why should He fast?

The son of God fasted because He knew there were supernatural blessings, indeed, unction for exploits that could not be released any other way.

The son of God fasted because He knew there were supernatural blessings, indeed, unction for exploits that could not be released any other way. How much more should fasting be a common practice in our lives? Fasting takes the believer from the ordinary realm to the extraordinary. Walking in favour is not a product of luck and coincidence! Breaking free from satanic forces, and life full of miseries, agony, mischiefs, shame and reproach, to the high life God has destined for you take more than prayer. This was the lesson the Master was trying to convey to the disciples who could not heal a demon possessed boy, when He said *"...this kind goeth not but by prayer and fasting"* (Matthew 17:20-21). Jesus says, *"If you will lose your life for my sake you will find it"* (Matthew 10:39). The Greek text says, *"If you will up that low life, you will find the *high life."* Fasting is one of the tools that help you shed the low life. As you begin to live a fasted life, the spirit of God begins to change your taste in life, urging you to reach out to 'that' high life in God; the place of excellence, perfection, abundance, and uncommon breakthrough! How does it work? You see, prayer and fasting will cause you to be much more spiritually sensitive to the Lord and His direction in your life.

Fasting is one of the tools that help you shed the low life. As you begin to live a fasted life, the spirit of God begins to change your taste in life, urging you to reach out to 'that' high life in God;

According to Mike Bickle,

"fasting is a means of intentional embracing of weakness for the purpose of uncovering greater grace. Fasting has a weakening effect on the human vessel. It makes us more vulnerable." Fasting gives the 'fas-ter' personal ownership of the principle, "My grace is sufficient for you, for my strength is made perfect in weakness" (2 Corinthians 12:9).

As we embrace weakness, His grace rushes in to strengthen us.

FASTING STRENGTHENS YOU TO DO EXPLOITS FOR GOD

"...but the people that do know their God shall be strong, and do exploits" (Dan. 11:32)

Anointing for exploits is different from the anointing that is needed by the believer for his day-to-day victorious living, as a child of God.

Anointing for exploits is different from the anointing that is needed by the believer for his day-to-day victorious living, as a child of God. There is an anointing within, and there is an anointing upon!

There is an anointing within, and there is an anointing upon! The anointing within is the most 'basic anointing' the believer is endued with upon giving his heart to the Lord. The 'anointing upon' is built on this anointing.

Let us examine this further:

The anointing within...

But the anointing which ye have received of him abideth in you, and ye need not that any man teach you: but as the same anointing teacheth you of all things, and is truth, and is no lie, and even as it hath taught you, ye shall abide in him (1 John 2:27).

The Spirit itself beareth witness with our spirit, that we are the children of God (Romans 8:16).

And the peace of God, which passeth all understanding, shall keep your hearts and minds through Christ Jesus (Philippians 4:7).

This "inner anointing", according to the above bible passages, abides in the believer and teaches him from within. It can provide peace or unrest. It bears witness in our spirits. I think all Christians have sensed it. You may feel a check in your spirit or a release in your spirit. I suppose it can be confused with other checks in our hearts at times.

The anointing upon...

But the anointing of the Holy Spirit UPON the believer is the anointing for exploits, anointing for warfare, anointing for ministry (Acts1:8). This is where there is a flow of the divine grace through the believer which overflows to others as he ministers God to them. It flows out from him. It often saturates your clothing, and it can be sensed leaving your body. It appears to be some form of spiritual energy.

The Bible says, as Jesus was ministering;

> *a woman who had a haemorrhage for twelve years, and had endured much at the hands of many physicians and had spent all that she had and was not helped at all but rather had grown worse after hearing about Jesus came up in the crowd behind Him, and touched his cloak, for she thought "if I just touch his garment, I shall get well. And immediately the flow of her blood was dried up; and she felt in her body that she was healed of her affliction. And from him had gone fourth, turned around in the crowd and said, 'who touched my garment? (Mark 5:25-30)*

Jesus, His Fasting and His Anointing

Jesus, without a shadow of doubt, stepped into a greater ministry after His forty days fast. A door of greater anointing - 'anointing without measure' was opened to Him. There was an anointing that launched Jesus into the ministry of the miraculous in His earthly ministry. The Bible says:

> *"For God giveth not the Spirit by measure unto him"* (John 3:34).

Jesus did not operate in the ministry of exploits, just because He was the son of God. No! The ministry of miracles, signs and wonders were a product of the price Jesus paid – 40 days fasting.

There was no mention of Jesus performing any miracles prior to His forty days and nights fasting experience. But after the fast, and as a result of the fast, the Bible says *"Jesus returned in the power of the Spirit into Galilee: and there went out a fame of him through all the region round about. And he taught in their synagogues, being glorified of all* (Luke 4:14-15).

The 'anointing without measure' is also available to us today. The way to greater anointing has been demonstrated to us by the Master. This is incredibly important! As seen in Acts 10:38, greater anointing is what qualifies us for greater ministry – a world-class, renowned ministry; a ministry of incredible exploits!

What a complete ministry Jesus had after His consecrated fast! He did not only go about healing the sick, raising the dead, etc, His teaching ministry stepped into prominence! He taught with profound wisdom, wisdom that defiled the intelligence of the greatest 'brains' of His time. How awe-stricken, even the Philosophers, teachers, and doctors of law of His days were at His teachings. *"He taught as one that had authority...",* was the commendation of His inspired audiences! (Mark 1:22).

EM Bound attributed this to the fact that:

"...the word depends on prayer that it 'may have free course and be glorified.' Praying apostles make preaching apostles... Sermons conceived by prayer and saturated with prayer are weighty sermons. **For Jesus it went beyond just prayer;** conceived by prayer, His teachings were rocket-fired into the hearts of men with the incredible **power of fasting!**" (Emphasis added).

Jesus fulfilled the words of the prophet Isaiah about the Lord's powerful life and ministry:

The Spirit of the Lord God is upon Me, Because the Lord has anointed Me To preach good tidings to the poor; He has sent Me to heal the brokenhearted, To proclaim liberty to the captives, And the opening of the prison to those who are bound; To proclaim the acceptable year of the Lord, And the day of vengeance of our God; To comfort all who mourn (Isaiah 61:1-2).

Like Jesus, fasting must deepen our exploits for God. Remember, *"... the people that do know their God shall be strong, and do exploits"* (Daniel 11:32b).

William Carey once said, "Expect great things from God; attempt great things for God." When you know the power of a covenant relationship with God and walk in His ways, you will experience a radical change in your life. Knowing God, and appreciating that in Him all things are possible, will release you into a deeper and more powerful walk with Him.

Men of faith are men of action! Their strength is not in the arm of flesh, but in the mighty arm of God who is strong to deliver and mighty to save. It is one thing to know God, but yet, another to do exploits for Him. For when you live in Covenant relationship with Him, you will rise with a new found faith, a new and fresh enthusiasm, inspired, touched by the hand of God, to do great exploits of faith.

FASTING HELPS TO STIR THE GIFTS OF GOD IN THE BELIEVER

This section has two important dimensions: First is the realisation that everyone- child of God has spiritual gifts invested in him:

> For I say, through the grace given to me, to every man that is among you, not to think of himself more highly than he ought to think; but to think soberly,

according as God has dealt to every man the measure of faith (Romans 12:3).

According to Jamieson-Fausset-Brown Bible Commentary:

"Faith…is the inlet to all the other graces, and so, as the receptive faculty of the renewed soul—that is, "as God hath given to each his particular capacity to take in the gifts and graces which He designs for the general good."

The truth here is that, God has given to every man "the measure of faith" (spiritual gifts); so we should consider what gifts, abilities, and knowledge we have, not of ourselves, but from God.

The second dimension has to do with the deployment, utilisation or usage of the grace which we have received of the Lord. It makes sense to argue that the deployment of the grace of God in our lives only comes into play when we realise that have been endued with such grace.

In 1 Timothy 4:6-14, we see Paul admonishing his spiritual son – Timothy, in essence, on 'the mark of a good minister of God'. In it, he turned the spotlights on the issue of Spiritual Gifts.

Neglect not the gift that is in you, which was given

you by prophecy, with the laying on of the hands of the presbytery (verse 14).

Notice, after a very lengthy admonition, Paul did not forget the all-important matter of spiritual gifts – drawing Timothy's attention to this vital issue that was needed to make his ministry fulfilling. He said to him in the succeeding verse:

Meditate on these things; give yourself wholly to them; that your profiting may appear to all (verse 15).

If this matter was of such importance to Timothy then, it should be for us today.

THE WONDERS OF FASTING

16

FASTING DEEPENS YOUR UNDERSTANDING OF THE WORD OF GOD AND INCREASES YOUR ABILITY TO HEAR FROM GOD

In Isaiah 33:6, the prophet declared, *"And wisdom and knowledge shall be the stability of thy times,..."* This scripture is as applicable today as it was when Isaiah first spoke it concerning the sins that plagued Judah centuries ago.

Today, the threat of murder, acts of terrorism, and nuclear mishaps dominates our media headlines and tries to instil fear in our hearts. It is comforting to know that God has promised to provide stability in these precarious times through knowledge and wisdom.

One of the personal rewards of fasting as promised by God is: *"Then [after you have fasted] shall thy light break forth as the morning..."* (Isaiah 58:8).

The Bible says,

The entrance of thy word giveth light, and giveth **understanding** *to the simple* (Psalm 119:130).

This impacts, not only your ability to receive revelations from God, but your ability in the delivery of God's word.

Bible revelation comes as a result of a conscious 'downloading' from the source – God, through His word.

God said to Moses' successor- Joshua:

This book of the law shall not depart out of thy mouth; but thou shalt meditate therein day and night, that thou mayest observe to do according to all that is written therein: for then thou shalt make thy way prosperous, and then thou shall have good success (Joshua 1:8).

Note that the above scripture does not say the book of the law should be on the believer's bookshelf, or in his library; but in his mouth. God's children are mandated to study and confess scriptures:

Study to shew yourself approved unto God a workman that needeth not to be ashamed, rightly dividing the word of truth (2 Timothy 2:15).

We having the same Spirit of Faith, according as it is written, I believed, and therefore have I spoken we also believe, and therefore speak (2 Cor. 4:13).

Michael Youssef was highly philosophical when he said, "a tattered Bible belongs to a life that cannot be tattered," and I fully endorse it.

Fasting gives an edge, 'bigger' entrance, and weight to the word of God. As you get intimate with God through fasting, your spirit-man is ignited to receive deep insight, and such profound revelation from God that you would not receive otherwise. It was while Moses was settling the destiny of Israel with God, through fasting that God gave him a powerful revelation that became known as – the Ten Commandments. Fasting lightens up your inner-man to hear and receive from God with clarity. I am always amazed at the depth of revelations I receive when undergoing a fast.

"…one of the greatest spiritual benefits of fasting" according to Elmer Towns, "is becoming more attentive to God – becoming more aware of our own inadequacies and His adequacy, our own contingencies and His self-sufficiency – and listening to what He wants us to be and do…"

This impacts, not only your ability to receive revelations from God, but your ability in the delivery of God's word. Fasting puts you in the realm where you practically *"rightly divide the word of God"* (2 Timothy 2:15).

If you must operate in power, fasting must be a common practice in your life.

In Ecclesiastes 10:10, the Bible says,

If an axe is dull, And one does not sharpen the edge, then he must use more strength; But wisdom brings success.

Fasting gives you that cutting edge of the anointing for kingdom service.

FASTING, A CATALYST FOR SPIRITUAL GROWTH

When you fast, you feed your spirit-man to grow. If you must operate in power, fasting must be a common practice in your life. Indeed, those who seek God through the discipline of fasting are open to reservoir of God's power because, fasting creates a deep hunger after God. When you get hungry for God, He gets closer. Spiritual hunger will move God, and open doors. The question is:

how hungry are you for God? Notice, I did not ask, how hungry you are for blessings and His provision, but how hungry are you for Him? His face, not just His hands! Does your soul long, even faint, for the presence of the Lord? We very much need to be hungry if we are going to see God move in our lives. Again, how hungry are you for God's presence in your life? David expressed deep hunger for God with the following words:

> *How lovely are Your tabernacles, O Lord of hosts! My soul yearns, yes, even pines and is homesick for the courts of the Lord; my heart and my flesh cry out and sing for joy to the living God… For a day in Your courts is better than a thousand [anywhere else]; I would rather be a doorkeeper and stand at the threshold in the house of my God than to dwell [at ease] in the tents of wickedness* (Psalm 84:1,2,10; Amp).

Deep hunger for God shuts down the influence of the flesh, so that the spirit man can take dominance. As you live a fasted life, you will not be flesh-ruled, and, the power to commit sin is broken! Why? Because when you fast, you are bringing your body into subjection.

In 1 Corinthians 9:27, Paul asserts: *But I keep under my body, and bring it into subjection: lest that by any means, when I have preached to others, I myself should be a castaway.*

According to Jentezen Franklin: "Fasting "dethrones" the rule of our demanding fleshly appetites, so that we can more easily follow the leading of the Holy Spirit".

This has the consequent effect of causing the believer to develop and produce the fruit of the spirit, according to Galatians 5:22.

FASTING BRINGS GREAT DELIVERANCE

There are times of emergency or serious crisis, when the believer is under a severe attack - desperate situations- a life or death situation; fasting has proven to be a formidable weapon for overcoming such onslaughts of the devil.

Every great crisis in life should be confronted that way. There is something about fasting that get demons very uncomfortable. It is without, controversy that many of the diseases, ailments, mental problems, and chronic behavioural problems afflicting mankind are instigated or perpetuated by unseen forces that intend to wreck the destiny of God's people.

> According to R.A. Torrey, "If we would pray with power, we should pray with fasting".

The simple truth about spiritual warfare is that most battles we try to fight in the flesh are better fought spiritually, employing the formidable weapons God has given to us. Spiritual warfare is a spiritual battle that must be fought and won in the spirit realm. Fasting is a weapon, infallible weapon "... *mighty through God to the pulling down of strongholds,*" (2 Corinthians 10:4). Fasting is designed to be used in times of fierce conflict with Satan, and Satan and his cohort know and respect the power of the believer's fast. In giving us the privilege of fasting, God has added a powerful weapon to our spiritual armoury beyond prayer. According to R.A. Torrey, "If we would pray with power, we should pray with fasting". In fasting great power is released for warfare. Fasting is God's appointed means for the release of His grace and power.

Fasting Lengthens Life Expectancy

Christians often quote Psalm 90:10, as a basis to claim that your life span is only seventy or eighty years.

The days of our years are threescore years and ten; and if by reason of strength they be fourscore years, yet is their strength labour and sorrow; for it is soon cut off, and we fly away (Psalm 90:10).

This is never the case! There is no scriptural basis to justify such claim. In fact, the context of this verse explains that, because of God's wrath and judgement, the years of our life are only seventy or eighty.

Fasting is God's appointed means for the release of His grace and power.

I do not believe that this scripture describes the believer's life expectance; definitely not mine! It all depends on what you bargain for. As will be seen in this book, fasting has been very instrumental in averting such judgments. As a matter of fact we have a covenant of longevity with God:

And the Lord said, My spirit shall not always strive with man, for that he also is flesh: yet his days shall be an hundred and twenty years (Gen. 6:3)

And one of the covenant blessings God gave to (Abram) Abraham was:

You, however, will go to your ancestors in peace and be buried at a good old age (Gen. 15:15).

It has been said that one who regularly fasts is likely to live much longer. This truth was vividly demonstrated in the life of Prophetess Anna. Her husband died after seven years of marriage. She did not choose to marry again, but dedicated her life to serving the Lord in the temple. Her service was accompanied by fasting, prayer, and godly service. She did this for eighty-four years!

When she was about 84, she recognised the baby Jesus, and then travelled throughout Jerusalem proclaiming the Messiah had come. Anna's life is the longest of any that is recorded in the New Testament. There is strong evidence that her length of life was related to her fasting (Luke 2:36.)

Part Five

The Mystery Of Fasting

17

CHANGING THE DESTINY OF NATIONS THROUGH FASTING

FASTING BRINGS VICTORIES IN DIFFICULT SITUATIONS

As seen in the life of Jesus, and other cases that would be considered shortly, fasting often brings victories in difficult situations. In the first chapter of Joel, we read,

> *The vine is dried up and the fig tree is withered; the pomegranate, the palm and the apple tree – all the trees of the field- are dried up. Surely the joy of mankind is withered away. Put on sackcloth, O priests, and mourn; wail, you who minister before the altar. Come; spend the night in sackcloth, you who minister before my God; for the grain offerings and drink offerings are **withheld from the house of your God. Declare a holy fast; call a sacred assembly. Summon the elders and all who live***

in the land to the house of the LORD your God, and cry out to the LORD (Joel 1:12-14, emphasis added).

In this passage of scripture, we are presented with a very gloomy situation that had engulfed and overwhelmed the very people of God. Indeed, a very depressing situation, only reminiscent of the times we live in now. Everything that could go wrong had, indeed, gone wrong. Israel was in a crisis situation: acute lack, famine, despondence, and bewilderment, all describe the situation in the land. Notice, there was no solution anywhere humanly-speaking. However, the Lord pointed the people in the right direction - as a way out of their predicament - the Lord told the people to "…sanctify a holy fast…" (Joel 2:15).

Child of God, at such a time that it appears the heavens are closed, and all you can see and feel are the very elements that result from a closed heaven, be rest assured that the supernatural holds the answer! The supernatural must be scaled and accessed for solution in times of crisis, be it in personal life, family, business or ministry. The lesson is very clear in this passage: when things are though, and nothing seems to be working for you in life, or the devil seems to be making a ridicule of you and your destiny, God says, "stop everything and fasts." You may have prayed all kinds of prayers, but to no avail. Jesus says, *"... this kind goeth not out but by prayer and fasting" (Matthew 17:21).* The nation of Israel said, *"...Our bones are dried, and our hope is lost: we are cut off for our part..." (Ezekiel 37:11).* Does this describe your situation today? Have you been praying and believing God for certain breakthroughs in life for a long while? You have done everything humanly possible, but there does not seem to be any notable breakthrough, or at best, you are constantly faced with solutions that 'appear for a while and disappear'; Jesus offers fasting as a solution to overcoming such situations. This is consistent with the instruction God gave Israel in Joel 2: 12-13:

> *Even now," declares the LORD, "return to me with all your heart, with fasting and weeping and mourning. Rend your heart and not your garments. Return to the LORD your God, for he is gracious and compassionate, slow to anger and abounding in love, and he relents from sending calamity.*

Then in Joel 2: 18 -32, we have a long list of what God promised to do in response to the fasting of His people, Israel:

> *Then will the Lord be jealous for his land, and pity his people. Yea, the Lord will answer and say*

unto his people, Behold, I will send you corn, and wine, and oil, and ye shall be satisfied therewith: and I will no more make you a reproach among the heathen: But I will remove far off from you the northern army, and will drive him into a land barren and desolate... Fear not, O land; be glad and rejoice: for the Lord will do great things. Be not afraid, ye beasts of the field: for the pastures of the wilderness do spring, for the tree beareth her fruit, the fig tree and the vine do yield their strength. Be glad then, ye children of Zion, and rejoice in the Lord your God: for he hath given you the former rain moderately, and he will cause to come down for you the rain, the former rain, and the latter rain in the first month. And the floors shall be full of wheat, and the vats shall overflow with wine and oil. **And I will restore to you the years that the locust hath eaten, the cankerworm, and the caterpiller, and the palmerworm, my great army which I sent among you. And ye shall eat in plenty, and be satisfied, and praise the name of the Lord your God, that hath dealt wondrously with you: and my people shall never be ashamed.** *And ye shall know that I am in the midst of Israel, and that I am the Lord your God, and none else: and my people shall never be ashamed.*

And it shall come to pass afterward, that I will pour out my spirit upon all flesh; and your sons and your daughters shall prophesy, your old men shall dream dreams, your young men shall see visions: And also upon the servants and upon the handmaids in those days will I pour out my spirit. And I will shew wonders in the heavens and in the earth, blood, and fire, and pillars of smoke. The sun shall be turned into darkness, and the moon into blood, before the great and terrible day of the Lord come. And it shall come to pass, that whosoever shall call on the name of the Lord shall be delivered: for in mount Zion and in Jerusalem shall be deliverance, as the Lord hath said, and in the remnant whom the Lord shall call. (Joel 2 18-32, emphasis added).

This is amazing!

Vital lessons from the Joel fast

Lesson 1:

A divine connection between the Church and the nation.

Scripture teaches a connection between the church and the nation. The nation needs the spiritual backing of the church to overcome its predicaments. In the events surrounding the dedication of the temple of Solomon, this connection between the people of God and their nation appeared at least twice. Asking for God's divine habitation of the temple just built, Solomon prayed:

When your people Israel are beaten by an enemy because they've sinned against you, but then turn to you and acknowledge your rule in prayers desperate and devout in this Temple, Listen from your home in heaven;   forgive the sin of your people Israel, return them to the land you gave to them and their ancestors (2Chronicles 6:24-25, The Message Bible)

When your people Israel have been defeated by an enemy because they have sinned against you and when they turn back and confess your name, praying and making supplication before you in this temple, Then hear thou from the heavens, and forgive the sin of thy people Israel, and bring them again unto the land which thou gavest to them and to their fathers. (2 Chronicles 6: 24-25, NIV).

After the temple was completed, God answered Solomon's prayer:

If my people, which are called by my name, shall humble themselves, and pray and seek my face, and turn from their wicked ways; then will I hear from heaven, and will forgive their sin, and will heal their land. (2 Chronicles 7:14).

Charles Spurgeon was remarkable in his comments - linking the role of the Church with the salvaging of a nation in crisis – he said,

You would just as soon expect a wounded soldier on the battlefield to heal himself without medicine, or get himself to a hospital when his arms and legs have been shot off as you would expect to [salvage] a nation without the help of God.

A common theme keeps appearing in relation to the connection between God's body - the church - and a nation in crisis. We see a parallel in Jeremiah 9:17-18:

Thus saith the LORD of hosts, Consider ye, and call for the mourning women, that they may come, and send for cunning women, that they may come: and let them make haste, and take up a wailing for us, that our eyes may run down with tears, and our eyelids gush out with waters.

It is very clear from this passage that these were spiritual women who were instructed to take up a wailing for the land, in a time of national emergency that was spelling disaster! Sense the urgency in God's tone: *"...and let them make haste..."* Spiritual weapons are to be applied in times of severe disaster or crisis without delay. The following verses: 19-22, spell out the urgency of the matter!

> *For a voice of wailing is heard out of Zion, How are we spoiled! we are greatly confounded, because we have forsaken the land, because our dwellings have cast us out. Yet hear the word of the LORD, O ye women, and let your ear receive the word of his mouth, and teach your daughters wailing, and everyone her neighbour lamentation.* **For death is come up into our windows, and is entered into our palaces, to cut off the children from without, and the young men from the streets.** *Speak, Thus saith the LORD, Even the carcases of men shall fall as dung upon the open field, and as the handful after the harvestman, and none shall gather them."* (Emphasis added).

Again, God's people were relied on to access the supernatural realm for a solution for the nations crisis.

Paul enjoins the believers in 1 Tim. 2 1-2:

> *I exhort therefore, that,* **first of all,** *supplications, prayers, intercessions, and giving of thanks, be made for all men; For kings, and for all that are in authority; that we may lead a quiet and peaceable life in all godliness and honesty. For this is good and*

acceptable in the sight of God our Saviour; Who will have all men to be saved, and to come unto the knowledge of the truth. (Emphasis added).

Notice, Paul says, "…first of all…"

Kenneth E. Hagin (Snr) said,

"…in life we suffer many times because we don't put first things first. We let secondary things predominate and neglect thing that should be first. In our spiritual life we blame God for our failures. We wonder why certain things don't go right, when really we are not putting first thing first…many times prayers are not answered for yourself because you are putting yourself first…"

It is very clear that if Christians were praying for the nation, and the leaders things would not be as bad as they are in our nations.

Lesson 2:

The healing that is needed in our nation must be orchestrated by the Ministers of God.

It is noteworthy that as a solution to the calamity that had engulfed the whole nation, God called on His ministers to take up the challenge, and pay the ultimate price for a divine intervention, as means of averting the crisis. It is a well-known principle that the church set the pace for the nation; where the church goes, the nation goes, and where the pulpit leads, societal culture follows.

God places onerous and special responsibilities upon three categories of spiritual leaders in this Bible account:

Joel 1:12-14 states:

Gird yourselves, and lament, ye priests: howl, ye ministers of the altar: come, lie all night in sackcloth, ye ministers of my God: for the meat offering and the drink offering is withholden from the house of your God. Sanctify ye a fast, call a solemn assembly, gather the elders and all the inhabitants of the land into the house of the Lord your God, and cry unto the Lord (Joel 1:13)

In Joel 2:16-17, God's instructions are:

Gather the people, sanctify the congregation, assemble the elders, gather the children, and those that suck the breasts: let the bridegroom go forth of his chamber, and the bride out of her closet. Let the priests, the ministers of the Lord, weep between the porch and the altar, and let them say, Spare thy people, O Lord, and give not thine heritage to reproach, that the heathen should rule over them: wherefore should they say among the people, Where is their God?"

The lessons are very clear: God wants His spiritual leaders to pave the way in a heart-felt, intensive seeking of His grace and mercy for the land – in an act of united prayer and fasting.

His invitation is still open today:

Let us therefore come boldly unto the throne of grace, that we may obtain mercy, and find grace to help in time of need (Hebrews 4:16).

God will not only show Himself mighty on behalf of those who are upright before Him, He will intervene on a nationwide scale if the Church and its leaders would rise to the challenge.

These are desperate times in our cities and nations; times of incredible economic challenges across the globe. Evils are perpetuated at an alarming rate beyond precedence! Weapons of mass destruction are frequently employed to wreak havoc on the planet God has given mankind to enjoy. In the face of these desperate and challenging times God has promised, *"If my people, which are called by my name, shall humble themselves, and pray, and seek my face, and turn from their wicked ways; then will I hear from heaven, and will forgive their sin, and will heal their land."* (2 Chronicles 7:14)

God will not only show Himself mighty on behalf of those who are upright before Him, He will intervene on a nationwide scale if the Church and its leaders would rise to the challenge. May we not be found wanting! May God not find cause to call us as He did in the Garden of Eden, asking us the pathetic question: "...WHERE ART THOU?"

Lesson 3:

If we refuse to wage war against the enemy, both the nation and the church will bear the consequences.

The crisis that befalls our nations, unless there are people who, like Deborah, would arise in the land to take appropriate action in the spirit realm, have a tendency to spill over to the church. Notice, in our original text, it is clearly stated:

> "...for the grain offerings and drink offerings **are withheld from the house of your God**..." (Joel 1:13, emphasis added).

Remember, Jesus' Sermon on the Mount, describes the people of God as 'salt of the earth, and light of the world.' *"Ye are the salt of the earth..." (Matthew 5:13), "Ye are the light of the world..." (Matthew 5:14).* Notice the passage says further, *"...the city that is set on a hill cannot be hid."* That is what the church of God, truly is. The church is God's battle axe, and His weapon of war – (Jeremiah 51:20).

Lesson 4:

Fasting is a pre-condition for the latter rain

God promises that he would send His people the much needed former and latter rain in response to the united prayer and fasting of His people. In a spiritual application of the rain, God says,

> And it shall come to pass **afterward**, that I will pour out my spirit upon all flesh; and your sons and your daughters shall prophesy, your old men shall dream dreams, your young men shall see visions: And also upon the servants and upon the handmaids in those days will I pour out my spirit (Joel 2:28-29 emphasis added).

Notice the word "afterward" in verse 28, which indicates that something happened as an aftermath of a previous action. The obvious question is: after what? After we have consecrated a fast, call a solemn assembly, seek God with corporate prayer and fasting. Then God promises, not only to avert the crises the nation faces, but commission the ministry of the Holy Spirit, whose work is to outlast the immediate generation that Prophet Joel served.

On the day of Pentecost, apostle Peter, addressing the crowed that assembled, made reference to the prophecy of prophet Joel, indicating that the phenomenon of the outpouring of the Holy Spirit that was seen of the day of Pentecost was a fulfilment of the prediction (prophecy) of prophet Joel.

But this is that which was spoken by the prophet Joel; And it shall come to pass in the last days, saith God, I will pour out of my Spirit upon all flesh: and your sons and your daughters shall prophesy, and your young men shall see visions, and your old men shall dream dreams: And on my servants and on my handmaidens I will pour out in those days of my Spirit; and they shall prophesy: And I will shew wonders in heaven above, and signs in the earth beneath; blood, and fire, and vapour of smoke (Acts 2:16-18)

So here we see God, not only seeking a fast as a remedy to the present predicament of the people, but as a springboard to letting loose the floodgate of heaven - for the beginning of the release of the most powerful presence of God on earth- through the ministry of the Holy Spirit. Fasting opens the great door of the supernatural – the place where the Church is better positioned to exercise power, dominion and authority.

The position of the Church today is reminiscent of the days in which Elijah prophesised rain upon earth, after a long period of draught. At first, it appeared there was no response whatsoever from heaven, but thank God, kept praying and believing God. The Church must show the same level of resilience.

After a long period of draught in the Church, we must set our minds on using the key God has given the Church to finally unlock the heavens in order to experience the "abundance of rain" again in the land.

And Elijah said unto Ahab, Get thee up, eat and drink; ***for there is a sound of abundance of rain.*** *So Ahab went up to eat and to drink. And Elijah went up to the top of Carmel; and he cast himself down upon the earth, and put his face between his knees, And said to his servant, Go up now, look toward the sea. And he went up, and looked, and said, There is nothing. And he said, Go again seven times. And it came to pass at the seventh time, that he said, Behold, there ariseth a little cloud out of the sea, like a man's hand. And he said, Go up, say unto Ahab, Prepare thy chariot, and get thee down that the rain stop thee not. And it came to pass in the meanwhile, that the heaven was black with clouds and wind, and there was a great rain…* (1 Kings 18: 41-45, emphasis added).

The Church would not only hear the "sound of the abundance of rain" as a result, but would move swiftly; in the spirit of Elijah, to overcome the onslaught of the Jezebels of our time that want to vex the church of God.

18

JEHOSHAPHAT GAINED VICTORY OVER HIS ENEMIES

Jehoshaphat, King of Judah was faced with a monumental situation – a large powerful army from the neighbouring territories of Moab, Ammon, and Mount Seir were invading his kingdom from the east. Total annihilation was imminent without the Lord's intervention! Realising that he had no military might to meet this challenge, Jehoshaphat turned to God for help. Scripture records that, *"Jehoshaphat feared, and set himself to seek the lord and proclaimed a fast throughout all Judah."* 2 Chronicles 20:3. God's people were called to unite in public, collective fasting and prayer for God's divine intervention.

The people of Judah fasted - men, women, and children. Desperate situations require desperate measures; they desperately needed to know God's battle plan to defeat this great enemy's army.

From the initial call to fasting,

"...all Judah gathered themselves together, to ask help of the LORD: even out of all the cities of Judah they came to seek the LORD (2Chronicles 20:4)

With the people of God thus assembled, Jehoshaphat led them in prayer, reminding God of His covenant with Abraham. Jehoshaphat's prayer received an immediate, response from heaven; because, as observed by Mahesh Chavda:

"...When the corporate prayers of many joined in the name of [Jesus] are mounted on the booster rocket of our corporate fasting, our prayers suddenly take on a supernatural power that few on earth have ever seen! You can be sure that Satan fears this holy combination as no other. Every time God's people have dared to lay aside their differences or personal concerns long enough to seek God in prayer and fasting together in one mind and one accord, terrible things have happened to his dark kingdom, while wonderful and miraculous things have happened to mankind!"

In the midst of the assembly of fasting people, God spoke through one of the prophets present - Jahaziel a powerful prophetic utterance, combining encouragement, assurance and direction. Said God:

Do not be afraid nor dismayed because of this great multitude, for the battle is not yours, but God's. You will not need to fight in this battle. Position yourselves, stand still and see the salvation of the LORD, who is with you, O Judah and Jerusalem!' Do not fear or be dismayed; tomorrow to out against them, for the LORD is with you (2 Chronicles 20: 15-17).

God had already put in place a master-plan for the defeat of the enemies of His people. Unknown to Judah, God was already making things happen behind the scene. God works the same way today; it takes faith to realise that our God is moving miraculously in our lives, even when we do not even know it.

How you would like to receive such comforting words in the midst of crisis in your life? But never forget, God spoke after the entire nation had spent time praying and fasting. God moves only in response to the cries of His people!

"Position Yourselves..." (verse 16)

However, due consideration must be given to this brief, but highly significant instruction, right in the middle of the prophetic word Judah received from God. It unravels God's mind, not just for Judah, but for the present day church. There is a place beyond victory called triumph that God is taking His saints. Indeed, we are told in scriptures that we are not just conquerors but MORE THAN conquerors.

"Nay, in all these things we are more than conquerors through him that loved us" (Romans 8:37). So God is taking us beyond the sphere of victory to the glorious place of triumph. Mahesh Chavda puts the position succinctly when he said:

"Victory is being able to defeat your enemies. But triumph goes far beyond mere victory. When you triumph, you come out of the battle with more than you had before! God wants to give you more."

Was not that what happened in this case? It is recorded that after the battle with the enemies, Judah spent the next three days gathering spoils – the enemies' possessions in battle.

Jehoshaphat and his people came to gather the spoils, and they found an abundance of cattle and personal property, garments and precious vessels. They took so much that they were unable to carry it all; it took them three days to gather the spoils, there was so much of it. (2 Chronicles 20: 25).

By no means would such astonishing miracles end with the people of old; it is still available for us - the church today! However, it would require a price. It would require a divine positioning of the church to scale beyond the limits of victory to that of triumph. The church has got to **prepare** herself for this level of breakthrough; it would not come on the platter of gold. The Bible says, "So Jotham became mighty, because he prepared his ways before the LORD his God." 2 Chronicles 27:6. Second, it would demand a greater level of unity in the Body of Christ than there is right now. Notice, in crisis, Judah pulled together! Hence they attracted God's astonishing response. What a mighty God we serve!

Events in the Household of Faith seem to point to the contrary; people in crisis situations seem to find more sympathy out in the world than in the church. The Church seems to be more prepared to attack and devour the wounded soldiers than to offer the needed assistance. We must stick together if we are ever going to transcend our level of victory into triumph. It is in the place of unity that God commands His blessings. Very authoritatively, the Psalmist shared the inestimable value of unity among brethren:

Behold, how good and how pleasant it is for brethren to dwell together in unity! It is like the precious ointment upon the head, that ran down upon the beard, even Aaron's beard: that went down to the skirts of his garments; As the dew of Hermon, and as the dew that descended upon the mountains of Zion: for there the Lord commanded the blessing, even life for evermore (Psalm 133).

In response, the Bible says, "And Jehoshaphat bowed his head with his face to the ground: and all Judah and the inhabitants of Jerusalem fell before the Lord, worshipping the Lord. And the Levites, of the children of the Kohathites, and of the children of the Korhites, stood up to praise the Lord God of Israel with a loud voice on high. And when he had consulted with the people, he appointed singers unto the Lord, and that should praise the beauty of holiness, as they went out before the army, and to say, Praise the Lord; for his mercy endureth for ever." (2 Chronicles 20:18-19, 21 KJV)

Jahaziel's prophetic utterance gave Judah, not only the assurance that God was with them in the crisis situation, but a sense of victory ahead of the battle. This was what gave Jehoshaphat the impetus to lead Judah to the battlefield with High Praise on their lips. They believed that God spoke to them without reservation whatsoever. In verses 22 – 30, we read the most fascinating outcome of this battle: the entire enemies' army destroyed themselves, without Jehoshaphat or his people having to resort to any military combat with them. God did not only give His people victory over their enemies, He turned the wealth of the enemies over to them (Prov. 13:22). Judah spent the next three days gathering the spoils and returning to Jerusalem amidst thunderous praise and thanksgiving. And the fame of Jehoshaphat spread to all the neighbouring nations.

This demonstrates the supremacy of spiritual power over carnal powers. While his enemies relied on carnal weapons (the arm of flesh), Jehoshaphat and his people utilised spiritual weapons. This was vividly demonstrated in yet, another battle the children of Israel were involved in. Just reminiscent of the account we're considering, God again assured His people victory over their enemies ahead of the battle. God told His people:

Be strong and courageous, be not afraid nor dismayed for the king of Assyria, nor for all the multitude that is with him: for there be more with us than with him: With him is an arm of flesh; but with us is the Lord our God to help us, and to fight our battles. And the people rested themselves upon the words of Hezekiah king of Judah (2 Chronicles 32:7-8).

David says, *"Some nations boast of their armies and weapons, but we boast in the LORD our God"* (Psalm 20:7, New Living Translation).

The two passages quoted above highlight the outright superiority of spiritual weapons over carnal (physical weapons), and the outcome of the battle Judah was in vividly demonstrates this. In 2 Corinthians 10:4, Paul says, *"... the weapons of our warfare are not carnal, but mighty through God to the pulling down of strongholds"*. Notice, according to Paul, spiritual weapons are formidable because God is involved in their usage. They are applied through God.

It would, no doubt, be beneficial to identify and highlight the spiritual weapons that Jehoshaphat used in this battle, as they are both relevant and applicable to present day believers.

They may be summarised as follows:

1. United prayer – Matthew 18:19-20

2. Collective public fasting – Esther 4:16

3. The Gift of prophecy – 1 Cor. 14:3

4. Biblical Praise and Worship – Psalm 149:6-9:

The Bible says, *"On the fourth day they held an assembly in the Valley of Berakah—for there they blessed the Lord; that is why the place is called the Valley of Berakah to this day. Then all the men of Judah and Jerusalem, with Jehoshaphat at their head, returned to Jerusalem with joy; for the Lord had given them joy over their enemies. They came to Jerusalem, with harps, lyres, and trumpets, to the house of the Lord."* (2 Chronicles 20: 26-28).

As said, these weapons are still as potent as they were when Jehoshaphat used them in the battle against the enemies of Judah.

FASTING FOR DIVINE PROTECTION: EZRA AND THE EXILES MIRACULOUS JOURNEY

Then I proclaimed a fast there, at the river Ahava, that we might humble ourselves before our God, to seek from him a safe journey for ourselves, our children, and all our goods. So we fasted and besought our God for this: and he was intreated of us. Then we departed from the river of Ahava on the twelfth day of the first month, to go unto Jerusalem: and the hand of our God was upon us, and he delivered us from the hand of the enemy, and of such as lay in wait by the way. (Ezra 8: 21, 23, 31).

Again and again, we see the nation of Israel resort to fasting in times of national emergency, and what appeared to be certain disasters were, without fail, averted.

Ezra, like Jehoshaphat, encouraged the Jews to fast before their perilous journey from Babylon. Ezra was leading an exodus of returning exiles from Babylon, carrying a large consignment of gold and silver to the temple in Jerusalem along a route infested with bandits.

The question arose as to how they were to be protected on their way to Jerusalem. Notice this was not going to be a journey undertaken by Ezra and a few Jewish men and women. As stated this was an exodus of the whole Jewish race that had lived in Babylon in the last 70 years. One can imagine the vast number of people that were to undertake the journey. Ezra had the option of going to the king to ask for an escort of soldiers to guide them on the way. Had Ezra chosen this option, no doubt, the king would have graciously granted the request. However, Ezra felt reluctant to make the request because he had already testified to the King that 'his' God – the Almighty God – does protect those that serve and trust in Him. This was Ezra's opportunity to live out his faith in God. Notice, doing otherwise would have compromised the testimony he had earlier given to the heathen king about the infinite power of God to save, in a seemingly hopeless situation.

Though, there would have been nothing morally wrong in accepting an escort from the king, Ezra would have, nonetheless, been depending on carnal means – *the arm of flesh* (11 Chronicles 32:8).

The powerful words of Hezekiah to Judah in yet, another battle, resonates in every situation of this kind.

He said:

Be strong and courageous. Do not be afraid or discouraged because of the king of Assyria and the vast army with him, for there is a greater power with us than with him. With him is only the arm of flesh, but with us is the Lord our God to help us and to fight our battles. And the people gained confidence from what Hezekiah the king of Judah said.

Instead, by collective prayer and fasting, Ezra and his people committed themselves to seeking help and protection solely from God.

As in the case of Jehoshaphat (the King of Judah), Ezra, as the leader of God's people proclaimed a fast. What an example for today's leaders!

Once again, hear the reason Ezra gave for leading his people in fasting:

> *that we might afflict ourselves before our God, to seek of him a right way for us, and for our little ones, and for all our substance* (Ezra 8: 21-22).

The outcome?

> *So we fasted and besought our God for this: and he was intreated of us* (verse 23).

After they had fasted (as a result of their fasting), the returning exiles had a safe and perfect journey; there was no opposition whatsoever.

19

ESTHER AVERTED NATIONAL CRISIS THROUGH FASTING

Go gather together all the Jews that are present in Shusham, and fast ye for me and neither eat nor drink three days, night or day: I also and my maiden will fast likewise, and so will I go into the king, which is not according to the law; and if I perish, I perish (Esther 4:16)

The crisis averted through this fast was the greatest the Jewish race had had to go through in their entire history. It has been said that it superseded, in form and scope, the crisis the Jewish people faced under Adolph Hitler; in that, Hitler had only one-third of all Jewish nation; but the Persian emperor had the entire Jewish nation.

In this crisis, a day had been set for the total annihilation of all the Jews in Persia. The Prime Minister of the land – Haman- had succeeded in

THE WONDERS OF FASTING

> **The crisis averted through this fast was the greatest the Jewish race had had to go through in their entire history.**

passing a law of genocide to kill all the Jews in the entire kingdom because Mordecai, a Jew, did not bow down to him. He instigated King Ahasuerus to issue a decree to wipe out the Jews and was even willing to pay 10,000 talents of silver into the king's treasuries to finance the work. Refusing the silver, the king nevertheless agreed with Haman and gave him his signet ring to seal the decree (Esther 3:10,12). This was a very serious matter because even the king himself could not revoke any decree sealed with his signet ring. A death sentence thus hung over the Jews as they waited for the date set by their enemy to kill them. When Mordecai learnt what had happened,

> *He tore his clothes and put on sackcloth and ashes as a sign of mourning for personal and national disaster. Indeed, everywhere the decree was sent, there was "great mourning among the Jews, and fasting, and weeping, and wailing; and many lay in sackcloth and ashes (Esther 4:3b).*

Mordecai went into the city, crying with a loud and bitter cry and stood outside the palace gate. Deeply distressed when told of this, Queen Esther sent Mordecai garments to replace the sackcloth. But Mordecai, the cousin who had raised her as his own daughter after her parents died, refused the garments.

Only the people of God can come before the King of kings and the Lord of grace to intercede and plead for His mercy on behalf of the endangered.

So Esther called Hathach, one of the king's eunuchs whom he had appointed to attend to her, to inquire of the whole matter. He returned with news about the impending destruction of the Jews, a copy of the decree and a message from Mordecai urging her to appear before the king to plead for her people. It had been in obedience to Mordecai that Esther had been taken to the palace and had not revealed her Jewish nationality.

There the king had chosen her to be his queen. Now her people were in great danger and Mordecai was asking her to go to the king and beg for mercy on their behalf.

However, anyone who came before the king without being summoned was in danger of losing his life unless the king held out his golden sceptre. And the king had not called for Esther for 30 days.

She might die if she appeared before the king without being called. But Mordecai would not take "no" for an answer. He was determined to save the Jews and sent word to Esther.

> *Then Mordecai commanded to answer Esther, Think not with thyself that thou shalt escape in the king's house, more than all the Jews. For if thou altogether holdest thy peace at this time, then shall there enlargement and deliverance arise to the Jews from another place; but thou and thy father's house shall be destroyed: and who knoweth whether thou art come to the kingdom for such a time as this?* (Esther 4:13-14)

If Esther did not act, deliverance could come from another source. But she and her family would perish anyway. Do you know why many households are destroyed? Because Christians do not fulfil the will of God in prayer and fasting. Only the people of God can come before the King of kings and the Lord of grace to intercede and plead for His mercy on behalf of the endangered. We are in God's unique time and place, just as Esther was.

Esther had not wanted to go before the king but when she received Mordecai's message, she knew that her only help was from God. She had to intensify her prayers with fasting and so she had all her people fasting for her.

> *Then Esther bade them return Mordecai this answer, Go, gather together all the Jews that are present in Shushan, and fast ye for me, and neither eat nor drink three days, night or day: I also and my maidens will fast likewise; and so will I go in unto the king, which is not according to the law: and if I perish, I perish. So Mordecai went his way, and did according to all that Esther had commanded him. (Esther 4:15-17)*

Satan knows that if he can threaten you with death, you are of little help to the kingdom of God. But praise the Lord that Jesus has conquered the last enemy -death.

Esther was willing to die. Satan knows that if he can threaten you with death, you are of little help to the kingdom of God. But praise the Lord that Jesus has conquered the last enemy -death (Rom 8:11). Once you know God, you are not afraid.

> *And they overcame him by the blood of the Lamb, and by the word of their testimony; and they loved not their lives unto the death. (Rev 12:11)*

When Esther said, "If I perish, I perish," she overpowered the enemy by the word of her mouth.

Her fasting gave her the boldness to risk her life and, if necessary, die for her people. When God saw this He had no choice but to intervene. So God turned everything around. He wrought a great victory for them. The impossible became possible. Death was turned into life, defeat into victory and mourning into rejoicing. Armed with the assurance of having fasted and prayed three days without food and water,

> Esther put on her royal apparel, and stood in the inner court of the king's house, over against the king's house: and the king sat upon his royal throne in the royal house, over against the gate of the house (Esther 5:1).

> And it was so, when the king saw Esther the queen standing in the court, that she obtained favour in his sight: and the king held out to Esther the golden sceptre that was in his hand. So Esther drew near, and touched the top of the sceptre. Then said the king unto her, What wilt thou, queen Esther? And what is thy request? it shall be even given thee to the half of the kingdom. (Esther 5:2-3)

Because of her fast, the king not only raised the sceptre but he also showed her sudden favour, offering her up to half his kingdom. Esther did not have to fight for such a vast kingdom. She merely fasted three days. However, her interest was not in a worldly kingdom but in her people. All she asked was for the king and Haman to be her guests at a banquet. An overjoyed Haman returned home and gathered his friends and wife together to boast about his great wealth, his many children, his honours from the king and his promotion over all others in the king's service. Why, even the queen invited only him and the king to her banquet. The only thing that made him angry was that his enemy, Mordecai, was still around. So his wife and friends suggested that he make a gallows, and in the morning ask the king to hang Mordecai on it before going to the banquet. At that time, Haman was so powerful that the king allowed him to do whatever he wanted. Even when he asked to kill all the Jews in the kingdom, he consented.

But Haman did not know that God was working out something.

That night, God intervened. The king could not sleep, so he asked for the historical records of his kingdom to be read to him. He discovered the report that Mordecai had saved him by exposing a plot by two of his eunuchs to kill him. Just as the king was wondering how to reward Mordecai, Haman arrived to ask the king's permission to hang Mordecai.

The king consulted Haman on how he could honour a man who pleased him. He thought to himself "who else would the king honour but me?" So Haman suggested what he personally wanted. He recommended that one of the king's most noble princes dress the person in one of the king's royal robes, seat him on one of the king's horses with a royal crest on its head and lead him on a parade through the city square.

Haman was so happy. Then the king asked him to do for Mordecai exactly what he had suggested. He had come to tell the king to send Mordecai to the gallows. Instead, he now became a 'king maker' for Mordecai.

So fasting can bring you a lot of surprises. It makes your life a pleasure to God, and brings amazing deliverance out of crisis situations. Mordecai did not know about Haman's plot to hang him. His good work had been forgotten but fasting brought it back to the king's remembrance. Fasting saved him from the gallows.

> Mordecai would not bow down to Haman. He chose to fast rather than compromise. Because he honoured God, God honoured him.

As a Jew, Mordecai would not bow down to Haman. He chose to fast rather than compromise. Because he honoured God, God honoured him. Fasting puts your enemy to shame and puts you in God's favour. A lot of Christians live in disgrace because they do not know how to fast. To them, it is always food, food, and food. Fasting brought Mordecai honour. He was the focus of a city parade. Dejected and humiliated, Haman went home to tell his wife and friends what had happened. But soon, the king's eunuchs arrived and he had to go to the banquet.

This time around, Esther pleaded for her life and for the lives of her people. The king demanded to know who would do such a thing as to plot their annihilation. When Esther revealed that it was Haman, the angry king strode out into the palace garden. Haman was terrified. He knew that his time was up and pleaded with the queen for his life. In his despair, Haman fell on the queen's couch just as the king came back in from the garden. The king was furious, thinking that Haman was trying to molest the queen in front of him. Haman was hanged on the very gallows he had prepared for Mordecai because he had tried to destroy the Jews (Esther 8:7). His ten sons later came to the same end.

Because the earlier decree sent out by Haman could not be revoked, the king gave Esther and Mordecai permission to write another decree as they pleased, in the king's name and sealed with the king's signet ring. Effective on the same day as the earlier decree, this new decree was sent to every level of authority under the king, giving the Jews the right to defend their lives and to destroy all those who would try to destroy them.

Instead of a day of great mourning, it was for the Jews a day of great rejoicing. Instead of their living in fear, their enemies were in fear and many became Jews themselves. Instead of being destroyed, the Jews had the opportunity to destroy their enemies. It had been an impossible situation. The decree to annihilate the Jews in Persia had been sealed with the king's signet ring. It could not be revoked. Just three days of fasting turned everything around. Just like all our previous examples, the Jews resorted to fasting as a means of averting, what was going to be a national disgrace. They understood that God would do nothing, except in response to the cries of His people. And Jesus said, "This kind goest out not, except by prayer and fasting (Matthew 17:21). A measure, greater than prayer, was needed to overcome this national disaster. Esther opted for fasting. And this brought God into the scene! The nature of the battle shifted the moment God people chose fast, as a means of overcoming the enemy's threat, it was no longer a battle of a political nature, but warfare to be fought, supernaturally with spiritual weapons – fasting and prayer! This clearly demonstrates that the weapon to be used in any battle is determined by the nature and intensity of the battle itself. With this choice, the battle line had been drawn! God intervened, just as Haman came to ask the king for permission to hang Mordecai, the Lord had already stirred the king to honour Mordecai for saving his life. God worked individual miracles for Esther and Mordecai - the very details of their lives, things they never imagined could happen. Why did God do it? Because they offered their lives and chose to fast and pray. God did powerful things that no man could do. He intervened. Do you know why God cannot intervene in the details of our lives? Because we give Him only part of our lives. After that, we try to find an earthly solution. There is no better solution than God's. There is no trouble, sickness, disease or difficulty that we cannot overcome through fasting. God is the same yesterday, today, and forever (Heb.

13:8), and He can do the same for us if we would fast and pray like they did.

The fast of Esther is still being commemorated today among the Jewish in a feast called Purim (meaning casting "lots"). According to Derek Prince, the feast is so called because Haman cast lots to determine the day the Jews would be exterminated. In this case casting lots is associated with a form of divination. Further, while Haman relied on unseen spiritual powers; Esther relied absolutely on God and sought Him through fasting. And God 'showed up'! May the God of battle show up on your case!

The fast is observed on the 13th day of the Hebrew month of Adar. The 13th of Adar was a fast day for the Jewish warriors while going out to battle, as it is believed to have been customary to fast during the battle in order to gain divine favour. There is definitely, a lesson for today God's warriors to learn from this. This appears to be consistent with all the cases we have considered so far – entering into a fast to avert 'actual and specific' crisis.

FASTING – THE WEAPON THAT TURNED DEFEAT INTO TRIUMPH.

The Nation of Israel and the Tribe of Benjamin in Battle

In the book of judges we find an account of Israel engaging in a battle with the tribe of Benjamin for its atrocity. God gave the rest of the tribes of Israel directives to fight against the tribe of Benjamin.

> *The children of Israel asked God, "Which of us shall go up first to battle against the children of Benjamin? And the LORD said, Judah shall go up first"* (Judges 20:18).

Mysteries unfolded in this battle. Even though Judah went into battle with the tribe of Benjamin at the express instruction of God, the former faced a woeful defeat in the hands of their enemies. Scripture records that the children of Benjamin killed twenty-two thousand men of the Israelites (verse 21). Those who survived the onslaught or massacre had a story to tell! However, with bitter tears, they enquired again from God, *"Shall I go up again to battle the children of Benjamin my brother? And the LORD said, Go up against him"* (verse 23).

With God's approval they headed for battle again, "And Benjamin went forth against them out of Gibeah the second day…"

Sadly, this battle ended with Israel being defeated again with loss of lives – this time - eighteen thousand men (verse 25).

Israel had lost a total of forty thousand military men in just two days. At the second catastrophic defeat, and in a desperate move to avert this national disaster, Israel decided to seek God with fasting before another attempt. The Scriptures says,

> *Then all the children of Israel, and all the people, went up, and came unto the house of God, and wept,* **and sat there before the LORD***, and fasted that day until evening, and offered burnt offerings and peace offerings before the LORD* (Judges 20:26 KJV, emphasis added)

> *All the Israelis, including its army, went up from there to Bethel and wept,* **remaining there in the LORD's presence***, fasting throughout the day until dusk, when they offered burnt offerings and peace offerings in the LORD's presence* (Judges 20:26 NIV, emphasis added)

There is great power in "remaining ...in the LORD's presence..." until victory is obtained. With fasting, Israel did something rather different from the two previous occasions; their desperation had led them to set everything aside to seek the Lord, all day with fasting.

They should have known to fast in the first place, yet they waited until two catastrophic defeats before they saw the need to fast for deliverance.

One of the leaders stood before the Ark of the Covenant and asked God:

Shall I yet again go out to battle against the children of Benjamin my brother, or shall I cease? And the LORD said, Go up; for tomorrow I will deliver them into thine hand (verse 28).

Notice there was something different with the response Israel received from God after they had sought Him with fasting: God, not only gave Israel permission to go to battle, as in the two previous cases, but gave them a firm assurance of victory over their enemies. Further, God told them precisely, when the battle would be won. Fasting will always make God's mind clearer, in any situation to you. With this assurance, the Israelites braced themselves for the greatest supernatural intervention they had had in battle for a long time. Fasting made the difference! God kept His promise. The Word says, "The Lord smote [defeated] Benjamin before Israel" (verse 35).

They should have known to fast in the first place, yet they waited until two catastrophic defeats before they saw the need to fast for deliverance. In adverse situations believers do everything, but the very thing that is needed to overcome the problem- fasting. On their first two attempts, the Israelites tried to fight the battle by themselves. They suffered defeat, they encountered loses! But when they fasted, the story changed - the Lord won the battle for them! Warfare cannot be engaged in casually. Neither can carnal weapons be employed in fighting spiritual battles. Paul says,

> *For the weapons of our warfare are not carnal, but mighty through God to the pulling down of strongholds* (2 Cor. 10:4, KJV)

> *The weapons we use in our fight are not made by humans. Rather, they are powerful weapons from God...* (2 Cor. 10:4, God's Word Translation).

As we use these weapons, we are guaranteed victory in whatever situation that warrants their usage.

FASTING TO AVERT GOD'S IMPENDING JUDGMENT

Prophet Jonah and the Nation of Nineveh

So the people of Nineveh believed God, and proclaimed a fast, and put on sackcloth, from the greatest of them even to the least of them. For word came unto the king of Nineveh, and he arose from his throne, and he laid his robe from him, and covered him with sackcloth, and sat in ashes. And God saw their works, that they turned from their evil way; and God repented of the evil, that he had said that he would do unto them; and he did it not. (Jonah 3:5, 10 KJV)

The Ninevites believed God. They declared a fast, and all of them, from the greatest to the least, put on sackcloth. When the news reached the king of Nineveh, he rose from his throne, took off his royal robes, covered himself with sackcloth and sat down in the dust. When God saw what they did and how they turned from their evil ways, he had compassion and did not bring upon them the destruction he had threatened (Jonah 3:5, 10 NIV)

The power to prevail with God was never more clearly demonstrated in the Bible that when a pronouncement of divine judgement was averted through repentance, prayer and fasting. *"Yet forty days"*, declared Jonah, *"and Nineveh shall be overthrown!* (Jonah 3:4)

The reaction of the Ninevites was spontaneous; and God, I believe, viewed this as a sign of repentance: The King of Nineveh proclaimed a national fast, not just for human, but also for beast, and the people cried unto God for mercy.

And the people said, "Who knows God may yet repent (change His mind) and turn from His fierce anger, so that we perish not."

The Ninevites' repentance, expressed through fasting, moved God to repent of the judgement He had said He would bring upon them; and He did not do it." In other words, God changed His mind regarding the judgment He had earlier pronounced against them.

Jonah's message of impending judgment was therefore, averted by the repentance of the people of Nineveh. This is very much in keeping with the nature of God. God has already said this of Himself:

At what instant I shall speak concerning a nation,

and concerning a kingdom, to pluck up, and to pull down, and to destroy it; If that nation, against whom I have pronounced, turn from their evil, I will repent of the evil that I thought to do unto them (Jeremiah 18:7, 8).

Our bodies are capable of instigating their own perfect healing if we allow them the opportunity - Fasting is such an opportunity.

The position of God on the subject is very clear, when man repents from his sins, God repents in respect of His judgment. The repentance of man provokes God's repentance concerning judgment! The Old Testament abounds with instances of this kind. It therefore, stands to reason that whenever God finds 'a faithful few' who stand in the gap, even in the eleventh hour, and humble themselves with prayer and fasting, He is ever ready to change His mind in relation to any judgment He might have intended to execute. This is vividly demonstrated in the conversation Abraham had with God about the impending judgment on Sodom and Gomorrah:

The men turned away and went toward Sodom, but Abraham remained standing before the Lord. Then Abraham approached him and said: "Will you sweep away the righteous with the wicked? What if there are fifty righteous people in the city? Will you really sweep it away and not spare the place for the sake of the fifty righteous people in it? Far be it from you to do such a thing—to kill the righteous with the wicked, treating the righteous and the wicked alike. Far be it from you! Will not the Judge of all the earth do right?

The Lord said, If I find fifty righteous people in the city of Sodom, I will spare the whole place for their sake.

Then Abraham spoke up again: Now that I have been so bold as to speak to the Lord, though I am nothing but dust and ashes, what if the number of the righteous is five less than fifty? Will you destroy the whole city for lack of five people? If I find forty-five there, he said, I will not destroy it. Once again he spoke to him, What if only forty are found there?" He said, For the sake of forty, I will not do it. Then he said, May the Lord not be angry, but let me speak. What if only thirty can be found there? He answered, I will not do it if I find thirty there. Abraham said, "Now that I have been so bold as to speak to the Lord, what if only twenty can be found there? He said, For the sake of twenty, I will not destroy it. Then he said, May the Lord not be angry, but let me speak just once more. What if only ten can be found there? He answered, For the sake of ten, I will not destroy it. When the Lord had finished speaking with Abraham, he left, and Abraham returned home (Genesis 18:16-33).

All that God is looking for is a man, if he can find more than one, that is even better (Deut. 32:30), that would make up the hedge, and stand in the gap before God for the land, that He would not destroy it (Ezekiel 22:30). We can see that clearly demonstrated in this accounts.

A condition for not destroying the land was God finding people (intercessors) to stand in the gap, pleading for mercy from God for the land. God has already covenanted, *"If my people, which are called by my name, shall humble themselves, and pray, and seek my face, and turn from their wicked ways; then will I hear from heaven, and will forgive their sin, and will heal their land (2 Chronicles 7:14).*

This, no doubt, speaks of the nature and character of God, and it is profoundly encouraging and of immense benefit in the midst of an impending judgment!

However, Arthur Wallis takes this subject to a significant dimension, and argues,

> "This action on the part of God presents us with a theological problem. God is revealed as omniscient, as One Who seers the end from the beginning. His foreknowledge

is complete and infallible. His character and counsel are immutable. 'I the Lord do not change.'"

Wallis argues further that scripture affirms that these are the attributes of the Almighty, and our common sense tells us that without them God would not be God. And he asks "Why, then, do so many Old Testament Scriptures affirm that "The Lord repented" or changed His mind?

No doubt, God foreknew when He sent Jonah that Nineveh would repent and its judgment would be averted. This then appears to be God's purpose for sending him, that He might extend mercy towards them. This nature of God is sufficiently demonstrated in 2 Peter 3:9:

> "…but is longsuffering toward us, not willing that any should perish, but that all should come to repentance" (KJV).

> "… Rather, he is patient for your sake. He does not want to destroy anyone but wants all people to have an opportunity to turn to him and change the way they think and act" (God's Word Translation).

God's Response to King Ahab's fast

These unique attributes of God are clearly demonstrated in God responding to the fasting of, even, a heathen king – Ahab to avert imminent judgment. King Ahab, the husband of Jezebel, had committed abomination before God.

No previous king of Israel was as wicked as Ahab. In a swift move to unleash His judgement against Ahab, God voiced His displeasure against his evils and that of his wife – Jezebel.

This prompted Ahab to seek forgiveness with fasting. Fasting and repentance are often associated, because true fasting brings about a spirit of repentance.

God said:

And it came to pass, when Ahab heard those words, that he rent his clothes, and put sackcloth upon his flesh, and fasted, and lay in sackcloth, and went softly. And the word of the Lord came to Elijah the Tishbite, saying, Seest thou how Ahab humbleth himself before me? because he humbleth himself before me, I will not bring the evil in his days: but in his son's days will I bring the evil upon his house (I Kings 21:29).

So we can see that fasting lifted God's judgment from the life of Ahab.

This powerful spiritual principle still applies today, and is consistent with God's promise to Israel:

> *Say to them, 'As surely as I live, declares the Sovereign LORD, I take no pleasure in the death of the wicked, but rather that they turn from their ways and live. Turn! Turn from your evil ways! Why will you die, O house of Israel?' "Therefore, son of man, say to your countrymen, 'The righteousness of the righteous man will not save him when he disobeys, and the wickedness of the wicked man will not cause him to fall when he turns from it. The righteous man, if he sins, will not be allowed to live because of his former righteousness.' If I tell the righteous man that he will surely live, but then he trusts in his righteousness and does evil, none of the righteous things he has done will be remembered; he will die for the evil he has done. And if I say to the wicked man, 'You will surely die,' but he then turns away from his sin and does what is just and right if he gives back what he took in pledge for a loan, returns what he has stolen, follows the decrees that give life, and does no evil, he will surely live; he will not die. None of the sins he has committed will be remembered against him. He has done what is just and right; he will surely live (Ezekiel 33:11 -16 NIV).*

20

THE DANIEL FAST: FASTING TO OVERCOME THE FLESH

In the third year of the reign of Jehoiakim king of Judah came Nebuchadnezzar king of Babylon unto Jerusalem, and besieged it. And the Lord gave Jehoiakim king of Judah into his hand, with part of the vessels of the house of God: which he carried into the land of Shinar to the house of his god; and he brought the vessels into the treasure house of his god. And the king spake unto Ashpenaz the master of his eunuchs, that he should bring certain of the children of Israel, and of the king's seed, and of the princes; Children in whom was no blemish, but well favoured, and skilful in all wisdom, and cunning in knowledge, and understanding science, and such as had ability in them to stand in the king's palace, and whom they might teach the learning and the tongue of the Chaldeans. And the king appointed them a daily provision of the king's meat, and of the wine which he drank: so nourishing them three years,

> *that at the end thereof they might stand before the king. Now among these were of the children of Judah, Daniel, Hananiah, Mishael, and Azariah: Unto whom the prince of the eunuchs gave names: for he gave unto Daniel the name of Belteshazzar; and to Hananiah, of Shadrach; and to Mishael, of Meshach; and to Azariah, of Abednego* (Daniel 1:1-5).

Daniel and the other Hebrew youths; Shadrach, Meshach and Abednego were Jews captivity in Babylon. These men were highly respected for their purity and absolute devotion to God. It was required that as people in captivity, and serving in the king's palace, that they be educated in the way of the Chaldeans.

Part of the process of training these young Jews for the Babylonian civil service was to rob them of their identities. They were given Babylonian names. They were taught the Babylonian language. They were to eat Babylonian food. And the Enemy of our souls uses the same tactics today. This was, particularly a testing time for these Hebrew men - their devotion to God was put to test.

It is not particularly known why Daniel accepted a Babylonian name and way of life but not the food. Daniel 1:5 records that the king's servants assigned them a daily amount of food and wine from the king's table (NIV). It was the intention of the King to keep them on this special rich diet of meats, fats, and sugary pastries and wine (the sort of unhealthy food gladly consumed in our society today) for three years, at the end of which they were to be presented to the king.

Just as we do not know how Daniel and his friends were feeling, we do not know why Daniel was so concerned about food. Some people think it was because the food would not conform to the Law of Moses - for example, it might contain pork. But, if that was the problem, why would Daniel refuse wine? Some think it is because the food would have been offered to idols. But would not the vegetables he was prepared to eat (see verse 12) also have been offered to idols? Some think that to accept food from the King's table would have been an expression of friendship that would not have been appropriate. But Daniel was prepared to accept other food, as well as clothing, accommodation, education and, I expect, money from the king. To repeat, we do not know.

In verse 8, we see the nature of the attitude that is generally needed to go through a fast. Daniel made up his mind that he would not defile himself with the king's rich and delicious meats or with the wine which he drank; so he sought permission from the commander of the officials that he might not defile himself.

But Daniel purposed in his heart that he would not defile himself with the portion of the king's meat, nor with the wine which he drank: therefore he requested of the prince of the eunuchs that he might not defile himself.

Just as the Holy Spirit is careful to include in scripture everything that He wants to be there, in the same way, He is careful to exclude from scripture everything He does not want to be there. When the Bible is vague, that's because it is supposed to be vague. It is enough for us to know that Daniel believed that it would have defiled him to eat food from the king's table. Daniel did what he believed was right - he acted with integrity. It has been suggested that Daniel could have rejected the king's food and wine because they did not meet the requirements of Jewish dietary laws or because these could have, first been offered to idols. This is in keeping with Apostle Paul's caution in Romans 12:1-2

Therefore, I urge you, brothers, in view of God's mercy, to offer your bodies as living sacrifices, holy and pleasing to God — this is your spiritual act of worship. Do not conform any longer to the pattern of this world, but be transformed by the renewing of your mind. Then you will be able to test and approve what God's will is—his good, pleasing and perfect will.

So Daniel made a request of the prince of the eunuchs:

Please test your servants for ten days: Give us nothing but vegetables to eat and water to drink. Then compare our appearance with that of the young men who eat the royal food, and treat your servants in accordance with what you see. So he agreed to this and tested them for ten days (verses 12-14 (NIV).

Accordingly, Daniel and the other three Hebrew youths lived a fasted life for three years on vegetarian diets instead of the king's food and water instead of the king's wine while learning and studying in the king's court. Heaven moved on their behalf to honour their partial fast.

At the end of the ten days fast, Daniel and his friends not only *"looked healthier and better nourished than any of the young men who ate the royal food"* (verse 15 NIV), but God granted them favour, wisdom and insight that could not be matched by their contemporaries who fed on the king's food.

We read in verses 18-20:

At the end of the time set by the king to bring them into his service, the chief official presented them to Nebuchadnezzar. The king talked with them, and he found none equal to Daniel, Hananiah, Mishael and Azariah; so they entered the king's service. In every matter of wisdom and understanding about which the king questioned them, he found them ten times better than all the magicians and enchanters in his whole kingdom.

This biblical account supports the notion that God honours those who honour Him with fasting. The Daniel fast eliminates rich and tempting food we easily want to reach for. Though not an absolute fast, God was greatly honoured nonetheless; Daniel and his Hebrew associates were greatly rewarded.

FASTING FOR REVELATION: INTERCEDING AGAINST THE POWER OF DARKNESS

The second account of Daniel's fast was to receive special revelation. Exceptional insights from God were sometimes given to the prophets and others during periods of fasting. In the book of Daniel we find an account in relation to prayer (intercession) and fasting for revelation about the future. This would, undoubtedly, challenge our prayer life if we can fully grasp it. Daniel sought God with fasting to ask God to fulfil His promise to restore Jerusalem (Daniel 9:9, 18 and compare with Jeremiah 29:10-13). He received through the angel Gabriel a wonderful unfolding of God's plan for Israel. If we have sought God in vain for the fulfilment of some promises, it could be that He is waiting for us to humble ourselves by fasting and seek Him as Daniel did.

> *And I set my face unto the Lord God, to seek by prayer and supplications, with fasting, and sackcloth, and ashes…, whiles I was speaking in prayer, even the man Gabriel … talked with me, and said O Daniel… at the beginning of thy supplications the commandment came forth…"* (Dan 9:3-21).

The Daniel fasting experience is replete with great lessons for today's believer. In the first place, this portion of scriptures make it abundantly clear that there are different ways to engage in a fast, and that fasting does not always have to involve total abstinence from food, as we see in Daniel 10:2,3.

> *In those days I Daniel was mourning three full weeks. I ate no pleasant bread, neither came flesh nor wine in my mouth, neither did I anoint myself at all, till three whole weeks were fulfilled.*

In the tenth verse he said,

> *And, behold, an hand touched me, which set me upon my knees and upon the palms of my hands. And he said unto me, O Daniel, a man greatly beloved, understand the words that I speak unto thee, and stand upright: for unto thee am I now sent. And when he had spoken this word unto me, I stood trembling. Then said he unto me, Fear not, Daniel: for from the first day that thou didst set thine heart to understand, and to chasten thyself before thy God, thy words were heard, and I am come for thy words.*

> *But the prince of the kingdom of Persia withstood me one and twenty days: but, lo, Michael, one of the chief princes, came to help me; and I remained*

there with the kings of Persia (verses 10-13).

It is worth noting that the angel was not sent from heaven to Daniel with the message of restoration until he had prayed and fasted. It should be noted too, that there was an extended period of time between Daniel's fasting and the time he had the answer through. God heard from the beginning of his supplication. Indeed, God sent the answer on the very first day, but the answer was delayed for twenty-one days. Here lies a valuable lesson: sometimes when we pray and the answer does not get through instantly, it does not mean that God does not answer us or has not responded to our request. In this case, God had sent the answer Daniel needed from Heaven, but it did not get through; why? The Bible says that the Prince of Persia withstood the angel:

Arthur Wallis observes that, in spite, of the resistance Daniel experienced in the spirit realm, his "earnest, desperate cry would not stop until the answer came." "Thus", continues Wallis, "we see that fasting was sometimes involved in earnest and prolonged supplication. When the heavens remained as brass despite earnest and persistent prayer, men were sometimes driven in their desperation to fasting as the only solution."

This biblical account confirms, more than anything else, the reality and intensity of spiritual warfare. This scripture, no doubt, refers to the existence of a spiritual kingdom of darkness that dominated, in the heavenly, over the earthly kingdom of Persia with a Satanic Prince heading it. It was this Satanic Prince that held up the answer that God had dispatched to Daniel. He did not want the angel to get through with the answer because of its significance to the Persian kingdom. The message that God dispatched had to do with the dissolution of the Medo-Persian kingdom; and the institution, in its stead, of the Grecian Kingdom that would, ultimately be replaced by the Roman Kingdom which would rule over Jerusalem.

Thank God, with the reinforcement from another angel, the message finally got through on the twenty-first day to Daniel. Notice what the angel said, "... *now will I return to fight with the prince of Persia: and when I am gone forth, lo, the prince of Grecia (Greece) shall come*" (verse 20).

We are given a clear picture of the nature of the battle we (believers) very often contend with, by Paul, in Ephesians 6:12:

For we wrestle not against flesh and blood, but against principalities, against powers, against the rulers of the darkness of this world, against spiritual wickedness in high places.

With fasting victory is guaranteed!

THE WONDERS OF FASTING

21

ELIJAH'S FAST: BREAKING NEGATIVE EMOTIONAL HABITS

The Elijah fast is to break negative emotional habits. You can rely on God to help you break free from specific habits as you apply the principles that can be gleaned from the Elijah Fast. Some of the mental and emotional habits that often serve as signs of needing the Elijah's fast, according to Elmer Towns are: negative self-image, low-self-image, self – rejection, threatening self-image; and he remarks:

It is without doubt that bad habits are so easy to develop and extremely difficult to break? Most of us have asked that question at one time or another. As creatures of habit, we tend to do the same thing we've always done even when we know it wrong and say we want to stop. We struggle week after week, month after month, desperately trying to break a bad habit, but realizing little or no success.

He went on to describe 'a habit' as "a behaviour pattern acquired by frequent repetition that is reflected in regular or increased performance."

For Elijah, and many people, involvement in ministry seems an open-gate for some of the negative emotions to manifest; even though involvement in God's work is often a source of significant joy in the life of a believer. Perhaps, that is why we are so surprised when we find ourselves discouraged or depressed while in God's service.

Though God used Elijah in a significant way, he was, nonetheless, subject to some emotional problems. We could find explanation in the fact that he described was a *"man subject to like passion"* (James 5:17). Elijah was the prophet who stood boldly alone on Mount Carmel and challenged 450 prophets of Baal. Many Israelites had begun to worship the false god Baal, but Elijah challenged them: *"How long will you waver between two opinions? If the Lord is God, follow him; but if Baal is God, then follow him"* (I Kings 18:21).

Elijah defied the prophet s of Baal and challenged them to have their god light the fire on the sacrificial altar. When they could not, Elijah had his altar soaked with water, then challenged God:

Lord God of Abraham, Isaac, and Israel, let it be known this day that You are God in Israel and I am Your servant, and that I have done all these things at Your word (v. 36).

God honoured Elijah's bold faith and fire fell from heaven, igniting the altar of the Lord. It was such a powerful display of power that the people rose up and killed the false prophets.

Queen Jezebel had sponsored Baal worship in Israel through her husband, King Ahab. This so enraged her that she swore to kill Elijah. Elijah was afraid and ran for his life (19:3).He fled to the wilderness and fell into extreme despondency. Elijah's problem was not Jezebel; it was his emotional state. He was an extrovert who was in great command in public, but when alone lapsed into terrible depression and despondency. Elijah's problem was himself.

Elijah left his servant in Judah and went a day's journey into the desert. He deliberately chose to go where there was no food. There Elijah asked God to take his life. Queen Jezebel's threat had exposed Elijah's lack of control over his own life.

Many Believers today have the same response to life's circumstances. Our lack of control over our future causes us to feel abandoned, to withdraw and become worried and depressed. We are victims of negative emotional habits.

God promises that fasting can break self-destructive habits. *"Is not this the fast that I have chosen: ...that you break every yoke?"* (Is. 58:6). The Elijah fast invites God into the problem of our negative emotional habits. In Christ's strength, victory is possible.

People who have negative mental and emotional habits like Elijah often struggle with self-image issues. They have either a low, negative or threatened self-image or they suffer from self-rejection. Due to his negative emotional habits, when problems threatened Elijah's control over his circumstances, or his self-image, Elijah had a tendency to withdraw from people and run from his problems. He would slide into despondency and depression. He would suffer from either emotional burn out or self-pity.

Does any of this sound familiar? If you cycle through bouts with pessimism and despondency, God can break your negative emotional habits through prayer and fasting.

22

LESSONS FROM ELIJAH'S FAST

Elmer Towns and Natalie Nichols share some valuable thoughts on the Elijah's fast I find extremely helpful to people struggling with emotional problems. This section contains some wealth of wisdom gleaned from their work.

1. Defeat Can Easily Overcome Victory

Elijah was a mighty man of God; no doubt! He had just called down fire from heaven, led the execution of the prophets of Baal and he frustrated the plans of the enemy being executed through evil rulers - Ahab and Jezebel. However, because of his mental or emotional weakness, he easily succumbed to circumstances that appeared to have threatened his self-image. He easily slipped into depression, ran away and prayed to die when Queen Jezebel threatened to kill him.

I have had enough, LORD,' he said. 'Take my life; I am no better than my ancestors (19:4).

Scripture gives accounts of other men of God who suffered similar fate at different times, in the course of their exploits for God. According to Natalie Nichols,

"Noah preached against the drunkenness of a generation, yet his children were judged because of his own sin of drunkenness (Gen. 9:24, 25). Abraham trusted God by faith, yet lied about Sarah (Gen. 12:12). Moses was meek and humble (numbers 12:3), yet God did not allow him to enter the Promised Land because he struck the rock for water. Peter insisted he would never deny Christ, however, within 24 hours he denied him with cursing (John 13:37, 38)."

We need to be careful when we have great success for God. Such success makes us prime target for severe satanic attacks. Apostle Paul admonishes, *"Wherefore let him that thinketh he stands take heed lest he fall"* (I Cor. 10:12).

2. We can get depressed doing the work of God

It must be noted that the service of God very often makes the believer a prime target for the enemy.

God used Elijah mightily. He stood alone for God when others compromised and worshipped Baal. Elijah boasted, "I alone am left" (v. 10). But Elijah was wrong. God told him that there were 7,000 in Israel who had not bowed the knee to Baal. Elijah's problem was that he was too self-centred.

Elijah was so focused on himself that he could not see what God was doing in the lives of others. He could not see the greater picture. God had to distance Himself from the problem so Elijah could see the big picture. The Elijah Fast can enable you to see the big picture.

This is of great significance to those in any aspect of ministry work today. It is also true that very often we fail to realise that the work that is entrusted to our care belongs to God in the first place. That puts us in the position to always involve Him in the discharge of the assignment. Closely related is again the unfortunate reality of taking on far more than has been committed to us by God. The Bible clearly states that:

> *The secret things belong unto the LORD our God: but those things which are revealed belong unto us and to our children forever, that we may do all the words of this law (Deuteronomy 29:29).*

Like Elijah, we can be focused like a laser beam on the negative. We can be so shackled to a negative emotional habit and response that we can't see what God is doing for us or what He is done for others. Our habit can absolutely blind us to the power and work of God.

3. Remember that God Knows the Heart

God knew all along what was in Elijah's heart. Elijah's emotional tendencies did not keep God from using Him. Here lies another invaluable lesson for 'the today's Elijahs.' The Bible says,

> *God has chosen the foolish things of the world to confound the wise; and God has chosen the weak things of the world to confound the things which are mighty* (1 Cor. 1:2).

Perhaps, greater solace for today kingdom's worker lies in the astonishing revelation that though, earthen vessels, tremendous treasures fit for the master's use reside in us (2 Cor. 4:7; 2 Timothy 2:12), and that is what the Lord is after in our lives. A treasure is a quantity of precious metals, gems, or other valuable objects or a very valuable object - something of great worth to be sought after. Things of great value are normal housed in special and expensive boxes, cases or containers. Being "earthen vessels" speaks of our dependability (depending on God's grace and mercy). And of course, the content of the vessel - the unction of the Holy Spirit - is precious.

This explains why, though a great man of God, mightily used of God, Elijah still had to grapple with issues that are common to ordinary man. Do not forget, the Bible says, *"Elias was a man subject to like passions as we are…" (KJV)*. *"Elijah was human like us…" (God's Word Translation)*.

It is interesting to note that the one thing we think will fix the problem – success – only exacerbated it for Elijah, and indeed, a good number of today's believers. When we cycle through negative emotions we feel we are justified because in our mind "nothing is going right." We think if only the tide would turn in our favour and we could experience a little success, then our negative emotions would improve. If we have negative emotional habits, no amount of victory and success will change them. The problem is not the circumstance, but the heart. Allow God to address your heart during the fast.

4. In dealing with negative mental or emotional habits, set realistic goals

It is a fact of life that if the devil cannot get us discouraged through inaction; he very often brings about discouragement through getting us set unrealistic goals. Whatever negative emotional habits you are seeking God to overcome, using the Elijah's fast, took decades to develop; consequently, it would take time and patience to overcome them. Set achievable goals in dealing with the situations.

There are no quick and easy solutions to some of these problems. There are no instant spirituality that can be utilised without discipline and patience. The Bible says, *"Praying always with all prayer and supplication in the Spirit, and watching thereunto with **all perseverance** and supplication for all saints"* (Ephesians 6:18, emphasis added). With all perseverance? Indeed! It means you should never be discouraged or disheartened. Compare this with Luke 18: 1:

> "Then Jesus told his disciples a parable to show them that they should always pray and not give up. He said: "In a certain town there was a judge who neither feared God nor cared what people

thought. And there was a widow in that town who kept coming to him with the plea, 'Grant me justice against my adversary." (NIV, emphasis added).

5. Fast to Hear God's Word

After Elijah prayed to die, he fell asleep. Then an angel touched him and told him to get up and eat. Bread and water were by his head. *"He ate and drank and then lay down again" (v. 6).* The angel came back again, touched him and said; *"Get up and eat, for the journey is too much for you" (v. 7).* Elijah got up and ate and drank. The Bible says, *"Strengthened by that food, he travelled forty days and forty nights until he reached Horeb, the mountain of God" (v. 8).*

Mount Sinai in Horeb was where God appeared in fire to Moses, and where He gave Moses the Ten Commandments. Elijah sought a fresh touch from God, so he returned to the place where God revealed Himself to Moses. It was there that *"the word to the LORD came to [Elijah]" (v. 9).* God had a word for him, but Elijah had to obey and travel to Sinai to get the word.

If we want God to break negative emotional habits from our lives through fasting, we must travel to a place of visitation. We need to embark on a journey with God. We cannot merely do without food and expect a miracle. You may want to revisit a place where God has spoken to you in the past, a place where you felt His anointing. Or you may simply visit your place of daily prayer - and meet Him with an open heart.

It takes new facts to break negative emotional habits. These new facts come from the Truth of God's Word. "And ye shall know the truth, and the truth shall make you free" (John 8:32). Knowing the truth often takes a discovery; an expedition with God. As a matter of fact, the word 'know' in the above scripture is rendered 'discover' in the original Hebrew Bible. New facts are introduced into our thinking by careful study of God's Word. Study Scriptures about faith, hope, the power and indwelling of God. The strength and truth from Scripture is what gives the ability to break negative emotional habits.

The wrong desires that come into your life aren't anything new and different. Many others have faced exactly the same problems before you. And no temptation is irresistible. You can trust God to keep the temptation from becoming so strong that you can't stand up against it, for he has promised this and will do what he says. He will show you how to escape temptation's power so that you can bear up patiently against it (I Cor. 10:13, TLB).

6. Let the Word Reveal Your Weakness

Reading the word of God causes us to question where we are spiritually. The light of the Word exposes our fleshly, sinful ways. When Adam sinned, God asked him *"Where art thou?" (Gen. 3:9)*. God knew where Adam was. He only asked the question to cause Adam to reflect on where he was. Until we realise and question our habitual patterns of thought, the bondage remains unbroken.

When Elijah got to Mount Sinai, the Word of the Lord came to him. *"What are you doing here, Elijah?" God asked (1Kings 19:9)*. God used the question as a mirror to make Elijah view himself from outside his inner compulsions. God does the same with us. During the Elijah fast, use the Word as a mirror to expose your weaknesses.

7. Confess and Agree with God about Your Weakness

When the Word came to Elijah on Mount Sinai, God began to pierce Elijah's soul. Elijah was embarrassed and attempted to justify himself. *"I have been very zealous for the Lord God of hosts; for the children of Israel have forsaken Your covenant"* (v. 10).

This seemed like a great self-defence, but in reality, it was Elijah's admission of failure. Self-justification keeps us from confessing our needs. Elijah disguised his need with the claim to be defending God. He did not see that God could defend Himself. Do not attempt to defend your weakness; instead confess and agree with God about it.

> *If we confess our sins, he is faithful and just to forgive us our sins, and to cleanse us from all unrighteousness* (1 John 1:9).

8. Listen for the Still, Small Voice

> *And behold the Lord passed by, and a great and strong wind rent the mountains, and brake in pieces the rocks before the Lord; but the Lord was not in the wind; and after the wind an earthquake; but the Lord was not in the earthquake: And after the earthquake a fire; but the Lord was not in the fire; and after the fire a still small voice. And it was so, when Elijah heard it, he wrapped his face in his mantle, and went out* (vv. 11-13, KJV).

Elijah's answer was in the still, small voice. The power was not in the wind, the earthquake or the fire; it was in the Word of God.

We go to the altar and beg, "God take this negative habit from me!" Pleading for an external force to miraculously whisk it away, we put the ball in God's court. Elmer Towns writes,

> People want to put the ball in God's court, when all along God wants to give them the ball to empower them to be more responsible. Habits are broken not by external forces, but from within. They must be broken the way they are formed, one act at a time—by submitting to discipline—by repeatedly choosing not to behave according to habit. Just as the habit of overeating was established one meal at a time, conquering that habit will require submitting to disciplined eating one meal at a time.

A habit is "frequent repetition." We must frequently repeat God's revealed discipline over our negative emotions, just as overeating is defeated with one meal at a time. An athlete is well acquainted with the fact that muscles are trained and built by repetition. They must exercise discipline to go to the gym or the track repeatedly in order to train muscles and acquire new habits and skills.

Fasting and prayer build the discipline that is required to overcome the flesh. Through fasting you submit your flesh, your appetites, and negative thoughts to the authority of your spirit-man. This discipline translates to other areas of your life, if you let it.

The Elijah fast involves looking into the Word of God and listening to what He is saying to you. God might want to use His power to break your habit externally. Or He might want to build up our inner strength through Christ so that in Him you can break your habit.

> *I have strength for all things in Christ Who empower me [I am ready for anything and equal to anything through Him Who infuses inner strength into me; I am self-sufficient in Christ's sufficiency]"* (Philippians 4:13, AMP).

9. Look for the Positive through God's Eyes

Often, we enter a season of fasting focused on the negative, trapping ourselves in the problem. Elijah's depression and pessimistic tendency trapped him in the problem as well. He continually reminded God, "I am the only one left." This statement was a manipulative way of bragging to God that he was faithful. All the while Elijah was boasting in his faithfulness, he should have been seeking to view the problem from God's perspective.

God came to Elijah with good news—with positive facts. "I reserve seven thousand in Israel—all whose knees have not bowed down to Baal and all whose mouths have not kissed him" (v. 18).

The truth is that when we focus on our problems, we exercise faith in our problems. We are admitting that our problems are bigger than we are and even bigger than God. Fear takes over! Fear is as much an exercise of faith, but in a wrong thing! As we focus on God's power, we develop more faith in His power than in our problems.

10. Take Positive Actions as God Instructs

Habits are broken by initiating positive actions rather than focusing on stopping negative ones. God did not tell Elijah, *"Stop being depressed."* He gave Elijah specific things to do. Go...*anoint Hazael as king over Syria"* (v. 15). Next He told him, *"You shall anoint Jehu the son of Nimshi as king over Israel" (v. 16).* Then He instructed Him to anoint Elisha to succeed him as prophet.

Even as you are fasting over specific issues, recognise God's power and listen for specific instructions as to definite steps you can take. Such steps might begin with new direction in prayer. Once we appreciate that God is greater than our greatest problem, our direction and momentum in prayer changes.

It was only after 40 days of fasting that God began to break negative emotional habits in Elijah. Fasting prepared him to hear from God, to recognise the still small voice. I encourage you to go to your "Mount Sinai," wherever that may be, and listen for God's still small voice. He will be faithful to speak, to reveal Himself to you, and to help you break your negative emotional feelings and habits.

FASTING FOR REEXAMINATION

No Christian discipline enables the believer to engage in self-examination as much as fasting. In the Old Testament, the need for re-examination was established by God as a duty to be observed once a year. The Day of Atonement was instituted by God for Israel to reflect on their spiritual state:

> *Also on the tenth day of this seventh month there shall be a day of atonement: it shall be an holy convocation unto you; and ye shall afflict your souls, and offer an offering made by fire unto the LORD* (Leviticus 23:27).

Also in Jeremiah 36:6, the Prophet Jeremiah wrote,

> *Therefore go thou, and read in the roll, which thou hast written from my mouth, the words of the LORD in the ears of the people in the LORD'S house upon the fasting day: and also thou shalt read them in the ears of all Judah that come out of their cities.*

In the process of self-denial, God wanted His people to examine their spiritual. The New Testament believer is expected to do likewise, albeit, not as a duty but as a means of drawing closer to God.

THE WONDERS OF FASTING

23

THE HEALING VALUE OF FASTING

"Fasting will detoxify your body, including your bloodstream, organs, and brain. With this detox you will see huge energy bursts. You will be able to think more clearly as the "brain fog" clears. Fasting has been shown to build immunity against diseases" – **Dr J. Harold Smith**

If done correctly, fasting has powerful and long-lasting health benefits. Part of the benefits God promises those that fast is:

"…thine health shall spring forth speedily…"
Isaiah 58

God has a passion to see us walk in health, and has made adequate provisions for this:

Surely he hath borne our griefs, and carried our sorrows: yet we did esteem him stricken, smitten of God, and afflicted But he was wounded for our transgressions, he was bruised for our iniquities: the chastisement of our peace was upon him; and with his stripes we are healed (Isaiah 53:4, 5).

How God anointed Jesus of Nazareth with the Holy Ghost and with power: who went about doing good, and healing all that were oppressed of the devil; for God was with him (Acts 10:38).

Fasting has been widely associated with healing for thousands of years.

Our bodies are capable of instigating their own perfect healing if we allow them the opportunity. Fasting is such an opportunity. Fasting is powerful therapeutic processes that can help people recover from mild to severe health conditions. Some of the most common ones are high blood pressure, asthma, allergies, chronic headaches, inflammatory bowel disease and a host of others

The reason fasting has such a powerful effect on healing the body, it is been alleged, is that in the fasting state, the body scours for dead cells, damaged tissues, fatty deposits, tumours and abscesses, all of which are burned for fuel or expelled as waste. Diseased cells are dissolved in a systematic manner, leaving healthy tissue. There is a remarkable redistribution of nutrients in the body through fasting.

In the first place, the process of digestion involves many bodily functions. In most cases the blood which is often required in the process of digestion is now liberated to work in other areas of the body. This gives the body more energy to divert to other activities given that so much energy is not being utilised in the digestion process. Consequently, a great deal of energy is released into your immune system as it works to detoxify your body, rebuild and refurbish your system.

Secondly, during an extended fast, you are not taking in foods that contain toxins. As a result the body has less foreign matters to grapple with. Fasting provides a period of concentrated physiological rest during which time the body can devote its self-healing mechanisms to repairing and strengthening damaged organs. The process of fasting also allows the body to cleanse cells of accumulated toxins and waste products.

It is amazing, the Bible says in Isaiah 58:8 that with fasting *"your health shall spring forth..."* Healing springs forth "speedily," from within our bodies, without any external interventions.

Dr Don Colbert, MD who is an expert in the field of nutritional health has this to say:

"Fasting allows your body to heal by giving it a rest. All living things need to rest, including you. Even the land must rest, which was a principle God gave to the ancient agrarian Jewish nation regarding their fields. Every seventh year they were not permitted to grow any crops at all. They had to let the land lie fallow so that it could re-establish its own mineral and nutrient content (Leviticus 25:1-7)... Every winter many animals will hibernate or rest for a season. Every night when you sleep, you give rest to your body and mind. Blessed rest is as much a law of the universe as gravity. It is also a powerful principle of healing. Think about it: when an animal is injured or sick, what does it do? It finds a resting place where it can lap up water, and it quits eating while it heals. This is natural, instinctual wisdom that God has placed within the animal Kingdom..."

Generally, fasting is associated with the following:

- help you lose weight and keep it off

- cleanse your body of metabolic wastes and toxins

- improve your skin tone and health, making you look younger

- stimulate new cell growth, making you feel younger

- strengthen your immune system and natural defences

- improve glandular health and hormonal balance

- increase mental clarity

- enhance your moods, enjoy a more positive outlook

- give you more energy and enthusiasm

- enhance your spiritual connection

- Rest to the digestive track

- Rejuvenate physically, mentally and spiritually

- Energizes cells

FASTING FOR THE BEGINNERS

Before going on a fasting program, check with your doctor to make sure you are in good health and that it is safe for you to carry out the program you are planning. This is especially important if you are on any prescription medications, as the lack of food could cause those drugs to be absorbed differently by your body.

Choose a fasting plan you can cope with. Start in moderation! Do not begin immediately with a 21 day or 40 day fast. Failure here would create such fear and discouragement that would make future attempts impossible. Success at, for instance, a 1 day fast would create a needed impetus to attempt longer and more rigorous fasts.

Further, beginning with a partial fast is a great boost. It might be unwise to start fasting with an absolute fast, unless it is just for a day. If it is a longer fast, I'd strongly advise a partial fast or a normal fast – of the type that Jesus did; which could be with water or juice. As stated, with time, you could gradually observe more rigorous fasts by withdrawing some of the "energy boosters" like juice or if a partial fast, some light diets. However, do not limit your fasting to partial fasts. Make progress. Get into complete fasts. You may begin with a forty-eight-hour complete fast, and increase it gradually. In his book, 'The Miracle of Fasting', health pioneer, Paul Bragg who spent decades supervising and practicing routine water fasting, outlines an incremental procedure for following water-only fasts. He suggests beginning with a twenty-four hour weekly fast of eight to ten glasses or more of pure water. Once this has been done successfully, the next fast can be extended to thirty-six hours. Short fasts of up to three days may be done monthly, after which time a longer fast of four to ten days, spaced at four-month intervals, may be implemented.

Vital Points for a beginner In Fasting

1. Check with your doctor that you are medically fit to fast

2. Start in moderation

3. Start with a partial fast

4. Understand what the purpose of a fast is before you embark on one

5. Study fasting scriptures, especially Isaiah 58 before commencing a fast

6. Meditate on scriptures throughout your period of fast

7. Spend quality time in prayer, remember fasting without prayer is an exercise in futility

8. Let your fasting be a matter between you and God.

9. If you violate your fast – break before the time appointed – do not get discouraged. Refresh yourself, give it sometime, and go for it again, remember the rule of moderation at this stage.

10. Have the goal(s) of your fast constantly before you.

Part Six

Fasting from the Legend's Perspective

THE WONDERS OF FASTING

24

QUOTES BY CHRISTIAN LEADERS ON FASTING

"Fasting is important – more important, perhaps, than many of us have supposed… when exercised with a pure heat and a right motive, fasting may provide us with a key to unlock doors where other keys have failed; a window opening up new horizons in the unseen world; a spiritual weapon of God's providing, "mighty, to the pulling down of strongholds." May God use this book to awaken many of His people to all the spiritual possibilities latent in the fast that God has chosen." – **Arthur Wallis**

"There are those who think that fasting belongs to the old dispensation; but when we look at Acts 14:23 and Acts 13:2-3, we find that it was practiced by the earnest men of the apostolic day. If we would pray with power, we should pray with fasting. This, of course, does not mean that we should fast every time we pray; but there are times of emergency or special crisis in work or in our individual lives, when men of downright earnestness will withdraw themselves even from the gratification of natural appetites that would be perfectly proper under other circumstances, that they may give themselves wholly to prayer. There is a peculiar power in such prayer. Every great crisis in life and work should be met that way. There is nothing pleasing to God in our giving up in a purely Pharisaic and legal way things which are pleasant, but there is power in that downright earnestness and determination to obtain in prayer the things of which we sorely feel our need, that leads us to put away everything, even things in themselves most right and necessary, that we set our faces to find God, and obtain blessings from Him." - **R. A. Torrey**

"The main reason that a proclaimed fast brings results is that it causes the people's minds to go in the same direction. That direction is toward God. They drop other things and centre their attention on Him. This brings the manifested presence in their midst." – **Kenneth Copeland.**

"A prepared heart is better than a prepared teaching, for a prepared heart will result in a prepared teaching. ...we do not meditate on God and his Word and watch and fast and pray enough… A season of fasting and prayer of deep humiliation and confession are the conditions from which a genuine and powerful work springs." – **E. M. Bounds**

"The reason many do not live in the power of their salvation is because 'there is too much sleep, too much meat and drink, too little fasting and self-denial, too much taking part in the world … and too little self-examination and prayer." - **William Bramwell**

"Our seasons of fasting and prayer at the Tabernacle have been high days indeed; never has Heaven's gate stood wider; never have our hearts been nearer the central Glory." – **Charles Spurgeon.**

"When we finish a fast, we cool into tempered Christians strong with self-control. The dross and cinders of our lustful cravings are skimmed off. Fasting produces a work of art - the tempered, selfless Christian - that can be created through no other process of refinement." – **Lee Bueno**

"Fasting is not to be some religious ritual we go through. When we fast, we should have a specific purpose in view, a reason for it, something we [want] to accomplish as a result of our fast. It can be for something very simple as well as for something complex and desperate." – **Gary Linton**

"More than any other discipline, fasting reveals the things that control us. This is a wonderful benefit to the true disciple who longs to be transformed to the image of Jesus Christ. We cover up what is inside of us with food and other things." - **Richard Foster**

"I was so taken back with my discovery that I trawled through scores of church history and revival books (electronically!) looking for references to fasting. What I found was astounding! There is clear, documented evidence that all the great leaders and revival movements of church history used this amazing key to add power to their prayers! In one collection of church history documents the software I used refused to reveal its findings, stating 'the search exceeds the 5,000 limit of this software!' Could it be that fasting is a vital, but missing ingredient in the 21st century church?... Men and women that God has used mightily throughout history, have similarly believed this. They saw God's glory manifest in their day. The possibility of joining their ranks is offered to every believer today. Right around the world thousands of believers are practicing prayer with fasting. The Lord is preparing his great army for a glorious and final outpouring of his Spirit to restore the glory to the church and in the world, before his return. Let's put fasting back on our menu!" - **Tony Cauchi.**

"It is right to fast frequently in order to subdue and control the body. For when the stomach is full, the body does not serve for preaching, for praying, for studying, or for doing anything else that is good. Under such circumstances God's Word cannot remain." – **Martin Luther**

"One obvious value of fasting lies in the fast that its discipline helps us keep the body in its place. It is a practical acknowledgment of the supremacy of the spiritual. But in addition to this flex value, fasting has direct benefits in relation to prayer as well. Many who practice it from right motives and in order to give themselves more unreservedly to prayer testify that the mind becomes unusually clear and vigorous. There are a noticeable spiritual quickening and increased power of concentration on the things of the spirit."
– **J. Oswald Sanders**

"Feeling somewhat of the sweetness of communion with God and the force of His love and how it captivates my soul and makes all my desires and affections to centre in God, I set apart this day for fasting and prayer to God, to bless me in view of preaching the Gospel. I had life and power in prayer this afternoon. God enabled me to wrestle ardently in intercession for my friends. The Lord visited me marvellously in prayer. I think my soul was never in such agony before. I felt no restraint, for the treasures of God's grace were opened to me. I wrestled for absent friends and for the ingathering of poor souls. I was in such agony from sun half an hour high till near dark that I was all over wet with sweat. Oh! my dear Saviour did sweat blood for these poor souls!

I longed for more compassion toward them. I was under a sense of divine love, and went to bed in such a frame of mind, with my heart set on God." - **David Brainerd**

"Fasting is a laudable practice and we have reason to lament that it is generally neglected among Christians." – **Matthew Henry.**

"I wonder whether we have ever fasted. I wonder whether it has even occurred to us that we ought to be considering the question of fasting. The fact is that this whole subject seems to have dropped right out of our lives and right out of our whole Christian thinking…As men and women are beginning to consider the days and times through which we are passing with a new seriousness, and as many are beginning to look for revival and reawakening, the question of fasting has become more and more important."– **D. Martyn – Lloyd-Jones.**

"The truth of fasting was one great contributing factor to the revival. One year before this we had read Franklin Hall's book, entitled 'Atomic Power with God through Fasting and Prayer.' We immediately began to practice fasting. Previously we had not understood the possibility of long fasts. The revival would never have been possible without the restoration of this great truth through our good brother Hall" - **George Hawtin**

"Do you have a hunger for God? If we do not feel strong desires for the manifestation of the glory of God, it is not because we have drunk deeply and are satisfied. It is because we have nibbled so long at the table of the world. Our soul is stuffed with small things, and there is no room for the great. If we are full of what the world offers, then perhaps a fast might express, or even increase, our soul's appetite for God. Between the dangers of self-denial and self-indulgence is the path of pleasant pain called fasting." - **John Piper**

"If you are serious enough about the personal and social tasks before you as a Christian to take up the discipline of fasting, you can expect resistance, interference and opposition. Plan for it, insofar as you are able. Do not be caught unawares. Remember that you are attempting to advance in your spiritual journey and to gain ground for the Kingdom. That necessitates taking ground away from the enemy – and no great movement of the Holy Spirit goes unchallenged by the enemy… one of the greatest spiritual benefits of fasting is becoming more attentive to God – becoming more aware of our own inadequacies and His adequacy, our own contingencies and His self-sufficiency – and listening to what He wants us to be and do… " - **Elmer L. Towns**

"…When the corporate prayers of many joined in the name of [Jesus] are mounted on the booster rocket of our corporate fasting, our prayers suddenly take on a supernatural power that few on earth have ever seen! You can be sure that Satan fears this holy combination as no other. Every time God's people have dared to lay aside their differences or personal concerns long enough to seek God in prayer and fasting together in one mind and one accord, terrible things have happened to his dark kingdom, while wonderful and miraculous things have happened to mankind." - **Mahesh Chavda**

"What are we salves to? What are our bottom-line passions? Fasting is God's testing ground - and healing ground. Will we murmur as the Israelites murmured when they had no bread? Will be leave the path of obedience and turn stones into bread? Or will we "live by every word that proceeds out of the mouth of God?" Fasting is a way of revealing to ourselves and confessing to God what is in our hearts... That's what I think fasting is at heart. It is an intensification of prayer. It is a physical explanation point at the end of the sentence, "We hunger for you to come in power." It is a cry with your body, "I really mean it, Lord! This much, I hunger for you... The absence of fasting is the measure of our contentment with the absence of Christ". - **John Piper**

"Learn from these men that the work which the Holy Ghost commands must call us to new fasting and prayer, to new separation from the spirit and the pleasures of the world, to new consecration to God and to His fellowship. Those men gave themselves up to fasting and prayer, and if in all our ordinary Christian work there were more prayer there would be more blessing in our own inner life...Prayer is reaching out after the unseen; fasting is letting go of all that is seen and temporal. Fasting helps express, deepen, confirm the resolution that we are ready to sacrifice anything, even ourselves to attain what we seek for the kingdom of God."- **Andrew Murray**

"Every time I fasted I establish a new spiritual dimension in my life and had new spiritual authority with people." - **George Pitt**

"One of the reasons I know that fasting is right is because there is such rebellion against it, even on the part of church people. The average preacher pokes fun at fasting and prefers the subject not to be discussed in his pulpit. Jesus made two statements that would convince any fair mind that fasting is right when He said, "They will fast." And then on the other occasion, in Matthew 17: 21, He said to His disturbed and embarrassed disciples, after a stinging rebuke about their inability to heal the child, "This kind goeth not out but by prayer and fasting."... I would suggest that you fast one day a week. However, this would be altered by the burdens that come, the leadership of the Spirit, and the spiritual needs you may face. Many times one needs to go on a semi-fast or maybe a fruit fast or natural food fast for a week just to tone up his physical system and give his body a chance to clean house. If I were to feel a sore throat coming on, I may fast three or four days. If I have an affliction of some sort that comes unannounced, I will fast and pray and read my Bible until it is gone and have God's people, of course, to pray for me and pray with me. If God leads you to go on an extended fast, don't be afraid of it. Fasting does not cause weakness primarily, but it is the poison in the system that rises forth. For instance, if you go without your cup of coffee or cola drink, you begin to get a headache. That's your system crying out for what it has been used to getting. A Christian has no need to be a slave to a habit like that when Jesus breaks every fetter and sets the captive free." – **Lester Roloff**

"This Man (Jesus) suddenly remarks one day, 'No one need fast while I am here.' Who is this Man who remarks that His mere presence suspends all normal rules?" – **C.S Lewis**

"As a Boomer, I have been conditioned to enjoy the best the world has to offer. Fasting speaks boldly to consumerism, one of my generational core values. To set aside what I want to encourage personal spiritual growth is what it means to deny myself and take up my cross daily in the nineties. I suspect it would be difficult for me to rise to the challenge of discipleship and live a consistently Christian lifestyle without practicing the discipline of fasting." – **Douglas Porter**

"If you say "I will fast when God lays it on my heart," you never will. You are too cold and indifferent to take the yoke upon you." – **D. L. Moody**

"The New Testament often links prayer with fasting. Abstinence from food can be a valuable aid in spiritual exercises. From the human side, it promotes clarity, concentration and keenness. From the divine standpoint, it seems the Lord is especially willing to answer prayer when we put that prayer before our necessary food." – **William MacDonald**

"A fast is not a hunger strike. Fasting submits to God's commands. A hunger strike makes God submit to our demands." - **Ed Cole**

"The purpose of such abstinence for a longer or shorter period of time is to loosen to some degree the ties which bind us to the world or material things and our surroundings as a whole, in order that we may concentrate all our powers upon the unseen and eternal things. To strive in prayer means in the final analysis to take up the battle against all inner and outward hindrances which would dissociate us from the spirit of prayer. It is at this point that God has ordained fasting as a means of carrying on the struggle against the subtle and dangerous hindrances which confront us in prayer." – **Ole Hallesby**

"One way to begin to see how vastly indulgent we usually are is to fast. It is a long day that is not broken by the usual three meals. One finds out what an astonishing amount of time is spent in the planning, purchasing, preparing, eating, and cleaning up of meals." – **Elisabeth Eliot**

"In Shansi I found Chinese Christians who were accustomed to spend time in fasting and prayer. They recognized that this fasting, which so many dislike, which requires faith in God, since it makes one feel weak and poorly, is really a divinely appointed means of grace. Perhaps the greatest hindrance to our work is our own imagined strength; and in fasting we learn what poor, weak creatures we are-dependent on a meal of meat for the little strength which we are so apt to lean upon." – **Hudson Taylor**

"Bear up the hands that hang down, by faith and prayer; support the tottering knees. Have you any days of fasting and prayer? Storm the throne of grace and persevere therein, and mercy will come down … The man who never fasts is no more in the way to heaven than the man who never prays." – **John Wesley**

"Inasmuch as fasting is before God, a practical proof that the thing we ask is to us a matter of true and pressing interest, and inasmuch as in a high degree it strengthens the intensity and power of the prayer, and becomes the unceasing practical expression of a prayer without words, I could believe that it would not be without efficacy, especially as the Master's words had reference to a case like the present. I tried it, without telling anyone, and in truth the later conflict was extraordinarily lightened by it. I could speak with much greater restfulness and decision. I did not require to be long present with the sick one; and I felt that I could influence without being present." - **Blumhardt**

"Our ability to perceive God's direction in life is directly related to our ability to sense the inner prompting of His spirit. God provides a special activity to assist us in doing this…Men through whom God has worked greatly have emphasised the significance of prayer with fasting…In an extended fast of over three days, one quickly experiences a great decrease in sensual desires and soon has a great new alertness to spiritual things." – **Bill Gothard**

"A lust for food has sent many an individual to an early grave: a grave dug with a fork…Fasting is not nearly so deadly as feasting." – **J. Harold Smith**

"The Scriptures bid us fast, the Church says now." - **George Herbert**

"Fasting has gone almost completely out of the life of the ordinary person. Jesus condemned the wrong kind of fasting, but he never meant that fasting should be completely eliminated from life and living. We would do well to practice it in our own way and according to our own need." – **William Barclay**

"Fastings and vigils without a special object in view are time run to waste. They are made to minister to a sort of self-gratification, instead of being turned to good account."
- **David Livingstone**

"If the solemnities of our fasting, though frequent, long, and severe, do not serve to put an edge upon devout affections, to quicken prayer, to increase Godly sorrow, and to alter the temper of our minds, and the course of our lives, for the better, they do not at all answer the intention, and God will not accept them as performed to Him." – **Matthew Henry**

"In my personal life, fasting has been for specific purpose and for a long duration. After three days, there are no hunger pains or desire for food. From twelve to fourteen days later, there seems to be a sense of cleanliness and mental clarity. After twenty-one days, there seems to be an outpouring of spiritual power and creativity that is indescribable, but continues until the fast is ended. It seems especially after the third week that one is no longer even remotely interested in the trivial physical world around. One's mind is filled exclusively with profound spiritual ideas and truths. One of the most profound things is that the mind will concentrate for hours on the same subject without once wavering or being distracted. There is no question that there is awesome power in fasting. If the fast is controlled by the Holy Spirit and Jesus is foremost, then it is a beautiful and powerful experience." - **Arthur Blessitt**

"Fasting in the biblical sense is choosing not to partake of food because your spiritual hunger is so deep, you determination in intercession so intense, or your spiritual warfare so demanding that you have temporarily set aside even fleshly needs to give yourself to prayer and meditation" - **Wesley L. Duewel**

"The greatest saint in the world is not he who prays most or fasts most; it is not he who gives alms, or is most eminent for temperance, chastity or justice. It is he who is most thankful to God." - **William Law**

"The reason why the Methodists in general do not live in this salvation is, there is too much sleep, too much meat and drink, too little fasting and self-denial, too much conversation with the world, too much preaching and hearing and too little self-examination and prayer." – **William Bramwell**

"By fasting, the body learns to obey the soul; by praying the soul learns to command the body." – **William Secker**
"I often felt myself weak in the presence of temptation and

needed frequently to hold days of fasting and prayer and to spend much time in overhauling my own religious life in order to retain that communion with God and that hold upon the Devine truth that would enable me efficiently to labor for promotion of revivals of religion." – **Charles G. Finney**

"The abstinence is not to be an end in itself but rather for the purpose of being separated to the Lord and to concentrate on godliness. This kind of fasting reduces the influence of our self-will and invites the Holy Spirit to do a more intense work in us." – **William Thrasher**

"When the devil, the foe and the tyrant, sees a man bearing this weapon [fasting], he is straight-away frightened and he recollects and considers that defeat which he suffered in the wilderness at the hands of the Saviour; at once his strength is shattered and the very sight of this weapon, given us by our Commander-in-chief, burns him." – **Isaac of Syria**

"Fasting is the change of every part of our life, because the sacrifice of the fast is not the abstinence but the distancing from sins. Therefore, whoever limits the fast to the deprivation of food, he is the one who, in reality, abhors and ridicules the fast. Are you fasting? Show me your fast with your works. Which works? If you see someone who is poor, show him mercy. If you see an enemy, reconcile with him. If you see a friend who is becoming successful, do not be jealous of him! If you see a beautiful woman on the street, pass her by. In other words, not only should the mouth fast, but the eyes and the legs and the arms and all the other parts of the body should fast as well. Let the hands fast, remaining clean from stealing and greediness. Let the legs fast, avoiding roads which lead to sinful sights. Let the eyes fast by not fixing themselves on beautiful faces and by not observing the beauty of others. You are not eating meat, are you? You should not eat debauchery with your eyes as well. Let your hearing also fast. The fast of hearing is not to accept bad talk against others and sly defamations. Let the mouth fast from disgraceful and abusive words, because, what gain is there when, on the one hand we avoid eating chicken and fish and, on the other, we chew-up and consume our brothers? He who condemns and blasphemes is as if he has eaten brotherly meat, as if he has bitten into the flesh of his fellow man. It is because of this that Paul frightened us, saying: "If you chew up and consume one another be careful that you do not annihilate yourselves." – **St. John Chrysostom**

"Our greatest victories are won on our knees and with empty stomachs." – **Julio C. Ruibal**

"Fasting can be a painful admission that I am not free, that my life is enslaved, obsessed or addicted to external things such as food, drink, co-dependent relationships, sex, television, privacy and the like." – **Albert Haase**

"Is fasting ever a bribe to get God to pay more attention to the petitions? No, a thousand times no. It is simply a way to make clear that we sufficiently reverence the amazing opportunity to ask help from the everlasting God, the Creator of the universe, to choose to put everything else aside and concentrate on worshiping, asking forgiveness, and making our requests known-considering His help more important than anything we could do ourselves in our own strength and with our own ideas." - **Edith Schaeffer**

"Fasting confirms our utter dependence upon God by finding in Him a source of sustenance beyond food." - **Dallas Willard**

"Everyone must study his own nature. Some of you can sustain life with less food than others can, and therefore I desire that he who needs more nourishment shall not be obliged to equal others, but that everyone shall give his body what it needs for being an efficient servant of the soul. For as we are obliged to be on our guard against superfluous food which injures body and soul alike, thus we must be on the watch against immoderate fasting, and this the more, because the Lord wants conversion and not victims." - **Francis of Assisi**

"Prayer is reaching out after the unseen; fasting is letting go of all that is seen and temporal. Fasting helps express, deepen, confirm the resolution that we are ready to sacrifice anything, even ourselves to attain what we seek for the kingdom of God." - **Andrew Murray**

"Bear up the hands that hang down, by faith and prayer; support the tottering knees. Have you any days of fasting and prayer? Storm the throne of grace and persevere therein, and mercy will come down." - **John Wesley**

"Suggestions for Fasting and Feasting: Fast from discontent; feast on thankfulness. Fast from worry; feast on trust. Fast from anger; feast on patience. Fast from self-concern; feast on compassion for others. Fast from unrelenting pressures; feast on unceasing prayers. Fast from bitterness; feast on forgiveness. Fast from discouragement, feast on hope. Fast from media hype, feast on the honesty of the Bible. Fast from idle gossip; feast on purposeful silence. Fast from problems that overwhelm; feast on prayer that undergirds."
– Anonymous

"A spiritually awake person would see everything as gift, even suffering. We deserve nothing and yet we so often act as though we deserve everything. Nothing should be taken for granted. We should say thank you every day to God and to each other for all that is provided for us. This is one reason why fasting is such an important spiritual discipline. Not just fasting from food, but also fasting from cars, shopping centres, the news - whatever we have an inordinate attachment to. Fasting can help re-kindle our gratitude for all that we have been given." - **Glen Argan**

"Jesus has many lovers of His kingdom of heaven, but he has few bearers of His Cross. Many desire His consolation, but few desire His tribulation. He finds many comrades in eating and drinking, but He finds few hands who will be with Him in His abstinence and fasting...But those who love Jesus purely for Himself, and not for their own profit or convenience, bless Him as heartily in temptation and tribulation and in all other adversities as they do in time of consolation. And if He never sent them consolation, they would still bless and praise Him." - **Thomas a Kempis**

Part Seven

Diverse issues about Fasting and Prayer

THE WONDERS OF FASTING

25

ANSWERS TO COMMON QUESTIONS ABOUT FASTING

This section is devoted to helping the believer understand some critical aspects of biblical fasting that have been greatly misunderstood, which has rendered the practice of fasting almost unthinkable for many.

Most of the problems often associated with fasting stern from the legalistic, rigid and ritualistic view of what biblical fast is and is not. Most people, for instance, are of the opinion that unless they engage in very lengthy fasts, they would not be able to gain God's attention. While some others think that they have to observe a certain kind fast in order to get God do what, perhaps, He would not do otherwise. We have established, as a matter of fact, that in no way does the fasting of man change God. Fasting, at its best, changes man and positions him spiritually to better receive from God. Second, no one can access the throne of grace successfully, even with the most lengthy and gruesome fast while living in sin. Again, I will like to stress that the sacrifice of man is an abomination to God if that man lives in enmity with his maker.

> "The sacrifice of the wicked is abomination: how much more, when he bringeth it with a wicked mind?" (Proverbs 21:27).

What is fasting?

Fasting is the abstention from food for a period of time, for spiritual purposes.

Fasting is not only an abstention from food; it is also a concentration on God's glory, God's holiness and His ways.

What are the purposes of fasting?

Primarily, the purpose of fasting is self-humbling. It is a scriptural means ordained by God for us to humble ourselves before Him. Denying oneself of food to seek God and His will shows humility. That is why fasting is also the equivalent of the phrase "to humble oneself before the Lord" (Psalm 35:13; 1 Kings 21:29; Ezra 8:21). When a person is truly concerned about the things of God, he will humble himself. There will be times when he will deny himself the pleasure and enjoyment of food to continue concentration and focus on that which is important to God.

Andrew Murray said:

Fasting helps to express, to deepen, and to confirm the resolution that we are ready to sacrifice anything – to sacrifice ourselves – to attain what we seek for the kingdom of God.

Why Should I fast?

You do not fast for the sake of fasting. You fast for specific purpose(s). You need to ask yourself the question: Why am I fasting? Is it for spiritual renewal, for guidance, for healing, for the resolution of problems, for special grace to handle a difficult situation? Ask the Holy Spirit to clarify His leading and objectives for your fast. This will enable you to pray more specifically and strategically. There are several reasons why a believer should decide to fast. Usually you fast as a means of seeking God. God said, "When you seek me with all your heart, I will be found by you" (Jeremiah 29:13, 14). When a man or woman is willing to set aside the legitimate appetites of the body to concentrate on the work of praying, they are demonstrating that they mean business; that they are seeking God with all their heart.

Fasting is an expression of wholeheartedness. This is clear from Joel's call to the nation of Israel: *"Yet even now," says the Lord, "return to me with all your heart, with fasting. . ."* (Joel 2:12).

Also you fast when you are faced with situations that prayers alone cannot deal with. There are stubborn situations that have demonic undertone that prove too extreme to avert with prayers alone. Jesus said: *"However, this kind does not go out except by prayer and fasting"* (Matthew 17:21).

Can I fast without necessarily having any reasons to?

Indeed. You can develop a fasted-life. Many believers I know fast one or two days a week and they do that faithfully as an act of worship to God.

How Should I Prepare For a Fast?

It is unwise to rush into any fast without adequate spiritual and physical preparations. Jesus emphasised the importance of preparation in all our endeavours:

For which of you, desiring to build a tower, does not first sit down and count the cost, whether he has enough to complete it? Otherwise, when he has laid a foundation, and is not able to finish, all who see it begin to mock him, saying, 'This man began to build, and was not able to finish.' Or what king, going to encounter another king in war, will not sit down first and take counsel whether he is able with ten thousand to meet him who comes against him with twenty thousand (Luke 14:28).

The way you begin your fast will largely determine its success. Do not rush into a fast. Prepare your body for the fast. Eat smaller meals before starting a fast. Eat raw fruit and vegetables for, at least, two days before starting a fast. Withdraw from high-fat, high-sugar diets, and coffee and tea, days before you commence a lengthy fast. People generally experience a significant drop in their blood sugar, resulting in headaches, dizziness and nausea during a fast. These are withdrawal symptoms of forgoing these items you may have been used to before the fast.

Apart from these valuable physical preparations, devote quality time in fellowship with God; studying scriptures that deal with God's rewards for fasting. These would help to focus your mind on your fast.

Confess every known sin in your life that the Holy Spirit calls to your remembrance and accept God's forgiveness (1 John 1:9).

How do you know when to pray and fast and when to just pray?

That is not a question that someone else can always answer for you. But here is a principle: In God's word we always find fasting connected with a very troubled spirit or a very anxious heart before the Lord. So a reason for fasting is not something you choose on the spur of the moment.

How do I know if I need to fast?

The answer to this question depends on your health status and goals. For many people, adopting an unprocessed, whole food diet, engaging in a sensible exercise program, acquiring restful sleep, and living in a relatively unpolluted environment will provide the necessary conditions to recover and maintain vibrant health. If a person is having a difficult time making necessary dietary and lifestyle changes, fasting can be a powerful way of accelerating health recovery. Fasting can also reset the sensitivity of the nervous system, providing an effective way of overcoming dependencies on caffeine, nicotine, alcohol, other recreational drugs, salt, sugar, and other stimulants. After fasting, many people marvel at how sweet romaine lettuce is, how refreshing apples are, and how wonderfully delicious baked potatoes are – without sour cream and butter! Many of us have been eating rich, salty, and sweetened foods for so long that we are unaware of how good foods taste in their natural, unprocessed states.

Some people choose to fast in the absence of overt symptoms of disease, knowing that a period of complete physiological rest can allow the body to rejuvenate itself from the toxins that build up in our tissues despite our efforts to live healthfully.

How long should I fast for?

When we were looking at the "normal fast" (see above), we noted that a fast was usually for one day. In addition to the Day of Atonement (Leviticus 23:32) you can see examples of one day fasts in Judges 20:26; 1 Samuel 14:24; 2 Samuel 1:12; and 2 Samuel 3:35. The Jewish day was counted from sunset to sunset, so this meant that the fast would be broken (that is, food could be eaten) after sundown. However, some fasts were longer. The fast of Esther continued 3 days, both day and night. At the burial of Saul the fast was seven days (1 Samuel 31:13) and David also fasted seven days when his child was ill

(2 Samuel 12:16-18). The longest fasts we find in the Bible are for forty days: Moses (Deuteronomy 9:9, 18; Exodus 34:28), Elijah (1 Kings 19:8), and Jesus (Matthew 4:2). The biblical principle here is that the length of time you fast is determined by your own desires and the occasion or purpose of the fast. The duration can be that which the individuals or groups feel led to set.

It has been stressed throughout this book that some fasting could be injurious to the body if wisdom is not applied. For instance, unless one is divinely sustained, fasting for more than three days without water is highly dangerous. It is to be discouraged!

Let me quickly add that you do not have to go on a particularly long fast in order to get the attention of God. Neither do long fasts get you more benefits than short ones.

However, I feel there is wealth of wisdom in the opinion shared by Arthur Blessitt that could be of immense benefit to the believer on the subject:

"In my personal life, fasting has been for specific purpose and for a long duration. After three days, there are no hunger pains or desire for food. From twelve to fourteen days later, there seems to be a sense of cleanliness and mental clarity.

ANSWERS TO COMMON QUESTIONS ABOUT FASTING

After twenty-one days, there seems to be an outpouring of spiritual power and creativity that is indescribable, but continues until the fast is ended. It seems especially after the third week that one is no longer even remotely interested in the trivial physical world around. One's mind is filled exclusively with profound spiritual ideas and truths. One of the most profound things is that the mind will concentrate for hours on the same subject without once wavering or being distracted. There is no question that there is awesome power in fasting. If the fast is controlled by the Holy Spirit and Jesus is foremost, then it is a beautiful and powerful experience."

If you choose to fast to recover from acute illness, you can fast until you feel well enough to eat again. In the case of a chronic health challenge, the length of the fast is determined by the progress of the fast. The healing processes that take place during a fast are predictable. Blood levels of cholesterol and uric acid tend to elevate during a fast, a result of the body stirring up stores of undesirable materials and expelling them into the circulation to be eliminated from the body. Shortly after the fast, these levels tend to be lower than they were before the fast, indicating a cleaner system. As a part of the detoxification process, some people experience headaches, dizziness, skin rashes, and other uncomfortable symptoms. Fasting under the supervision of a health care professional who is trained to distinguish healing responses from harmful processes can be helpful in allowing a person to deal with uncomfortable symptoms of detoxification.

It is not uncommon for people to experience significant improvement in their health from fasting between 3 and 30 days. The idea is to fast as briefly as possible, but as long as is necessary to allow the body to restore health.

I often encourage those just beginning the discipline of fasting to start with very short fasts, for instance, fast a meal, and get used to that, and gradually move on to a fairly longer fasts, say, a day, three days, before attempting longer fasts. Fasting with water is an added benefit for you. You can also consider some juice fasts.

Please note that fasting for too long can cause you very serious harm, especially if you are observing the absolute fast.

As a matter of fact, absolute fast should not, under any circumstances whatsoever, go beyond 72 hours (three days). Unless the subject is supernaturally sustained by God, as in the cases of Moses and Elijah, who both observed 40 days dried fasts, he could have some of his major organs severely damaged in the process.

Your decision to fast should be guided by the Holy Spirit. In addition, I highly recommend, especially if you have never fasted, that you seek both medical and spiritual counsel before embarking on any type of prolonged fast.

How often can I fast?

Fasting should be a regular part of a Christian's life, not just on God's Holy Day known as the Day of Atonement (Leviticus 23:32), but several times in a year. Periodic fasting is of immerse value. The Bible says that Paul did this often (2Corinthians 11:27). The Apostle Paul knew that fasting would be a way of life for Christians (1Corinthians 7:5). In His teaching on the subject Jesus said: "When ye fast..." (Matt. 6:18), and not if you fast, which presupposes that Jesus expects fasting to be part of our regular services to God. Jesus did not only teach fasting, He validated the practice by actually doing it at the highest level – forty days. Fasting is a formidable weapon of warfare!

As to the question of how often you should fast, you need to be guarded and led by the Holy Spirit. Apart from its valuable spiritual benefits, periodic fasting, according to Derek Prince, helps to eliminate some of the unpleasant body reactions such as headaches, in subsequent fastings.

How do I know what kind of fasting to observe?

This question takes into account the fact that there are different kind of fasting; majorly three. This knowledge can help deal with much of the misconceptions and, at times, frustrations that are very often associated with fasting. Further, this gives the believer a wide variety to choose from.

The three fasts dealt with in the word of God are:

The Absolute Fast - This is when no food and no liquids are consumed. It is the rare fast and only mentioned a few times in the Bible. Paul, during his Damascus Road experience "was three days without sight, and neither ate nor drank." We cannot tell for sure if this was because he was so shocked by what was happening with him or if it was for spiritual purposes.

In Ezra 10 we find the prophet so distraught over the actions of the people that he went into great mourning and praying before the Lord. At this time he neither ate nor drank for at least one night and perhaps longer.

There are a few examples of 40-day absolute fasts where the men must have been sustained supernaturally. Moses, on two separate occasions when he was before God, neither ate nor drank. Elijah seems to have travelled across the desert for 40 days while eating no food nor drinking any water. He was ministered to by an angel who gave him water and cakes.

Partial Fasting – Daniel engaged in a partial fast as recorded in Daniel 10:2, 3, "In those days I, Daniel, was mourning three full weeks. I ate no pleasant food, no meat or wine came into my mouth, nor did I anoint myself at all, till three whole weeks were fulfilled." We do not know for sure why Daniel did not totally abstain from food, because it appears that he did so in the fast recorded in Chapter 9. However, for some reasons, Daniel engaged in a partial fast to seek the Lord's wisdom.

The Daniel Fast is just one type of fasting that's modelled after accounts in the Bible. Biblical fasting is the restriction of food for spiritual reasons. And we find followers fasting throughout the Old and New Testaments.

Normal Fast - This is the fast that Jesus did when he went into the wilderness. He ate no food and appears to have had only water. The reason scholars conclude that he drank water while on this fast was because the Scripture says he was hungry, but did not say he was thirsty, after the fast. The devil tempted Jesus with bread, but not with water. So we assume this was a water only fast.

The kind of fast that is best for you or any other person is determined by a number of factors:

(1) Sickness- Many medical problems would disqualify a person from fasting. People with illness, such as diabetes and other health issues that particularly require constant food intake, should consult their physicians before they embark on any fast. If they have the permission, and perhaps the supervision of their doctors to fast, even with such assistance, I would not recommend anything beyond a partial fast of few days. Pregnant women should NOT fast.

(2) A beginner- As said, beginners should go into fasting gradually. I suggest you begin with a partial fast of one or few days. You could then try your hands on normal fast (i.e., going without food for a day).

How do I know when to fast?

The leading of the Spirit of God is very vital in knowing when to fast. The occasion for fasting is a totally voluntary decision. Some of the specific times when people in the Bible fasted are listed in the next section. But basically we can say a Christian may decide to fast whenever there is a spiritual concern or struggle in his or her life. Of course, there may be times when those in authority over us proclaim a fast, as was done by King Saul (1 Samuel 14:24) or Jehoshaphat (2 Chronicles 20:3). But normally and ultimately that decision is solely between us and the Lord.

Can I fast and not let my husband know?

Very clearly Jesus taught that we are to observe our fasts in secret.

"Moreover when you fast, be not, as the hypocrites, of a sad countenance: for they disfigure their faces, that they may appear to men to fast. Truly I say to you, They have their reward. But you, when you fast, anoint your head, and wash your face; That you appear not to men to fast, but to your Father which is in secret: and your Father, which sees in secret, shall reward you openly."

However, when it comes to fasting within the premise of husband and wife relationship, Paul's warning is to be taken into account. Paul cautioned Christian couples not to "Deprive ...one the other, except it be with consent for a time, that you may give yourselves to fasting and prayer; and come together again, that Satan tempt you not for your lack of self-control (1 Cor. 7:5, emphasis added). Within the context of Paul's reasoning, it is absolutely impossible for a party to a marriage to engage in a fast without the other party having knowledge of it. As a matter of fact, due consent of the 'non-fasting' partner is to be obtained well ahead of time.

Arguing this point beyond the frontier of sexual relationship in marriage, it could be said that in a proper family setting, it is expected that crucial matters as fasting would be thoroughly discussed at least between husband and wife, for adequate adjustments – perhaps in the area of food – and other vital areas in an average family setup to be made ahead of time.

Further, I strongly believe that who we choose to reveal our fasting to is entirely our decision. Motive, is no doubt, an issue that must be carefully considered.

There are occasions that make giving knowledge of our fasting to others quite legitimate or unavoidable.

I find pearls of wisdom in Zac Tanee Fomum thoughts as he identifies some of such situations which includes where the person fasting:-

1.   Feels that he is weak and cannot complete the fast without the prayers of the brethren. He therefore announces his fast to them so as to solicit their prayers.

2.   Is a leader who is setting example in fasting for those he is leading so that they may do likewise. He therefore, tells them not because he wants them to "see" him but because he desires their growth in this area.

3.   Has a major battle before him and wants people to fast with him for the overthrow of the enemy. He must therefore, tell them about his fast and solicit their cooperation.

4.   May want to demonstrate to young believers that God does honour fasting, that fasting is not something that has outlived its usefulness, and that they should commit themselves to a life of fasting. In doing this he might have to share how it has worked in his own life. He can therefore, talk about

his experience in fasting without seeking to draw attention to himself or to his record in fasting.

The golden rule, I believe, should be 'guard your heart and motive.' You can do any of the above without drawing attention to yourself. We know about the forty-days fast of the Lord Jesus because He told the disciples about it. His motive was clear and legitimate. Moses made his forty-day fasts public, the same goes for Paul who spoke quite openly about his fasted life; otherwise they would not have been sources of inspiration to us, yet none of these people suddenly became hypocrites because of that.

The admonition of Paul is of tremendous assistance on the subject:

> *But with me it is a very small thing that I should be judged of you, or of man's judgment: yea, I judge not mine own self. For I know nothing by myself; yet am I not hereby justified: but he that judgeth me is the Lord. Therefore judge nothing before the time, until the Lord come, who both will bring to light the hidden things of darkness, and will make manifest the counsels of the hearts: and then shall every man have praise of God (1 Cor. 4:3-5).*

Is there any relationship between prayer and fasting?

Although the connection between prayer and fasting is not specifically explained in Scripture, a common thread connecting the two seems to run through all the instances of prayer and fasting recorded in the Bible. In the Old Testament, it appears that fasting with prayer had to do with a sense of need and dependence, and of abject helplessness in the face of actual or anticipated calamity. Prayer and fasting are combined in the Old Testament in times of mourning, repentance, and deep spiritual need.

The first chapter of Nehemiah describes Nehemiah praying and fasting, because of his deep distress over the news that Jerusalem had been desolated. His many days of prayer were characterised by tears, fasting, confession on behalf of his people, and pleas to God for mercy. So intense was the outpouring of his concerns that it is almost inconceivable he could "take a break" in the middle of such prayer to eat and drink. The devastation that befell Jerusalem also prompted Daniel to adopt a similar posture: "So I turned to the Lord God and pleaded with him in prayer and petition, in fasting, and in sackcloth and ashes" (Daniel 9:3). Like Nehemiah, Daniel fasted and prayed that God would have mercy upon the people, saying, "We have been wicked and have rebelled; we have turned away from your commands and laws" (v. 5).

In several instances in the Old Testament, fasting is linked with intercessory prayer. David prayed and fasted over his sick child (2 Samuel 12:16), weeping before the Lord in earnest intercession (vv. 21-22). Esther urged Mordecai and the Jews to fast for her as she planned to appear before her husband the king (Esther 4:16). Clearly, fasting and petition are closely linked.

There are instances of prayer and fasting in the New Testament, but they are not connected with repentance or confession. The prophetess Anna "never left the temple but worshiped night and day, fasting and praying" (Luke 2:37). At age 84, her prayer and fasting were part of her service to the Lord in His temple as she awaited the promised Saviour of Israel. Also in the New Testament, the church at Antioch was fasting in connection with their worship when the Holy Spirit spoke to them about commissioning Saul and Barnabas to the Lord's work. At that point, they prayed and fasted, placed their hands on the two men and sent them off. So, we see in these examples that prayer and fasting are components of worshipping the Lord and seeking His favor. Nowhere, however, is there any indication that the Lord is more likely to answer prayers if they are accompanied by fasting. Rather, fasting along with prayer seems to indicate the sincerity of the people praying and the critical nature of the situations in which they find themselves.

The more critical the situation, the more appropriate it is to fast and pray. In Mark 9, Jesus casts a demon from a boy. The disciples had been unable to perform the exorcism, although they had previously been given authority over unclean spirits (Mark 6:7). Later, the disciples asked Jesus why they failed in their attempts to free the boy from the demon, and Jesus said, "This kind can come out only by prayer" (Mark 9:29). Matthew's account adds the phrase "and fasting" (Matthew 17:21). In this particular case, the demon was exceptionally malicious and obdurate (Mark 9:21-22). Jesus seems to be saying that a determined foe must be met with an equally determined faith. Prayer is a ready weapon in the spiritual battle (Ephesians 6:18), and fasting helps to focus prayer and give it resolve.

Finally in His discourse, Jesus spoke of fasting with the same expectation He employed in speaking of prayer. He said, *"When you pray,"* (Matt. 6:16)

Secondly, the theme of His teaching on both subjects centred on motive:

Moreover when ye fast, be not, as the hypocrites, of a sad countenance: for they disfigure their faces, that they may appear unto men to fast. Verily I say unto you, They have their reward. But thou, when thou fastest, anoint thine head, and wash thy face; That thou appear not unto men to fast, but unto thy Father which is in secret: and thy Father, which seeth in secret, shall reward thee openly (Matt. 6 : 16-18).

What can I expect during the fast?

Most people, within the first three days of their fast, experience some unpleasant reactions such as nausea, headaches, dizziness and a stiff neck. These are just early symptoms which gradually withdraw once you pass the threshold of the first three days. Reasons often attributed to feeling poorly during the first few days of a fast are that the body is eliminating toxic wastes that may have been stored for a long while. After this period, into your fifth to seventh day, you enter into a realm where you experience such focus and clarity of thoughts that you are able to seek God with passionate fervency.

However, while in such a high spiritual plane, it is common for the devil to try and attack you with depression, heaviness and negative emotion. This should be expected as a counter-attack for the act of aggression that is being committed against the enemy's kingdom. Do not give up! Engage in warfare still; he will not resist for long. Fear not. Use the word – the Sword of the Spirit – constantly against the enemy's attacks. You are being refined into a spiritual gold with these attacks; you are being listed into the highest ranks in the greatest army of all time! Remember, there is no General without bruises! But yours are bruises of gold!

It is usually after the fast that the release is manifested. As stated, in preparation, and in the course of the fast, read scriptures on fasting like Isaiah 58, focusing on the outstanding benefits of fasting, and reading books by seasoned authors on the subject. It is consistent with human nature to put up with what does not appeal to use easily if we know what we stand to gain therefrom. Finally, keep your work load light during the fast, if possible.

Let us examine some other way you may react to your fast:

Sleeplessness

This is a common problem with longer fasts and among those who have just started to do shorter fasts. With intermittent fasting, it may take a while to get used to going to bed without a dinner or an evening snack, but after an induction period, it is no problem. You may even find that you sleep better than you did before and need less sleep.

With fasts lasting several days, trouble falling asleep at night may persist. Especially if you are trying to sleep while you are experiencing one of the more serious hunger pangs, you would probably find it very difficult to fall asleep. You will just be tormented by vivid images of food, until you gain sleep. Rely on His grace, He will see you through.

Inability to sleep properly could continue throughout the fast despite the fact that many of the other hurdles are already behind. So you will spend your day feeling energetic and your night feeling, well, energetic. Some ways of relieving this problem are: drinking water to temporarily mask the hunger. And of course, you can simply try to use the time for something more productive than sleeping! You could spend the time ministering to the Lord. It was written of the elders in the early church:

> As they ministered to the Lord, and fasted, the Holy
> Ghost said, Separate me Barnabas and Saul for
> the work whereunto I have called them. And when
> they had fasted and prayed, and laid their hands on
> them, they sent them away (Acts 13:2, 3).

Further, you could spend the time in active prayer and intercession. I particularly attach greater significance to midnight prayers than those done at other time of the day.

> And at midnight Paul and Silas prayed, and sang
> praises unto God: and the prisoners heard them.
> And suddenly there was a great earthquake, so
> that the foundations of the prison were shaken: and
> immediately all the doors were opened, and every
> one's bands were loosed (Acts 16: 25-26).

If for anything, please enjoy the clarity of thoughts and focus such times offer to concentrate on some spiritual exercises. I am astounded at the volume of work I get done with great strength at such times.

What else could happen during a fast?

Low energy, weariness and emotional battle are all part of early days experiences of fasting. However, as part of the body detoxifying process, you may have foul breath, and foul body odours. Before embarking on a fast, one should be aware of possible unpleasant reactions. The first reaction would be hunger, as it takes the body three days to lose an appetite for food while fasting. More rest is sometimes necessary as energy levels may initially drop.

Other typical reactions include headaches and a white coating on the tongue as stored toxins are dislodged from organs and tissues. Depending on the individual's level of toxicity, blemishes, bad breath or body odour may be experienced as toxins are released through the skin.

These are all temporary responses that are followed by a feeling of well-being, clarity, emotional and physical balance - and occasionally euphoria - depending on the amount of cleansing accomplished. Experiencing unpleasantness in order to get well may sound absurd! However, in fasting, your body takes advantage of lack of food intake to engage in a total 'house cleansing'. The lasting benefits of fasting significantly offset the fleeting pleasantries.

During a fast, toxins will be flushed out of the body, primarily through the kidneys, lungs and skin. Bowel movements will be few or will stop completely as the body rests and rejuvenates itself.

ANSWERS TO COMMON QUESTIONS ABOUT FASTING

How do I know when to quit fasting?

Fasting that is pleasing to God also requires wisdom. Watch your body signs!

Some have erroneously advised for these signs to be ignored, and attribute them to part of the pranks of the enemy to get you to give up your fast. Undesired outcomes have, in many cases, been sadly resulted. Be warned! This caution is particularly for those that undertake very lengthy fasts. While it is normal, as we have already said, to experience some unpleasant reactions within the first few days of a fast, such as headaches, nausea, tight neck etc, which withdraw with hunger pangs as the fast progresses (usually after about three days), These hunger pangs do return after your body has burnt off all excess fat and detoxified. When it comes to the point of beginning to burn off tissue from vital organs, it will give signal of severe hunger pangs, at which time you should break your fast; in fact, immediately! Some have ignored these signs to their detriment. As said, this is a case for lengthy fasts.

It is also the case that at the beginning of a fast, the length of the fast is determined, as advised in this book. While that is perfectly normal, in fastings that go beyond fourteen, twenty-one into forty-days, please watch out for these signs! Once hunger pangs return, please break the fast; it does not matter whether you have covered the period you have set to fast for, or not.

I want to fast but cannot because of an illness, I feel ashamed every time members of my church fast and I cannot.

If your illness requires constant taking of medication, it is wise to abstain from fasting, until you have your physician's permission to do so.

If you cannot fast as a result of an illness, you should not feel ashamed.

Let these words of a father of faith speak and minister to you:

"If you cannot go without eating all day because of an ailment of the body, beloved one, no logical man will be able to criticize you for that. Besides, we have a Lord who is meek and loving (philanthropic) and who does not ask for anything beyond our power. Because he neither requires the abstinence from foods, neither that the fast take place for the simple sake of fasting, neither is its aim that we remain with empty stomachs, but that we fast to offer our entire selves to the dedication of spiritual things, having distanced ourselves from secular things... because human nature is indifferent and gives itself over mostly to comforts and gratifications, for this reason the philanthropic Lord, like a loving and caring father, devised the therapy of the fast for us, so that our gratifications would be completely stopped and that our worldly cares be transferred to spiritual works..."- **St John Chrysostom.**

Who Should Not Fast?

Fasting is not for everyone. Those who are unwilling or unable to eliminate caffeine, alcohol, carbonated beverages, or drugs of any type should not consider fasting. Pregnant or nursing women; children under eighteen years of age; and individuals with heart diseases, mental illness, or anyone in a debilitated or malnourished state should refrain from fasting. A health care provider should be consulted to clear up any question of whether or not one should begin a fast of any duration.

More energy comes from a purified body and fasting of all types contribute to health maintenance, mental clarity, and spiritual cleansing as it eases the daily burden of bodily processes, allowing rest and cellular healing to occur.

Graceful aging and reclaiming robust health in a toxic, contaminated world is possible when we give the body proper nourishment, exercise, and adequate opportunities to rest, purify and heal itself. The routine practice of fasting, and regular exercise such as rebounding, are but two strategies to achieve this goal.

How Do I overcome Satan's temptations to violate my fast?

If you have ever been tempted to violate your fast, you are not alone! Everyone that has ever fasted or lives a fasted life faces this temptation. Instead of giving-in to the temptation, be encouraged in the fact that your fast is causing the enemy some irritations and fierce disturbances, hence the attack to violate your fast! The enemy does not border himself with matters that do not hold significance before him.

Once again, use the word of God to overcome such temptations. Focus on the promised rewards to fasters. At such times make Isaiah 58 one of your favourite scriptures. Claim the promises in the face of Satan's cheap tricks.

How do I Break a fast successfully?

The way you break your fast is extremely important for your physical and spiritual well-being.

Properly breaking a fast is a vitally important consideration. Many bodily systems, especially digestion, have rested and need time to become accustomed to food again. It is imperative to gradually reintroduce food so as not to overburden the body after its period of rest and healing. Metabolism slows during a fast and requires time to re-adjust. This is achieved by carefully adding small amounts of easily-digested foods on the days following a fast.

Much of the body's toxins are stored in fat tissue. During a fast, toxic fats are released and eliminated; however, if too much food is reintroduced too quickly, the body will easily regain more than the lost fat. A good practice is to consume raw fruits and at least 64 ounces of filtered water on the first day following a fast.

Break your fast gradually. Begin eating gradually. Do not eat solid foods immediately after your fast. Suddenly reintroducing solid food to your stomach and digestive tract will likely have negative, even dangerous, consequences. Try several smaller meals or snacks each day. If you end your fast gradually, the beneficial physical and spiritual effects will result in continued good health.

Gradually return to regular eating with several small snacks during the first few days. Start with a little soup and fresh fruit such as watermelon and cantaloupe. Advance to a few tablespoons of solid foods such as raw fruits and vegetables or a raw salad and baked potato.

Fruits and vegetables, raw or lightly steamed may be eaten on the second day. By the third day the pre-fast diet may be resumed. Generally, the longer the fast, the longer it should take to return to the normal diet. It is also important to chew thoroughly and avoid overeating.

Your ability to experience bowel movement successfully (without some delivery pangs) depends largely on the way you start the fast. To achieve easy passing of stool at the end of the fast, you've got to see to it that few days before you commence the fast you consume a great deal of fruits and vegetables, preferably, broccoli etc.

26

FASTING SCRIPTURES: BIBLE REFERENCES OF BOTH INDIVIDUAL AND CORPORATE FASTS

INDIVIDUAL FASTS

MOSES

Moses twice spends forty days on Mount Sinai without eating or drinking, and in mourning over Israel's sin.

Then Moses entered the cloud as he went on up the mountain. And he stayed on the mountain forty days and forty nights. Moses was there with the Lord forty days and forty nights without eating bread or drinking water. And he wrote on the tablets the words of the covenant—the Ten Commandments.

Then once again I fell prostrate before the Lord for forty days and forty nights; I ate no bread and drank no water, because of all the sin you had committed, doing what was evil in the Lord's sight and so arousing his anger.

When I went up on the mountain to receive the tablets of stone, the tablets of the covenant that the Lord had made with you, I stayed on the mountain forty days and forty nights; I ate no bread and drank no water. I lay prostrate before the Lord those forty days and forty nights because the Lord had said he would destroy you.

Now I had stayed on the mountain forty days and forty nights, as I did the first time, and the Lord listened to me at this time also. It was not his will to destroy you. (Exod. 24:18, 34:28; Deut. 9:9, 18, 25, 10:10)

HANNAH

Hannah weeps and **refuses to eat** when her husband's other wife provokes her, and she prays for a son.

And as he did so year by year, when she went up to the house of the Lord, so she provoked her; therefore she wept, and did not eat. Then said Elkanah her husband to her, Hannah, why weepest thou? and why eatest thou not? and why is thy heart grieved? am not I better to thee than ten sons? (1 Sam 1:7-8, emphasis added)

FASTING SCRIPTURES: BIBLE REFERENCES OF BOTH INDIVIDUAL
AND CORPORATE FASTS

JONATHAN

Jonathan refuses to eat because of his grief over his father's mistreatment of David.

So Jonathan arose from the table in fierce anger, and did eat no meat the second day of the month: for he was grieved for David, because his father had done him shame (1 Sam 20:34).

SAUL

Saul eats nothing all day and night when he consults with the witch of En-dor (1 Sam 28:20)

DAVID

David refuses to eat food until evening when he heard of the death of Abner.

And when all the people came to cause David to eat meat while it was yet day, David sware, saying, So do God to me, and more also, if I taste bread, or ought else, till the sun be down (2 Sam 3:35)

David fasts and weeps seven days during the terminal illness of his son by Bathsheba. David therefore besought God for the child;

and David fasted, and went in, and lay all night upon the earth. And the elders of his house arose, and went to him, to raise him up from the earth: but he would not, neither did he eat bread with them. And it came to pass on the seventh day, that the child died. And the servants of David feared to tell him that the child was dead: for they said, Behold, while the child was yet alive, we spake unto him, and he would not hearken unto our voice: how will he then vex himself, if we tell him that the child is dead? But when David saw that his servants whispered, David perceived that the child was dead: therefore David said unto his servants, Is the child dead? And they said, He is dead. Then David arose from the earth, and washed, and anointed himself, and changed his apparel, and came into the house of the Lord, and worshipped: then he came to his own house; and when he required, they set bread before him, and he did eat. Then said his servants unto him, What thing is this that thou hast done? thou didst fast and weep for the child, while it was alive; but when the child was dead, thou didst rise and eat bread. And he said, While the child was yet alive, I fasted and wept: for I said, Who can tell whether God will be gracious to me, that the child may live?

But now he is dead, wherefore should I fast? Can I bring him back again? I shall go to him, but he shall not return to me. (2 Sam 12:16-23)

FASTING SCRIPTURES: BIBLE REFERENCES OF BOTH INDIVIDUAL
AND CORPORATE FASTS

David defends his honor by saying that he fasted and prayed when his enemies were sick.

But as for me, when they were sick, my clothing was sackcloth: I humbled my soul with fasting; and my prayer returned into mine own bosom (Ps 35:13)

David's fasting, weeping and prayer was an object of scorn by his enemies.

When I wept and chastened my soul with fasting, that was turned to my reproach (Ps 69:10)

The afflicted psalmist forgets to eat bread because of his great grief.

My heart is smitten, and withered like grass; so that I forget to eat my bread (Ps 102:4)

David says his knees are weak from fasting, and his flesh has grown lean during his affliction from his enemies.

My knees are weak through fasting; and my flesh faileth of fatness (Ps 109:24)

UNNAMED PROPHET

An unnamed prophet is instructed by God not to eat or drink while on a mission to prophesy against Jeroboam's idolatry.

For so was it charged me by the word of the Lord, saying, Eat no bread, nor drink water, nor turn again by the same way that thou camest. So he went another way, and returned not by the way that he came to Bethel (1Kgs 13:9-10)

ELIJAH

Elijah goes forty days on the strength of the food provided to him by an angel.

And he arose, and did eat and drink, and went in the strength of that meat forty days and forty nights unto Horeb the mount of God (1Kgs 19:8)

AHAB

Ahab eats no food because he is sullen after Naboth refused to sell his vineyard.

And Ahab came into his house heavy and displeased because of the word which Naboth the Jezreelite had spoken to him: for he had said, I will not give thee the inheritance of my fathers. And he laid him down upon his bed, and turned away his face, and would eat no bread (1Kgs 21:4)

AHAB

Ahab fasts and puts on sackcloth in repentance after Elijah rebuked him, and God recognized Ahab's humility.

And it came to pass, when Ahab heard those words, that he rent his clothes, and put sackcloth upon his flesh, and fasted, and lay in sackcloth, and went softly. And the word of the Lord came to Elijah the Tishbite, saying, Seest thou how Ahab humbleth himself before me? because he humbleth himself before me, I will not bring the evil in his days: but in his son's days will I bring the evil upon his house (1 Kings 21:27-29)

EZRA

Ezra eats and drinks nothing because of his mourning over the unfaithfulness of the exiles.

Then Ezra rose up from before the house of God, and went into the chamber of Johanan the son of Eliashib: and when he came thither, he did eat no bread, nor drink water: for he mourned because of the transgression of them that had been carried away (Ezra 10:6)

NEHEMIAH

Nehemiah mourns and fasts for days over the news of the state of Jerusalem, confessing national sin.

> *And it came to pass, when I heard these words, that I sat down and wept, and mourned certain days, and fasted, and prayed before the God of heaven,* (Neh. 1:4)

JOB

Job groans at the sight of food, and experiences great affliction and pain.

> *For my sighing cometh before I eat, and my roarings are poured out like the waters. He is chastened also with pain upon his bed, and the multitude of his bones with strong pain: So that his life abhorreth bread, and his soul dainty meat* (Job 3:24, 33:19-20)

GOD'S CHOSEN FAST

> *Wherefore have we fasted, say they, and thou seest not? wherefore have we afflicted our soul, and thou takest no knowledge? Behold, in the day of your fast ye find pleasure, and exact all your labours. Behold, ye fast for strife and debate, and to smite*

with the fist of wickedness: ye shall not fast as ye do this day, to make your voice to be heard on high. Is it such a fast that I have chosen? a day for a man to afflict his soul? is it to bow down his head as a bulrush, and to spread sackcloth and ashes under him? wilt thou call this a fast, and an acceptable day to the Lord? Is not this the fast that I have chosen? to loose the bands of wickedness, to undo the heavy burdens, and to let the oppressed go free, and that ye break every yoke?

EZEKIEL

Ezekiel is instructed in special mourning rites, that include fasting, for the death of his wife.

So I spake unto the people in the morning: and at even my wife died; and I did in the morning as I was commanded (Ezekiel 24:18)

DARIUS

Darius fasts from food, entertainment, and sleep through the night while worrying for Daniel in the lion's den.

Then the king went to his palace, and passed the night fasting: neither were instruments of musick brought before him: and his sleep went from him (Dan 6:18)

DANIEL

Daniel's choice of special diet (partial fast) in preference to the king's nutritious food and wine.

> But Daniel purposed in his heart that he would not defile himself with the portion of the king's food, nor with the wine which he drank: therefore he requested of the prince of the eunuchs that he might not defile himself. Then said Daniel to Melzar, whom the prince of the eunuchs had set over Daniel, Hananiah, Mishael, and Azariah, Prove your servants, I beseech you, ten days; and let them give us vegetables to eat, and water to drink. Then let our countenances be looked on before you, and the countenance of the children that eat of the portion of the king's meat: and as you see, deal with your servants. ... Daniel 1:1, 11-13

Daniel fasts, confessing Israel's sin, upon reading Jeremiah's prophecy of the seventy weeks.

> And I set my face unto the Lord God, to seek by prayer and supplications, with fasting, and sackcloth, and ashes (Dan 9:3)

Daniel mourns for three weeks, abstaining from tasty food, meat, wine, and ointment.

In those days I Daniel was mourning three full weeks. I ate no pleasant bread, neither came flesh nor wine in my mouth, neither did I anoint myself at all, till three whole weeks were fulfilled (Dan 10:2-3)

JESUS

Jesus fasts forty days in the wilderness, being tempted by the devil.

And when he had fasted forty days and forty nights, he was afterward an hungred (Matt. 4:2; Luke 4:2)

JESUS ON FASTING (1)

Jesus teaches that fasting should be done privately for God, not for the purpose of being seen to be fasting, like the hypocrites.

Moreover when ye fast, be not, as the hypocrites, of a sad countenance: for they disfigure their faces, that they may appear unto men to fast. Verily I say unto you, They have their reward. But thou, when thou fastest, anoint thine head, and wash thy face; That thou appear not unto men to fast, but unto thy Father which is in secret: and thy Father, which seeth in secret, shall reward thee openly (Matt 6:16-18)

JESUS ON FASTING (2)

Jesus taught the disciples that certain problems (demonic situations) could only be overcome by the combined weapons of prayer and fasting.

However, this kind does not go out except by prayer and fasting (Matt 17:21 Mark 9:29)

ANNA

Anna serves in the temple night and day with fastings and prayers.

So He said to them, "This kind can come out by nothing but prayer and fasting (Luke 2:37)

THE PHARISEE IN JESUS' PARABLE

The Pharisee in Jesus' parable shows his self-righteousness by boasting that he fasts twice a week and tithes.

I fast twice a week; I give tithes of all that I possess (Luke 18:12)

SAUL (PAUL)

Saul fasted from food and water three days after the Damascus Road experience.

And he was three days without sight, and neither ate nor drank (Acts 9:9)

CORNELIUS

Cornelius was fasting and praying when an angel instructed him to go to Peter.

So Cornelius said, "Four days ago I was fasting until this hour; and at the ninth hour[a] I prayed in my house, and behold, a man stood before me in bright clothing (Acts 10:30)

PAUL

Paul lists "fastings" among the hardships he suffered as a mark of his apostleship.

In weariness and painfulness, in watchings often, in hunger and thirst, in fastings often, in cold and nakedness (2 Corinthians 11: 27)

In beatings, imprisonments and riots; in hard work, sleepless nights and hunger (2 Corinthians 6:5)

THE WONDERS OF FASTING

27

FASTING SCRIPTURES 2

CORPORATE FASTINGS

Israel fasts until evening to inquire of YHWH after loss to Benjamin.

Then all the children of Israel, and all the people, went up, and came unto the house of God, and wept, and sat there before the LORD, and fasted that day until even, and offered burnt offerings and peace offerings before the LORD (Judges 20:26)

THE NATION OF ISRAEL

Israel fasts for a day to repent, Samuel prays, *YHWH delivers them from the Philistines.* And they gathered together to Mizpeh, and drew water, and poured it out before the Lord, and fasted on that day, and said there, We have sinned against the Lord. And Samuel judged the children of Israel in Mizpeh. (1 Sam 7:6)

SAUL's ARMY

Saul places the army under oath not to eat until evening on the day of battle with the Philistines.

And the men of Israel were distressed that day: for Saul had adjured the people, saying, Cursed be the man that eateth any food until evening, that I may be avenged on mine enemies. So none of the people tasted any food. And all they of the land came to a wood; and there was honey upon the ground. And when the people were come into the wood, behold, the honey dropped; but no man put his hand to his mouth: for the people feared the oath. (1 Sam 14:24-26)

MEN OF JABESH

Men of Jabesh fast seven days after recovering the bodies of Saul and Jonathan from the Philistines.

And when the inhabitants of Jabeshgilead heard of that which the Philistines had done to Saul; All the valiant men arose, and went all night, and took the body of Saul and the bodies of his sons from the wall of Bethshan, and came to Jabesh, and burnt them there. And they took their bones, and buried them under a tree at Jabesh, and fasted seven days (1 Sam 31:13, 1 Chr. 10:12)

DAVID AND HIS MEN

David's men fast until evening upon hearing the news of the death of Saul and Jonathan.

Then David took hold on his clothes, and rent them; and likewise all the men that were with him. And they mourned, and wept, and fasted until even, for Saul, and for Jonathan his son, and for the people of the Lord, and for the house of Israel; because they were fallen by the sword.

JEZEBEL'S CALL FOR FASTING

Jezebel calls a false day of fasting to accuse Naboth of cursing God.

And she wrote in the letters, saying, Proclaim a fast, and set Naboth on high among the people: And set two men, sons of Belial, before him, to bear witness against him, saying, Thou didst blaspheme God and the king. And then carry him out, and stone him, that he may die. And the men of his city, even the elders and the nobles who were the inhabitants in his city, did as Jezebel had sent unto them, and as it was written in the letters which she had sent unto them. They proclaimed a fast, and set Naboth on high among the people (1 Kgs 21: 27 – 29)

JEHOSHAPHAT AND JUDAH

Jehoshaphat proclaims a fast throughout Judah to seek God for fear of the armies of Ammon and Moab.

It came to pass after this also, that the children of Moab, and the children of Ammon, and with them other beside the Ammonites, came against Jehoshaphat to battle. Then there came some that told Jehoshaphat, saying, There cometh a great multitude against thee from beyond the sea on this side Syria; and, behold, they be in Hazazontamar, which is Engedi. And Jehoshaphat feared, and set himself to seek the LORD, and proclaimed a fast throughout all Judah. And Judah gathered themselves together, to ask help of the LORD: even out of all the cities of Judah they came to seek the LORD (2 Chr 20:1-4)

EZRA AND THE RETURNING EXILES

Ezra calls a fast to seek God's protection for those leaving Babylon for Israel.

Then I proclaimed a fast there, at the river of Ahava, that we might afflict ourselves before our God, to seek of him a right way for us, and for our little ones, and for all our substance. For I was ashamed to require of the king a band of soldiers and horsemen to help us against the enemy in the way: because we had spoken unto the king, saying, The hand of our God is upon all them for good that seek him; but his power and his wrath is against all them that forsake him. So we fasted and besought our God for this: and he was intreated of us (Ezra 8:21-23).

NEHEMIAH AND ISRAEL

The people of Israel assemble with fasting to confess their sin after Ezra reads from the law.

Now in the twenty and fourth day of this month the children of Israel were assembled with fasting, and with sackclothes, and earth upon them (NEH. 9:1)

THE JEWS FASTED TO DESTROY THEIR TURMENTOR

The Jews weep and fast when they hear of the king's decree for their destruction.

And in every province, whithersoever the king's commandment and his decree came, there was great mourning among the Jews, and fasting, and weeping, and wailing; and many lay in sackcloth and ashes (Esth 4:3).

ESTHER, HER MAIDENS AND THE JEWS

Esther, her maidens, and the Jews of Susa fast from food and drink for three days before she goes to the king.

> *Go, gather together all the Jews that are present in Shushan, and fast ye for me, and neither eat nor drink three days, night or day: I also and my maidens will fast likewise; and so will I go in unto the king, which is not according to the law: and if I perish, I perish* (Esth. 4:16)

PURIM – A DAY OF FASTING FOR THE JEWS

Purim is established for the Jews with instructions for fasting and lamentations, in commemoration of the three days fasted by Esther and Mordecai and those who joined them.

> *To confirm these days of Purim in their times [appointed], according as Mordecai the Jew and Esther the queen had enjoined them, and as they had decreed for themselves and for their seed, the matters of the fastings and their cry* (Esth 9:31).

GOD REJECTS ISRAEL'S FASTS

Israel's fasts are not heard by God because of their oppression and hypocrisy; He desires righteousness first.

When they fast, I will not hear their cry; and when they offer burnt offering and an oblation, I will not accept them: but I will consume them by the sword, and by the famine, and by the pestilence (Jer 14:12).

ISRAEL'S FASTING DAY

Israel's fasts are not heard by God because of their oppression and hypocrisy.

Therefore go thou, and read in the roll, which thou hast written from my mouth, the words of the Lord in the ears of the people in the Lord's house upon the fasting day: and also thou shalt read them in the ears of all Judah that come out of their cities (Jer 36:6).

ISRAEL'S FAST UNDER JEHOIAKIM

The people of Judah assemble in Jerusalem for a fast, and Baruch reads Jeremiah's prophecy to them.

And it came to pass in the fifth year of Jehoiakim the son of Josiah king of Judah, in the ninth month, that they proclaimed a fast before the Lord to all the people in Jerusalem, and to all the people that came from the cities of Judah unto Jerusalem (36:9)

ISRAEL NATIONAL FASTING

Joel calls for a nation-wide fast to overcome famine in the land.

Sanctify ye a fast, call a solemn assembly, gather the elders and all the inhabitants of the land into the house of the LORD your God, and cry unto the LORD (Joel 1:14)

ISRAEL CALLED TO RETURN TO GOD WITH FASTING

God calls the people to return to Him with fasting, rending their hearts, not garments; Joel again calls for a fast.

Therefore also now, saith the Lord, turn ye even to me with all your heart, and with fasting, and with weeping, and with mourning: And rend your heart, and not your garments, and turn unto the Lord your God: for he is gracious and merciful, slow to anger, and of great kindness, and repenteth him of the evil. Who knoweth if he will return and repent, and leave a blessing behind him; even a meat offering and a drink offering unto the Lord your

God? Blow the trumpet in Zion, sanctify a fast, call a solemn assembly (Joel 2: 12-15).

NINEVEH NATION-WIDE FAST

All of Nineveh fasts, repenting at the preaching of Jonah of the destruction of the city.

So the people of Nineveh believed God, and proclaimed a fast, and put on sackcloth, from the greatest of them even to the least of them (Jonah 3:5).

GOD EXPRESSED DISSATISFACTION AT THE PEOPLE'S FASTS

God rebukes the priests for their ritual fasts that were done more for themselves than for Him.

Speak unto all the people of the land, and to the priests, saying, When ye fasted and mourned in the fifth and seventh month, even those seventy years, did ye at all fast unto me, even to me? (Zech 7:5)

GOD BLESSES THE PEOPLE'S FASTS

God will transform the ritual fasts into feasts of joy when God's people have repented of sin and He grants them favour.

> *Thus saith the Lord of hosts; The fast of the fourth month, and the fast of the fifth, and the fast of the seventh, and the fast of the tenth, shall be to the house of Judah joy and gladness, and cheerful feasts; therefore love the truth and peace* (Zech 8:19).

JESUS DEFENDS HIS DISCIPLES

Jesus tells John's disciples that His do not fast because the bridegroom is present, but when He is taken away they will.

> *And Jesus said unto them, Can the friends of the bridegroom mourn, as long as the bridegroom is with them? but the days will come, when the bridegroom shall be taken from them, and then shall they fast* (Matt. 9:15).

JESUS AND THE CROWD

Jesus did not wish to send the crowd away fasting, since they had been with Him three days and have nothing to eat.

> *Then Jesus called his disciples unto him, and said, I have compassion on the multitude, because they continue with me now three days, and have nothing to eat: and I will not send them away fasting, lest they faint in the way* (Matt. 15:32)

THE LEADERS OF THE CHURCH IN ANTIOCH

Prophets and teachers in Antioch were ministering to the Lord and fasting before and after the Holy Spirit set apart Saul and Barnabas.

As they ministered to the Lord, and fasted, the Holy Ghost said, Separate me Barnabas and Saul for the work whereunto I have called them. And when they had fasted and prayed, and laid their hands on them, they sent them away (Acts 13: 2-3).

PAUL AND BANABAS

Paul and Barnabas appoint elders in the churches, having prayed with fasting.

And when they had ordained them elders in every church, and had prayed with fasting, they commended them to the Lord, on whom they believed (Acts 14:23).

SOME JEWS

Certain Jews bind themselves by oath not to eat or drink until they kill Paul.

And when it was day, certain of the Jews banded together, and bound themselves under a curse, saying that they would neither eat nor drink till they had killed Paul (Acts 23:12).

PAUL'S REFERENCE TO DAY OF ATONEMENT FAST

Paul's voyage to Rome takes place after "the fast" was over, a reference to the Day of Atonement.

Now when much time was spent, and when sailing was now dangerous, because the fast was now already past, Paul admonished them (Acts 27:9)

PAUL'S SHIP CREW

Paul encourages the ship's crew to eat, since they had gone 14 days fasting.

And while the day was coming on, Paul besought them all to take meat, saying, This day is the fourteenth day that ye have tarried and continued fasting, having taken nothing (Acts 27:33)

PAUL'S INSTRUCTION TO CHRISTIAN COUPLES ABOUT FASTING

Paul tells couples not to deprive one another sexually, except for brief periods devoted to prayer and fasting.

Deprive not one the other, except it be with consent for a time, that you may give yourselves to fasting and prayer; and come together again, that Satan tempt you not for your lack of self-control (1 Cor 7:58)

PAUL'S ACCOUNT OF HIS FASTING LIFE

In stripes, in imprisonments, in tumults, in labours, in watchings, in fastings (2 Cor 6:5)

In weariness and painfulness, in watchings often, in hunger and thirst, in fastings often, in cold and nakedness (2 Cor 11:27)

THE WONDERS OF FASTING

28

BIBLICAL RECORD OF WRONG FASTING

JEZEBEL

And she wrote in the letters, saying, Proclaim a fast, and set Naboth on high among the people: And set two men, sons of Belial, before him, to bear witness against him, saying, You did blaspheme God and the king. And then carry him out, and stone him, that he may die (1 Kings 21:9).

LEADERS OF JEZREEL

And the men of his city, even the elders and the nobles who were the inhabitants in his city, did as Jezebel had sent to them, and as it was written in the letters which she had sent to them. They proclaimed a fast, and set Naboth on high among the people. And there came in two men, children of Belial, and sat before him: and the men of Belial witnessed against him, even against Naboth, in the presence of the people, saying, Naboth did *blaspheme God and the king. Then they carried him forth out of the city, and stoned him with stones, that he died* (1 Kings 21: 11-13).

ISRAEL

Wherefore have we afflicted our soul, and thou takest no knowledge? Behold, in the day of your fast ye find pleasure, and exact all your labours. Behold, ye fast for strife and debate, and to smite with the fist of wickedness: ye shall not fast as ye do this day, to make your voice to be heard on high (Isaiah 58:3,4)

Then said the LORD unto me, Pray not for this people for their good. When they fast, I will not hear their cry; and when they offer burnt offering and an oblation, I will not accept them: but I will consume them by the sword, and by the famine, and by the pestilence (Jeremiah 14:11-12)

Speak unto all the people of the land, and to the priests, saying, When you fasted and mourned in the fifth and seventh month, even those seventy years, did you at all fast unto me, even to me?

And when you did eat, and when you did drink, did not you eat for yourselves, and drink for yourselves? Should you not hear the words which the LORD has cried by the former prophets, when Jerusalem was inhabited and in prosperity, and the cities thereof round about her, when men inhabited the south and the plain? And the word of the LORD came to Zechariah, And the word of the LORD came to Zechariah, saying, Thus speaks the LORD of hosts, saying, Execute true judgment, and show mercy and compassions every man to his brother (Zech. 7:5-8)

HYPOCRATES

Moreover when you fast, be not, as the hypocrites, of a sad countenance: for they disfigure their faces, that they may appear unto men to fast. Verily I say unto you, They have their reward (Matt. 6:16)

PHARISEES

The Pharisee stood and prayed thus with himself, God, I thank thee, that I am not as other men are, extortioners, unjust, adulterers, or even as this publican I fast twice in the week, I give tithes of all that I possess. (Luke 18: 11, 12)

CERTAIN JEWS PLOT TO KILL PAUL

And when it was day, certain of the Jews banded together, and bound themselves under a curse, saying that they would neither eat nor drink till they had killed Paul. And they were more than forty which had made this conspiracy. And they came to the chief priests and elders, and said, We have bound ourselves under a great curse, that we will eat nothing until we have slain Paul.

29

DURATION OF FASTS

DURATION OF FASTS

The teaching presented so far reveals that fasting, as seen in the word of God are of different durations, ranging from one day to days, even weeks. In this section, we will be examining the various fasting revealed in the word of God and their durations.

PART OF THE DAY FAST

Then the king went to his palace, and passed the night fasting: neither were instruments of music brought before him: and his sleep went from him – Daniel 6:18.

ONE DAY FAST

Also on the tenth day of the seventh month there shall be a day of atonement: it shall be an holy convocation unto you; and ye shall afflict your souls, and offer an offering made by fire unto the Lord. And ye shall do no work in that same day: for it is a day of atonement, to make atonement for you before the Lord your God - Lev. 23:27 KJV

The tenth day of this seventh month is the Day of Atonement. Hold a sacred assembly and deny yourselves, and present a food offering to the Lord. 28 Do not do any work on that day, because it is the Day of Atonement, when atonement is made for you before the Lord your God - Lev 23:27 NIV

And they gathered together to Mizpeh, and drew water, and poured it out before the Lord, and fasted on that day, and said there, We have sinned against the Lord. And Samuel judged the children of Israel in Mizpeh -1 Sam. 7:6.

And the men of Israel were distressed that day: for Saul had adjured the people, saying, Cursed be the man that eateth any food until evening, that I may be avenged on mine enemies. So none of the people tasted any food - 1 Sam. 14:24.

Therefore go thou, and read in the roll, which thou hast written from my mouth, the words of the Lord in the ears of the people in the Lord's house upon the fasting day: and also thou shalt read them in the ears of all Judah that come out of their cities -Jere. 36:6

Now in the twenty and fourth day of this month the children of Israel were assembled with fasting, and with sackclothes, and earth upon them (Neh. 9:1)

THREE DAYS

And they gave him a piece of a cake of figs, and two clusters of raisins: and when he had eaten, his spirit came again to him: for he had eaten no bread, nor drunk any water, three days and three nights (1 Sam. 30:12).

Many people may have difficulty regarding this as a fast, given our definition of fasting as a deliberate abstention from food for a spiritual purpose. In the first place, the subject of the supposed fast could not be said to have abstained from food deliberately (voluntarily). Had he had access to food he could have eaten and drank. Secondly, his abstention from food could not have been said to be for a spiritual purpose, given that he was not even an Israelite (or to be more specific from Judah) he was an Egyptian who was among the enemy's allies that evaded Ziglag, the habitant of the people of God at the time.

"And David said unto him, To whom belongest thou? and whence art thou? And he said, I am a young man of Egypt, servant to an Amalekite; and

my master left me, because three days ago I fell sick. We made an invasion upon the south of the Cherethites, and upon the coast which belongeth to Judah, and upon the south of Caleb; and we burned Ziklag with fire" (1 Sam. 30 13-14)

However, the discussion leads us to the question I'm so often asked: "Can one observe a fast involuntarily?"

Recently I found an interesting material on the topic by Arthur Wallis I would like to share with you.

These are his thoughts:

"...we should observe that fasting may also refer to abstaining from food involuntarily." "The two kinds of involuntary fasting", he adds "are:

1. Where there is no desire for food because of anxiety, sorrow or mental distress (Dan 6:18), and

2. Where persons find themselves in a situation where no food is available [as in the case of the Egyptian], also in Matt 15:32.

Paul evidently knew a good deal of this second sort. No doubt his mention of "fastings" in 2 Corinthians 6:5 and 11:27 refers to this kind of involuntary hardship. Evidently

Paul had no difficulty in reconciling such want with the promise, "My God will supply every need of yours." (Phil. 4:19). He knew that the experience of finding himself temporary without food, and without the means to obtain it, was a necessary trial of faith permitted by God for his ultimate blessing. "I have learned, in whatsoever state I am, to be content. I know both how to be abased, and I know how to abound: in any and all circumstances I have learned the secret of facing plenty and hunger, abundance and want" (Phil 4:11, 12). And he concludes, "If God should call us to walk 'the path of necessity', and we find ourselves on a fast that is not our choosing, let us not fear. He will yet "… turn our captivity… and bless our latter end more than our beginning" (Job 42:10)."

FURTHER RECORDS OF THREE DAYS FASTS

Go, gather together all the Jews that are present in Shushan, and fast for me, and neither eat nor drink three days, night or day: I also and my maidens will fast likewise; and so will I go in unto the king, which is not according to the law: and if I perish, I perish (Esther 4: 16)

Then Jesus called his disciples unto him, and said, I have compassion on the multitude, because they continue with me now three days, and have nothing to eat: and I will not send them away without food, lest they faint in the way. (Matt. 15:32, Mark 8: 2, 3)

And he was three days without sight, and neither did eat nor drink (Acts 9:9)

A) SEVEN DAYS

And when the inhabitants of Jabeshgilead heard of that which the Philistines had done to Saul; All the valiant men arose, and went all night, and took the body of Saul and the bodies of his sons from the wall of Bethshan, and came to Jabesh, and burnt them there. And they took their bones, and buried them under a tree at Jabesh, and fasted seven days (1 Sam. 31:11-13, 1 Chron. 10:11, 12).

And Nathan departed unto his house. And the Lord struck the child that Uriah's wife bare unto David, and it was very sick. David therefore besought God for the child; and David fasted, and went in, and lay all night upon the earth. And the elders of his house arose, and went to him, to raise him up from the earth: but he would not, neither did he eat bread with them. And it came to pass on the seventh day, that the child died. And the servants of David feared to tell him that the child was dead: for they said, Behold, while the child was yet alive, we spake unto him, and he would not hearken unto our voice: how will he then vex himself, if we tell him that the child is dead? Then said his servants unto him, What thing is this that thou hast done? thou didst fast and weep for the child, while it was alive; but when the child was dead, thou didst rise and eat bread. And he said, While the child was yet alive, I fasted and wept: for I said, Who can tell whether God will be gracious to me, that the child may live? But now he is dead, wherefore should I fast? Can I bring him back again? I shall go to him, but he shall not return to me (2 Sam. 12: 15-18, 21-23)

B) FOURTEEN DAYS

And while the day was coming on, Paul besought them all to take meat, saying, This day is the fourteenth day that ye have tarried and continued fasting, having taken nothing. Wherefore I pray you to take some meat: for this is for your health: for there shall not an hair fall from the head of any of you. And when he had thus spoken, he took bread, and gave thanks to God in presence of them all: and when he had broken it, he began to eat (Acts 27:33-35)

C) TWENTY -ONE DAY FASTS

I ate no pleasant food, neither came meat nor wine in my mouth, neither did I anoint myself at all, till three whole weeks were fulfilled (Dan. 10:2, 3).

D) FORTY DAY FASTS

And he was there with the Lord forty days and forty nights; he did neither eat bread, nor drink water. And he wrote upon the tables the words of the covenant, the ten commandments (Exod. 34:28)

When I was gone up into the mount to receive the tables of stone, even the tables of the covenant which the LORD made with you, then I abode in the mount forty days and forty nights, I neither did eat bread nor drink water (Deut. 9:9)

And I fell down before the LORD, as at the first, forty days and forty nights: I did neither eat bread, nor drink water, because of all your sins which ye sinned, in doing wickedly in the sight of the LORD, to provoke him to anger (Deut. 9:18)

And he arose, and did eat and drink, and went in the strength of that food forty days and forty nights unto Horeb the mount of God (1 Kings 19:8)

Then was Jesus led up of the Spirit into the wilderness to be tempted of the devil. And when he had fasted forty days and forty nights, he was afterward an hungred (Matt. 4:1-2)

And Jesus being full of the Holy Ghost returned from Jordan, and was led by the Spirit into the wilderness Being forty days tempted of the devil. And in those days he did eat nothing: and when they were ended, he afterward hungered.

THE WONDERS OF FASTING

30

PRAYER, WHAT IS IT?

For so many reasons, I have decided to devote the last chapters of this book to dealing with the all-important subject of prayer. Like fasting, prayer has been a much debated subject for so long; everyone trying to understand it from different angles, ranging from pure theological perspective to that where prayer is understood as a product of a particular religion i.e. a hybrid of a particular religious persuasion or denomination.

All the major religions of the world – Christianity, Islam, Hindu, Buddha etc, have their different conceptions; shaped by unique believes, about prayer. This is further the case as you consider prayer within the ambit of specific denominations - within the broad spectrum of various religions. For example, Christians and Muslims do not only relate with the concept of prayer from an entirely different perspective, even within the Christian circle, prayer is viewed differently amongst different denominations. Prayer holds something, somewhat different for the Roman Catholics than from the evangelical, for instance. While an overview description of prayer in both denominations might present something coherent, at least in form, in content, however, we are far apart.

Within the evangelicals, prayer is presented as an interesting topic of discussion, a hot topic for seminars, conventions, or conferences; also an easy-grab subject for the gospel minister to preach on.

While no attempt is made in this work to deal with all the misconceptions that are associated with the subject of prayer, a somewhat brief discourse is undertaken in an attempt to examine what prayer truly is, from a pure theological perspective.

This section seeks to answer the question: what is prayer? It focuses on the vital elements or ingredients that qualify any expression of one's heart towards God as prayer.

DEFINITION

Prayer has been widely defined, at least within the Christian circle, as 'communication between God and man'.

While the above definition, undoubtedly, contains some elements that describe what prayer is, it should be stressed that it leaves much to be desired.

My understanding of the subject, both from experience and in-depth study of scriptures reveals that Prayer is not just communication between man and his creator – God, but that prayer is both communication and communion (deep heart-to-heart intimacy and affection) between God and man.

Every communication with God must flow from the springboard of a pre-existing intimate relationship between God and man; such that if there is no relationship, any attempt by man to engage in any form of communication with God becomes an exercise in futility.

Accordingly, when a man that has no relationship, whatsoever, with God prays, his prayer becomes an abomination to God. Such prayer has communication (supposed talking to God) quite alright, but lacks the vital, essential ingredient (communion) that causes such communication to receive heaven's validation.

Prayers are answered, not on the basis of being communication, but on the basis of being both communication and communion! As a matter of fact, communion with God qualifies prayer for answers than communication. Heaven is inundated with barrage of communications (supposed prayers) but very little communication flows from the platform of communion with the father.

There are degrees or depths of communication. Whether we realise it or not, we engage in communication with different people based on different levels of intimacy we have with them. In essence, the degree of intimacy we have with people determines not just what we say or communicate with them but the extent to which we take such conversations. The underlying factor is intimacy!

This one element (intimacy), not only shapes the nature of the conversations I have with my wife, for instance, but it is what makes such conversations of a different kind from that which I hold with friends, even my best friend!

My top secrets are safely lodged in the custody of my wife; but only few friends know any such secrets. My wife knows virtually everything about me. Within the first few months of our marriage, I gave her access to the vaults that hold such information, and vice versa. But no friends of ours hold any such information about us - because the nature of our relationship with them does not call for it.

In the same vein, the manner in which, and the degree to which I respond, to the needs of my wife are different to the way and degree I give myself to meeting the needs of other people. Again, the nature of my relationship with her calls for this. Same principle governs my relationship with my children. I have four wonderful children (treasures, I call them); the very nature of our relationship places onus on me (their father) to feed them, clothe them, ensure their safety, and as often the case, take them to Chinese Restaurant – (their favourite restaurant) - periodically. Needless to say that nothing places such responsibilities on me in relation to my neighbour's children, not even my best-friend's children. Why? The nature of our relationship does not warrant such treatment; even though we share jokes occasionally, whenever we meet.

This is the underlying principle, indeed, the basis on which prayers are answered by God. Everything as far as our relationship with God is concerned, rises and falls on this one principle – intimacy, relationship, affections.

God said of Abraham:

> ... Shall I hide from Abraham that thing which I do; Seeing that Abraham shall surely become a great and mighty nation, and all the nations of the earth shall be blessed in him? For I know him, that he will command his children and his household after him, and they shall keep the way of the Lord, to do justice and judgment; that the Lord may bring upon Abraham that which he hath spoken of him (Gen. 18:17-19).

We could trace the genesis of this relationship to Gen.12: 1-3, when God established a covenant with Abraham:

> Now the LORD had said to Abram, Get you out of your country, and from your kindred, and from your father's house, to a land that I will show you: And I will make of you a great nation, and I will bless you, and make your name great; and you shall be a blessing: And I will bless them that bless you, and curse him that curses you: and in you shall all families of the earth be blessed...

The dealing of God with Abraham, from this humble beginning, was on the premise of a well-established relationship. God and Abraham were in intimate relationship. The testing of Abraham by God - demanding an offering in Isaac, further authenticated this relationship.

Remember, God said in the end, *"...for now I know that thou fearest God, seeing thou hast not withheld thy son, thine only [son] from me"* (Gen. 22: 12).

The principle, therefore, is that what qualifies a man to pray and have his prayers answered, is not his much talking, or his eloquence in the presence of God (communication), but his identity before God (communion).

Very succinctly, Jesus puts the position this way:

I am the good shepherd, and **know my sheep**, *and am known of mine* (John 10:14, emphasis added).

To that we may add another significant declaration of Christ, I believe that could help us build the picture that strengthens our line of thoughts in this regard.

In Matthew 7: 20 -22, Jesus says:

...by their fruits you shall know them. Not everyone that said to me, Lord, Lord, shall enter into the kingdom of heaven; but he that does the will of my Father which is in heaven. Many will say to

me in that day, Lord, Lord, have we not prophesied in your name? and in your name have cast out devils? and in your name done many wonderful works?

Communion and oneness with the father remain, as always, the underlying factor for a healthy relationship with God. On the basis of communion man can worship, and his worship receives God's approval, he can pray, and his prayers are heard, he can give of his substance to God, and it is accepted.

Beloved, "The sacrifice of the wicked is abomination: how much more, when he brings it with a wicked mind?" Proverbs 21:27.

"The sacrifice of the wicked is an abomination to the LORD: but the prayer of the upright is his delight." Proverbs 15:8

When God demands that, *"... the fire upon the altar shall be burning in it; it shall not be put out: and the priest shall burn wood on it every morning, and lay the burnt offering in order upon it; and he shall burn thereon the fat of the peace offerings... The fire shall ever be burning upon the altar; it shall never go out* (Leviticus 6: 12, 13), He was speaking more from the perspective of communion - our relationship with the Master - than mere communication with Him.

The above discourse does not; in any way diminish the place of communication in prayer. The communication of man with his maker occupies an integral part in his relationship with the divine. Without communication with his creator, man has lost contact with his source, and needless to say that such has far-reaching consequences. However, as said, what qualifies man for the rare privilege of finding audience with the King of Kings is his place in God; without which his prayer becomes *"the sacrifice of the wicked..."* (Prov. 15:8, Prov. 21:27).

In the Sermon on the Mount, Jesus spoke greatly, on the significance of communication with God:

Ask and it will be given to you; seek and you will find; knock and the door will be opened to you. For everyone who asks receives; the one who seeks finds; and to the one who knocks, the door will be opened. "Which of you, if your son asks for bread, will give him a stone? Or if he asks for a fish, will give him a snake? If you, then, though you are evil, know how to give good gifts to your children, how much more will your Father in heaven give good gifts to those who ask him! (Matt. 7: 7-10).

On another occasion, Jesus taught, not just how to engage in communication in prayer, but the place of importunity in prayer:

And He said to them, Which of you who has a friend will go to him at midnight and will say to him, Friend, lend me three loaves [of bread], For a friend of mine who is on a journey has just come, and I have nothing to put before him; And he from within will answer, Do not disturb me; the door is now closed, and my children are with me in bed; I cannot get up and supply you [with anything]? I tell you, although he will not get up and supply him anything because he is his friend, yet because of his shameless persistence and insistence he will get up and give him as much as he needs. So I say to you, Ask and keep on asking and it shall be given you; seek and keep on seeking and you shall find; knock and keep on knocking and the door shall be opened to you. For everyone who asks and keeps on asking receives; and he who seeks and keeps on seeking finds; and to him who knocks and keeps on knocking (Luke 11: 5-10 Amplified Bible).

The Lord enjoys our constant communication with him, no doubt! However, such communication must flow from pre-existing relationship with Him.

31

TYPES OF PRAYER

Just as there are different kinds of fasting, as earlier established, in the same vein, there are different kinds of prayer. This is what the bulk of this section is devoted to. Understanding of this vital topic will, not only revolutionise your prayer life, but would answer the question as to why some, if not most of your prayers are not receiving answers, as they should.

Sadly, most Christians are not aware that there are several types of prayers discussed in the word of God, and if you use one type when you should be using another, it would not work. You would be applying the wrong spiritual tool to your needs or request. God intends for each of the six forms of prayer mentioned in the Bible to have different functions, as described below. In essence, there is nothing like 'prayer is prayer.'

Like most things in life, different types of prayer are governed by different rules. Misunderstanding or misapplications of these rules could render your prayers of non-effect.

In practise, however, we all use different types of prayer during our prayer times. What may start out as a prayer of faith can soon develop into prayer of intercession or supplication.

If any of the above types of prayers are absent in your life then you should seek God's face about it. Ask Him to fill you with more of His love and make your prayer life richer. There is no reason why your prayer-life should be narrowed to one or few of the different prayers discussed in this book. On occasions, God places a demand on His saint to engage in any of the prayers outlined here, hence it is very important to develop a prayer-life that is extensive and all embracing.

The following three scriptures would act as a springboard to set out study:

Praying always with all prayer and supplication in the Spirit, and watching thereunto with all perseverance and supplication for all saints (Ephesians 6:18).

I exhort therefore, that, first of all, supplications, prayers, intercessions, and giving of thanks, be made for all men; For kings, and for all that are in authority; that we may lead a quiet and peaceable life in all godliness and honesty (1 Tim. 2:1-2).

Be careful for nothing; but in everything by prayer and supplication with thanksgiving let your requests be made known unto God (Philippians 4:6).

The different types of prayers there are in scriptures are well identified in these bible passages:

Here are the main types of prayers in the Bible:

Supplication

Supplication means to petition or entreat someone for something. A passionate zeal or hunger fuels the prayer of supplication. Supplications are requests that come from a heart, crying out to God for help. At times we are driven to praying the prayer of supplication because of imminent danger. The prayer of supplication can sometimes lead us into fasting (Nehemiah 1: 1-6). In 11 Chronicles 20: 4, 14, we read,

> *And Judah gathered themselves together,* **to ask help** *of the Lord: even out of all the cities of Judah*

they came to seek the Lord. O our God, wilt thou not judge them? for we have no might against this great company that cometh against us; neither know we what to do: but our eyes are upon thee (emphasis added).

Faced with the threat of invasion from armies of neighbouring nations, Judah assembled to pray to ask for God's intervention.

We are admonished in Philippians 4:6,

Do not be anxious about anything, but in everything by prayer and supplication with thanksgiving let your requests be made known to God." Part of winning the spiritual battle is to be "praying at all times in the Spirit, with all prayer and supplication (Ephesians 6:18).

A common characteristic of prayer of supplication is importunity. This is vividly illustrated in the teaching of Jesus:

"And He said to them, Which of you who has a friend will go to him at midnight and will say to him, Friend, lend me three loaves [of bread], For a friend of mine who is on a journey has just come, and I have nothing to put before him; And he from within will answer, Do not disturb me; the door is

> now closed, and my children are with me in bed; I cannot get up and supply you [with anything]? I tell you, although he will not get up and supply him anything because he is his friend, yet because of his shameless **persistence and insistence** he will get up and give him as much as he needs".
> (Luke 11:5-8: Amplified emphasis added).

Another bible passage that illustrates the connection between the prayer of supplication and importunity is Luke 18: 1-6:

> Then Jesus told his disciples a parable to show them that they should always pray and not give up. He said: "In a certain town there was a judge who neither feared God nor cared what people thought. And there was a widow in that town who kept coming to him with the plea, 'Grant me justice against my adversary.' "For some time he refused. But finally he said to himself, 'Even though I don't fear God or care what people think, yet because this widow keeps bothering me, I will see that she gets justice, so that she would not eventually come and attack me!'" And the Lord said, "Listen to what the unjust judge says. And will not God bring about justice for his chosen ones, who cry out to him day and night? Will he keep putting them off? I tell you, he will see that they get justice, and quickly. However, when the Son of Man comes, will he find faith on the earth?

Intercession

Intercession involves praying for others. It may involve praying in a general sense for such subject-matter as the church or the government, or praying for another, based on your knowledge of the person's needs.

Intercession generally means to plead or mediate on behalf of another person. The scripture references above show specific circumstances where intercession was being made. Intercession will involve various degrees of supplication. Intercession is not normally a one-off prayer. We are told to make intercession "for everyone" in 1 Timothy 2:1. Jesus serves as our example in this area. The whole of John 17 is a prayer of Jesus on behalf of His disciples and all believers.

A hallmark of prayer of intercession is that it requires persistence. Abraham demonstrated this clearly in the following scripture:

> And the men turned their faces from thence, and went toward Sodom: but Abraham stood yet before the Lord. And Abraham drew near, and said, Wilt thou also destroy the righteous with the wicked? Peradventure there be fifty righteous within the city: wilt thou also destroy and not spare the place for the fifty righteous that are therein? That be

far from thee to do after this manner, to slay the righteous with the wicked: and that the righteous should be as the wicked, that be far from thee: Shall not the Judge of all the earth do right? And the Lord said, If I find in Sodom fifty righteous within the city, then I will spare all the place for their sakes. And Abraham answered and said, Behold now, I have taken upon me to speak unto the Lord, which am but dust and ashes: Peradventure there shall lack five of the fifty righteous: wilt thou destroy all the city for lack of five? And he said, If I find there forty and five, I will not destroy it. And he spake unto him yet again, and said, Peradventure there shall be forty found there. And he said, I will not do it for forty's sake. And he said unto him, Oh let not the Lord be angry, and I will speak: Peradventure there shall thirty be found there. And he said, I will not do it, if I find thirty there. And he said, Behold now, I have taken upon me to speak unto the Lord: Peradventure there shall be twenty found there. And he said, I will not destroy it for twenty's sake. And he said, Oh let not the Lord be angry, and I will speak yet but this once: Peradventure ten shall be found there. And he said, I will not destroy it for ten's sake. And the Lord went his way, as soon as he had left communing with Abraham: and Abraham returned unto his place (Gen. 18: 22-33).

In Ephesians 1:15-18, Paul wrote: *"Therefore I also, after I heard of your faith in the Lord Jesus and your love for all the saints, do not cease to give thanks for you, making mention of you in my prayers; that the God of our Lord Jesus Christ, the Father of glory, may give to you the spirit of wisdom and revelation in the knowledge of Him, the eyes of your understanding being enlightened; that you may know what is the hope of His calling, what are the riches of the glory of His inheritance in the saints."*

Here Paul wrote that he prayed regularly for the church in Ephesus and for the individuals there to receive these blessings.

Likewise, in his greeting to the Philippians, he wrote, *"I thank my God upon every remembrance of you, always in every prayer of mine making request for you all with joy"* (Phil. 1:3-4). The fact that Paul said he made requests for these saints suggests that this also was an example of intercessory prayer.

You can see that not appreciating the different types of prayer can hinder our prayer life, as said. If you only recognise the prayer of supplication, for instance, you may fail to intercede for another believer who is in trouble of any kind or needs God to intervene in his or her life. Did you notice that

Elijah had to keep praying - seven times - before the rain that God had already promised came (1 Kings 18:41-46).

When we take it upon ourselves to pray earnestly for other people, we enter into the realm of intercession. To enter into intercession we must have a heart that really loves the Lord and cares about the things God cares about.

The Prayer of faith

For verily I say unto you, That whosoever shall say unto this mountain, Be thou removed, and be thou cast into the sea; and shall not doubt in his heart, but shall believe that those things which he saith shall come to pass; he shall have whatsoever he saith. Therefore I say unto you, What things soever ye desire, when ye pray, believe that ye receive them, and ye shall have them (Mark 11: 23-24).

James 5:15 says, *"And the prayer of faith shall save the sick..."*

All prayer relies on our faith in God. Although the phrase 'prayer of faith' is commonly used, the reality is that all prayer is by faith in God. The prayer of faith is rooted in our confidence in God's Word. The woman with the issue of blood (Matthew 9:18-30) knew that touching Jesus would get her healed. Her faith made way for her healing. When you are sure that what you are praying for is God's will for you, the prayer of faith should be utilised. Unforgiveness (Mark 11: 25) and doubt (James 1: 5-8) are the two greatest hindrances to the prayer of faith.

The rule to consider here is rooted in Mark 11:24,

"Therefore I say unto you, What things soever ye desire, when ye pray, believe that ye receive them, and ye shall have them."

Notice that the above scripture does not say when you will actually see the result of your prayer. It does not tell you how long it will take for that prayer result to appear. All it says is that believe that you have your needs met. This is often where most believers give up.

When you pray in faith, God immediately gives you what you prayed for—in the spirit realm. But in the natural world, due to a number of factors, it may take time for the answer to manifest itself. Remember Daniel's prayer in Daniel 10.

God answers prayers, and He will answer your specific prayer in line with His Word, but it is your faith that brings that answer out of the spirit realm into the physical world. How many times in

Scripture does Jesus say to someone, "According to your faith"?

He referred to peoples' faith constantly, and even though it was His power that healed them, He always credited their faith with being the catalyst. In fact, when Jesus went to His hometown, we are told that *"He did not do many mighty works there because of their unbelief"* (Matt. 13:58).

Did Jesus suddenly lose His power on that visit to Nazareth? No!

His power never changed. What changed? It was the people's level of faith mixed with His power.

There is a simple spiritual explanation for this. God will not do something against your will. God cannot violate free will. If you do not have faith to do something, He would not arbitrarily override your lack of faith.

Prayer of agreement

In Matthew 18:19, 20, Jesus introduced the prayer of agreement when He said,

> *Again I say to you that if two of you agree on earth concerning anything that they ask, it will be done for them by My Father in heaven For where two or*

three are gathered together in My name, I am there in the midst of them.

This is the bedrock of the prayer of agreement. Prayer of agreement is where two or more people are praying on the same issue together. These could be members of a church, two or more friends, or even more powerfully, a husband and wife; who stand on their pre-existing covenant relationship (marriage), to agree together in prayer on specific issues before God.

God has given power and authority to the Church and when we stand together in unity we can see more of God's power released (Matthew 28: 16-20). Unity is standing together with one purpose, sharing a joint vision and trusting God's Word to be fulfilled. We need to appreciate the power of unity if we are to see God's power released. The Bible says, *"How should one chase a thousand, and two put ten thousand to flight, except their Rock had sold them, and the LORD had shut them up?"* (Deut. 32:30).

CONDITIONS FOR PRAYER OF AGREEMENT

Agreement

For the prayer of agreement to work, the people involved must agree! There must actual, not implied agreement. If someone asks me to pray in agreement with them, I ask, "What specifically do you want me to pray for?" You absolutely must make sure you are in perfect agreement about what your prayer request is before you join with another believer in the prayer of agreement. Jesus says, "If any two of you on earth agree." You've got to make sure that the person you are praying with, first, understands the purpose of the prayer, and second, does agree with you on the subject matter of your prayer. It is vitally important to find someone who will agree with you in the spirit. Please test the spirit! It is got to be someone who believes in your vision.

Ask together

Another important consideration about Prayer of Agreement as seeing from the teaching of Jesus on the subject is that the people praying must ask together about the situation.

We find a good example of this in the book of Acts.

Peter therefore was kept in prison: but prayer was made without ceasing of the church unto God for him. And when he had considered the thing, he came to the house of Mary the mother of John, whose surname was Mark; where many were gathered together praying (Acts 12: 5, 12).

Jesus says, *"For where two or three are gathered together in my name, there am I in the midst of them" (Matthew 28: 20).* There is power in agreement!

When we agree together in prayers, a power is released from heaven to bring about results on earth.

Prayer of dedication or consecration

Jesus shows us example of prayer of consecration in Luke 22:39-42:

Coming out, He went to the Mount of Olives, as He was accustomed, and His disciples also followed Him. When He came to the place, He said to them, "Pray that you may not enter into temptation. And He was withdrawn from them about a stone's throw, and He knelt down and prayed, saying, "Father, if it is Your will, take this cup away from Me; nevertheless not My will, but Yours, be done.

Sometimes, prayer is a time of setting ourselves apart to follow God's will. Jesus made such a prayer the night before His crucifixion: "And going a little farther he fell on his face and prayed, saying, 'My Father, if it be possible, let this cup pass from me; nevertheless, not as I will, but as you will'" (Matthew 26:39).

The prayer of consecration is a humble submission to the will of God. This is not always easy. After the Apostles had just been whipped for their faith they immediately rededicated themselves to God's will with prayer (Acts 4:29-31).

If God leads you into an area of ministry or work that is difficult it will take the prayer of consecration for you to fulfil it. The same is true of living a holy life. The prayer of consecration is asking for the strength to accomplish His will with His power. The prayer of consecration is expedient for all maturing Christians.

In Luke 22:41-42, we see outlined the prayer of consecration and dedication: *"And He [Jesus] was withdrawn from them [Peter, James and John] about a stone's throw, and He knelt down and prayed, saying, 'Father, if it is Your will, take this cup away from Me; nevertheless not My will, but Yours, be done.'"*

He was praying, in effect, "If there is any other way to do this, let us do it that way." But the key for Jesus, and for us, is, "Nevertheless not My will, but Yours, be done."

You pray that God's will would be done when you do not know His will or do not know if an alternative path that appears is equally "correct" or godly. In the absence of direct instructions, the prayer of consecration and dedication says you will allow God to set your direction or make your decisions.

The prayer of consecration and dedication works when you have two (or more) godly alternatives before you, and you are not getting a clear sense at that time about which option God wants you to take. When the direction is unclear—but any of the options appear to be legitimate, righteous options—that is the perfect time to say, "Lord, if it be your will, I am going to go with option A."

The Prayer of Praise, Worship and thanksgiving

Let the high praises of God be in their mouth, and a two-edged sword in their hand; To execute vengeance upon the heathen, and punishments upon the people; To bind their kings with chains, and their nobles with fetters of iron; To execute upon them the judgment written: this honour have all his saints. Praise ye the Lord (Psalm 149:6-9).

The prayer of biblical praise is a formidable weapon in warfare; it brought down the walls of Jericho. The army marched around seven times, and the priests blew their horns. At the end of the seventh time, the priests blew the horns long and hard. Joshua shouted to his people, *"Shout aloud, for the Lord has given us this city." (Joshua 6:16).* So the people shouted and the walls of Jericho fell to the ground.

It was what gave Jehoshaphat and Judah victory over their enemies:

And they rose early in the morning, and went forth into the wilderness of Tekoa: and as they went forth, Jehoshaphat stood and said, Hear me, O Judah, and you inhabitants of Jerusalem; Believe in the LORD your God, so shall you be established; believe his prophets, so shall you prosper. 21And when he had consulted with the people, he appointed singers to the LORD, and that should praise the beauty of holiness, as they went out before the army, and to say, Praise the LORD; for his mercy endures for ever. 22And when they began to sing and to praise, the LORD set ambushes against the children of Ammon, Moab, and mount Seir, which were come against Judah; and they were smitten (2 Chronicles 20:20-22).

The prayer of worship is similar to the prayer of thanksgiving. The difference is that worship focuses on who God is; thanksgiving focuses on what God has done. Church leaders in Antioch prayed in this manner with fasting: *"While they were worshiping the Lord and fasting, the Holy Spirit said, 'Set apart for me Barnabas and Saul for the work to which I have called them.' Then after fasting and praying they laid their hands on them and sent them off"* (Acts 13:2-3).

Praise and worship brings us into the presence of God. When we praise God in the mist of seemingly negative situations we are affirming our faith in Him. This pleases God and helps our faith. Thanking God in the good times also keeps our eyes focused on the source of our strength.

Thanksgiving should be a regular part of our talking to God. Thanksgiving is an all-inclusive act that involves praise, worship and honour of God.

In this prayer, you are not asking God to do something for you or to give you something. You are not even asking for direction and dedicating your life to whatever it is God has called you to do.

Rather, you just want to praise the Lord, to thank Him for His many blessings and mercy. You want to tell Him how much you love Him.

Paul wrote to the Philippians: *"Be anxious for nothing, but in everything by prayer and supplication, with thanksgiving, let your requests be made known to God" (Phil. 4:6, emphasis added).* This says that even when we pray the prayer of faith, we should always intersperse worship and praise.

The Prayer of Binding and Loosing

Assuredly, I say to you, whatever you bind on earth will be bound in heaven, and whatever you loose on earth will be loosed in heaven. Again I say to you that if two of you agree on earth concerning anything that they ask, it will be done for them by My Father in heaven (Matthew 18: 18-19).

There are several important nuggets in Jesus' statements here, the first being that we have authority on earth by virtue of our covenant rights through Jesus. The second thing we notice is the direction of the action. Things do not begin in heaven and come to earth, but rather the action starts here on earth and flows to heaven. Notice that it says, "Whatever you bind on earth will be bound in heaven, and whatever you loose on earth will be loosed in heaven."

This type of prayer is particularly useful in warfare! You bind satanic or demonic forces that are hindering people's progress, causing sicknesses and diseases in the body, and causing outright wreckage of people's destiny.

When you pray in this manner, God affirms it in heaven and puts His seal of approval on your prayer. Binding and loosing have to be based on the authority God has granted you in Scripture, not on some desire you have.

God has provided each type of prayer for a specific purpose. Though you may use more than one at any given time, it is important to be clear about which type you are using and why, and to be aware of its limitations. If you follow the examples in the Bible, you'll be sure to use them properly and have the desired results.

Praying in the Spirit

Likewise the Spirit also helpeth our infirmities: for we know not what we should pray for as we ought: but the Spirit itself maketh intercession for us with groanings which cannot be uttered. And he that searcheth the hearts knoweth what is the mind of the Spirit, because he maketh intercession for the saints according to the will of God (Romans 8:26-27).

The above scripture can be analysed as follows:

God has given us His Holy Spirit to help us in our weakness(s). The word for "help" is a rich word that carries with it the idea of a person who comes alongside another to take part of the heavy load and help him bear it. God has given us the Holy Spirit to help us in our prayer lives.

Further, the Holy Spirit intercedes for us. When one person intercedes for another, they literally take the position of the one for whom they are interceding, and argues his case. This is like the work of an advocate in court. For the past two thousand years, Jesus has been doing the job of an advocate on the behalf of His saints before God. Jesus is our parakletos (Advocate)! He is the one who comes to our aid when we sin; He stands by us and pleads our case before God, as we confess our sins (1 Jn. 1:8-2:2). In this sense, the Holy Spirit is said to go to the Father on our behalf to interpret and give voice to the prayers of our heart.

The Holy Spirit intercedes with groaning that words cannot express. He communicates with the Father in a deep, intimate, and wordless language that we can't comprehend or express.

Finally, Holy Spirit prays effectively on our behalf because the Spirit prays in accordance with God's will. The Holy Spirit knows what is best for our life. He knows God's plan for us. He knows the purpose of every event and situation in our life. The Holy Spirit prays for God to accomplish His work in us.

For if I pray in an unknown tongue, my spirit prayeth, but my understanding is unfruitful. What is it then? I will pray with the spirit, and I will pray with the understanding also: will sing with the spirit, and I will sing with the understanding also (1 Cor. 14:14-15).

Epilogue

Fasting is a joyous opportunity God has given the believer to access the miraculous! Every door that is meant to act as a means of security also requires a key or keys to both strengthen the door and unlock it for passage.

Fasting plays both roles. Fasting is the mystery key that provides access to the world of impossibilities and metamorphoses miracles out of that realm for the believer.

In Matthew 16:19 Jesus promises,

"I will give you the keys of the kingdom of heaven; whatever you bind on earth will be [a] bound in heaven, and whatever you loose on earth will be [b] loosed in heaven."

Fasting is one of those infallible keys that turn defeat into triumph, failure into success, rejection into admiration and acceptance. Use this key today and be celebrated!

With fasting, eternity has, literarily been given to the believer in Christ Jesus. The Saint is placed in a position where he could determine, shape and reshape his destiny, at will. What a rare privilege!

JESUS IS LORD

EPILOGUE

You need to know Jesus personally

Do not gamble with your eternal destination!

Religion, good works, good intentions are not good enough to get you into heaven.

Jesus said:

"Behold I stand at the door and knock: if any man hear my voice and open the door, I will come into him, and will sup with him he with me"

Revelations 3:20

If you have not yet given your life to the Lord Jesus please do so by praying the following Prayer of Salvation:

Lord Jesus I come to you just as I am

Thank you for dying on the cross for my sins

Thank you for being the substitute for all my wrong doings

Today I open my heart to you

Lord come in and be my Master, Be my Lord

I surrender the rest of my life to you

Satan I refuse you today

I refuse all your operations my life

I reject all the works of the flesh I have been used to

Jesus I Surrender all to you

I am born again by your grace

Amen

I rejoice with you and the angels in heaven rejoicing over your salvation. Please find a living bible believing Church where you can grow and fellowship with other Christians.

If you have prayed this prayer, please we will very much like to hear from you. Kindly contact us through the following address:

Hope of Glory International Christian Centre
54b Mineral Street
Off Plumstead High Street
LONDON
SE18 1QR
Tel: 02036893603
Email: hopeofglory@btinterent.com

Website: www.hopeofgloryinternational.com

BIBLIOGRAPHY

1. D. Prince, Experiencing God's Power, (Whitaker House, USA, 1998)
2. D. Prince, How to Fast Successfully, (Whitaker House, USA, 1976)
3. D. Prince, Fasting, (Whitaker House, USA, 1976)
4. D. Y. Cho, Prayer that Brings Revival, (Creation House, 1984)
5. D. Colbert, Toxic Relief, (Siloam, USA, 2001)
6. E. Town, Fasting For Spiritual Breakthrough, (Regal, USA, 1996)
7. E. Towns, Fasting For A Miracle, (Regal, USA, 2012)
8. J. Kilpatrick, When the Heavens Are Brass, (4th Edition, Revival Press, USA, 1997)
9. M. Chavda, The Hidden Power of Prayer and Fasting, (3rd Edition, Destiny Image, USA, 1998).

OTHER BOOKS BY PASTOR ANN IRUOBE

God did not plan for you to be in a joy-less marriage where you only experience "weeping and gnashing of teeth". His desire is that you and your husband live joyfully together. Ecclesiastes 9:9. "The joyful wife" will open your eyes to ways in which the joy of the Lord on YOUR life can transform your marriage. I don't know why God said "a wise woman builds her home", but I know that a deep revelation of that scripture puts the key of the success of your home in your hand as a joyful wife. A woman is powerful enough to tear down the home with her own hands. In this book the Lord will open your eyes to know how to:

- "Break the ice" in your home
- Win your husband's favour
- Foster "joyful communication"
- Be a "joyful mother"
- Be a "joyful minister's wife" etc.

The "joy pills" at the end of the book are daily scriptures you can read and meditate on to inspire you to experience the joy of the Lord every day of the month.

Get ready for a "joyful" marriage!

You don't have to be married or even have a child of your own to be a mother. What do you need? The answer is a "mother-heart", a heart that can have compassion and "feel" for people in the world, a heart that will cry to God about the condition of the world today.

God has a great need in these end times for women with "mother-hearts" "Thus saith the LORD of hosts, Consider ye, and call for the mourning women,…And let them make haste, and take up a wailing for us, Jeremiah 9:17-18. Do you want to be such a woman? I hope your answer will be "yes". Then you are holding a book that will fire you up and prepare you to be such a vessel. Women have to arise on behalf of their husbands and children, their nation, the Church of God and even the world as a whole.

It is time for mothers to arise!

"Why did God decide to make me a woman?" "I'm only human, I'm just a woman" what possibly can I contribute to God's world?" If these are the questions in your heart, this book is for you. When you know your purpose as a woman you will confidently pursue it and get results that will make your life fruitful. As a woman, you have been called to be a mother. This is your primary calling – whatever your niche in life. Whether you are a bank manager, a nurse or a house wife. You are the "mother of all living", blessed to give life to the nations of the world. How do you affect your family, local church or community? How do people feel after they come in contact with you? As you read this book I pray the Lord will challenge you to be a mother indeed, as you learn:

- What a mother heart is
- How to develop a "mother heart"
- How to be a mother even before you get married
- How to win your husband's trust
- None shall be barren among you etc.

Its time for you to manifest your "motherhood"!!!

To order any of these books please contact:
Hope of Glory International Christian Centre,
54b Mineral Street, off Plumstead High Street, London, SE18 1QR
Tel: **0203 689 3603/ 07950 707 133** Email: **hopeofglory@btinternet.com**

www.ingramcontent.com/pod-product-compliance
Lightning Source LLC
Chambersburg PA
CBHW021050080526
44587CB00010B/197